Victorious Eschatology

A Partial Preterist View

Third Edition

Dr. Harold R. Eberle

&

Dr. Martin Trench

***Victorious Eschatology:* A Partial Preterist View**
Dr. Harold R. Eberle and Dr. Martin Trench

First Edition: 2006
Second Edition: 2007
Third Edition, First Printing: 2021
Second Printing: 2023
Third Printing: 2025 (with minor revisions)

ISBN 978-1-953087-26-3

Worldcast Publishing®, P.O. Box 10653, Yakima, WA 98909-1653
www.worldcastministries.com® • office@worldcastministries.com
(509) 248-5837

Underlining within quotations is the author's own, added for emphasis.

Cover by Chris Ritchie

Printed in the United States of America

What Others Are Saying

When I first read *Victorious Eschatology*, a light bulb went on in a dim part of my brain! I realized that my previous *Scofield Bible* eschatology would no longer cut it. However, while I knew what I wasn't, I didn't quite know what I was until Harold Eberle and Martin Trench came along. This is one of the most important books I have read in a long time!

C. Peter Wagner
Founder, *Global Harvest Ministries*
Colorado Springs, CO

For someone looking to make sense of biblical end times, this is a must read! Theology is very complex but Dr. Eberle and Dr. Trench have a way of sharing, that challenges difficult perspectives, while bringing us all along. *Victorious Eschatology* is certainly no exception. Dr. Eberle along with Dr. Trench simplify the complicated and lead the reader into foundational biblical perspectives of a hopeful future.

Ben Nichols
Director, *All People Free*
Lynden, WA

What Harold Eberle and Martin Trench have written here will cause a shift in your thinking of eschatology or end-time events. We need a shift that will move the Church from a rapture mentality to a harvest theology . . . We are not the Church in failure, running out the back door while the devil kicks in the front door. We are the Church of Luke 10:19 that has authority over all the power of the enemy.[1]

Cal Pierce
Director, *Healing Rooms Ministries, International*
Spokane, WA

1. This is an excerpt from the foreword that Cal Pierce wrote for the first edition of *Victorious Eschatology*.

What Others Are Saying

God is NOT a pessimist. God did not create a pathetic world waiting for permanent destruction. He is a Glorious God. He created you and me capable of delivering to Him a Victorious Kingdom! The end defines the means! This book shall change the fate of the Church and the face of the Earth. Every Christian leader should read it, and every Christian University should teach this course.

Benny Yang
CEO and Vice Chancellor, *Wagner University*
Claremont, CA

We need a reformation in the area of eschatology, and I believe Harold Eberle and Martin Trench's book is a step in that direction. It gives a clear understanding of the Olivet Discourse and corrects present teaching that has taken the words of Jesus out of context. *Victorious Eschatology* will help shift your paradigm concerning the end times, and I highly recommend it as a foundational book in the present reformation.

John J. Eckhardt
Presiding Apostle, *IMPACT Network*
Chicago, IL

If you, like myself, were brought up with an end-times prospective that left you pessimistic and fearful about the future, then you also may find *Victorious Eschatology* extremely liberating and faith building. Dr. Harold Eberle and Dr. Martin Trench do a brilliant job of examining Scripture, reviewing historical evidence and presenting an optimistic perspective of a victorious return of Jesus Christ and His rule and reign on the Earth. We are called to be disciples (students) of Jesus, and His primary teaching, parables, and illustrations were centered on the Kingdom of God and its advancement in the earth. It is for this very reason I highly recommend *Victorious Eschatology* to everyone!

Dave Collins
COO | International Dean, *Wagner University*
Claremont, CA

When I first read Harold and Martin's book ,*Victorious Eschatology,* I was struck by how straightforward it was laid out, taking me to conclusions that I have always believed at a heart level but had never heard expressed before. It was the first book of its kind that my heart said, "Yes!" page after page. I gave a copy to one young mother who had been often tormented with fears about the last days. She said these vanished as she read the book, giving her a new expectation, for whatever lay ahead.

Penn Clark
Author and Senior Leader, *Word of Grace Network*
Penn Yann, NY

Victorious Eschatology helps give a broader perspective on the predominant historical Christian eschatological views. Harold Eberle and Martin Trench are modern-day reformers that God uses to wake the Church out of slumber. God has used this book to deliver the body of Christ from fear-based eschatology and to see the world from a Kingdom perspective. I love that this book is insistent that the Kingdom of God is increasing in the earth and permeating every realm of society until the physical return of Jesus. Powerful truths like these will cause the Church to rise in glory and victory in the earth today!

Zack Wechsler
Senior Leader, *Encounter Church NY*
Chili, NY

Harold and Martin answer so many questions that I wrestled with for 50 years of Christian life and ministry. Aligning Scripture with historical New and Old Testament events, they clearly present ideas that both challenged and strengthened my end-times understanding and expectations. Unlike any eschatology book I have ever read, I recommend it to anyone who wonders what the future holds for believers.

Tim Matteson
Founding Pastor, *Hope City Church*
Reno, NV

What Others Are Saying

I cannot imagine getting up every morning with a defeatist attitude about life. Nor can I imagine serving a God who cannot overcome evil, but simply snatches away a few poor souls. Harold Eberle and Martin Trench's book, *Victorious Eschatology*, gives us a clear understanding of what to expect as kings of the King.

Don Atkins
President, *Kingdomquest International Ministries*
Charlotte, NC

When I talk with millennial and generation Z Christians, I see them come alive when discussing a victorious view of the end times. The old "left behind" scenarios do not seem to connect with them. I can relate to their excitement as I reflect on the content in this book. It presents an optimistic view that will make your heart leap with joy for the future of the Church, but it is also solidly Bible-based and rooted in the views of the historical Church. The reader will understand, maybe for the first time, key Scriptures about the end times and see hope for the future of the Church.

Brian Sauder
Director, *Training Schools, DOVE International*
Lititz, PA

Victorious Eschatology not only brings a more accurate view of end-time biblical prophecy, but it also inspires believers to walk forward in victory and hopeful expectation of God's expanding Kingdom on Earth. Thank you, Harold and Martin, for helping us break out of an unhealthy, defeated view of the end times. With a victorious interpretation of Scripture, we are empowered to actively participate in the Father's plan for our future. I am thankful that these teachings are bringing spiritual energy to many East African ministers.

Ryan Helbling
Director, *Ezekiel's River School of the Kingdom*
East Africa

Victorious Eschatology was my personal catalyst for rethinking the future and the mission of the Church. This wonderful book is a great user-friendly resource for understanding the cultural and historical context of Matthew 24 and Revelation. As always, Dr. Eberle and Dr. Trench write in a way that makes the Scriptures come alive!

Rob Covell
Provost, *Wagner University*
Pasadena, CA

Victorious Eschatology is the right book at the right time. Much has been said to produce fear, complacency, and selfishness in the Church when it comes to end times. Like all of Harold's books, *Victorious Eschatology* roots us in the Bible and history, plus stirs our heart to faith, hope and love. Let the Church read and arise in victory.

Kevin Taylor
Lead Pastor, *ember church*
Chester, SC

Harold Eberle is one of the brightest minds of our time and his book, *Victorious Eschatology,* might possibly be his greatest work. His insights into the end times are profoundly accurate. Brick by theological brick, he exposes the fallacies of the rapture mentality that has rendered the Church of Jesus Christ powerless and ineffective for decades.

I have given this book to our staff and we use it in our *Bethel School of Ministry* to teach our students about the end times. I highly recommend *Victorious Eschatology* to every Believer. It will change your life!

Kris Vallotton
Senior Associate Leader, *Bethel Church* Redding, CA
Co-Founder, *Bethel School of Supernatural Ministry*
Author of more than a dozen books, including:
Spirit Wars and *Spiritual Intelligence*

Victorious Eschatology validated perceptions and beliefs that I have had for much of my life . . . but now they are firmly anchored in a biblical and historical context. Scripture was clearly and convincingly tied to copious documented historical evidence from the Early Church time period. As a result, *Victorious Eschatology* has become a solid reference book in many of my serious conversations about "end times." You will be surprised and grateful as Harold Eberle and Martin Trench liberate you from a defeatist and escapist mentality. The victorious new day is dawning. Enjoy!

Mark Hendrickson
Dwelling Place Ministries - www.dpmkc.org
Author of *Supernatural Provision–Where God Guides He Provides*
Kansas City, MO

One of the important works of our time, *Victorious Eschatology* by Harold Eberle and Martin Trench invites you to a biblical, theological discussion that will encourage you to partner with what the Father is doing now and equip you to think about the future with hope.

In church, theological ideas are often presented as irrefutable dogma, rather than simply the speaker's perspective, based on their study of the Word and the topic being presented.

Harold and Martin are leaders who are creating a culture where the Church within the context of community can search the Scriptures and consider such topics with critical thinking and discussion, seeking to understand differing perspectives with humility and honor.

I heartily recommend *Victorious Eschatology* as a primer on the topic of end-times theology, one which will hopefully create a victorious view of the future, thereby increasing understanding of the Father's love for this world and releasing the Church to partner with Him in serving it with the compassion and devotion of a loving parent.

James Bradburn
Senior Leader, *Rock Creek Church*
Portland, OR

Several years ago, a good friend asked if I had read the book on end times that our mutual friend, Dr. C. Peter Wagner, recommended. My response was that I did not think Peter had an opinion on the topic. But he clearly did.

My friend showed me the book, *Victorious Eschatology, A Partial Preterist View,* written by Harold Eberle and Martin Trench. I started reading and found myself nodding in agreement as question after question in my mind was answered. I bought that book off my friend as I had to travel and could not get another copy quick enough. I read it through twice in two days.

When I returned home, I contacted Dr. Eberle's ministry for further copies and then went to Yakima to meet Dr. Eberle to invite him and his wife Linda to come and teach in New Zealand. He and Linda Eberle taught at our three main conferences, so hundreds of Kiwis have now been exposed to a better understanding of these issues.

The book explains the various options on end-time issues and shows the biblical and historic information as to why this particular view is more in line with God's Word. I highly recommend *Victorious Eschatology, A Partial Preterist View,* in part because it will put to an end some of the non-biblical views shared on Christian television and bookstands.

Selwyn Stevens, Ph.D., D. Min.
President, *Jubilee Resources International*
New Zealand

We had been introduced to many divergent views of eschatology over the years and had grown skeptical of the subject altogether. But when challenged to read this book, we were hesitant to consider one more time the subject of "last things." We were completely surprised and delighted as we were encouraged to study what the Scriptures had to say about last things rather than what we had been taught. We invite you to open your heart to do the same.

Randy and Deborah O'Dell
Senior Leaders and Apostles, *Freedom Gateway Center*
Farmington, MI

What Others Are Saying

Harold Eberle and Martin Trench's *Victorious Eschatology* is exactly what the Church needs. A breakthrough book that reveals hope for the future and provides a biblical understanding of popular themes like the Great Tribulation and the reign of anti-Christ. Once we embrace a reshaped eschatology (victorious) it changes our lives, changes how we raise our children and transforms the vision of the local church. Few books have this ability; *Victorious Eschatology* does. This is an important book with a vital message.

Dr. Stan Newton
President, *Crown Institute of Theology*
Omak, WA

Personally, this book has been the most practical and helpful manual to create hope filled theology about the end times that I have come across. This book has been like a personal professor helping me shape healthier beliefs and practices as a human and leader in this amazing entity called Church. I am indebted to Harold and Martin for the sacrifice and work that they have done to produce this work that has so changed me and the community around me. You will find fear and dread about the future leaving your life as you read.

Matt Stutzman
Senior Pastor, *Church of Baltimore*
Baltimore, MD

Besides the Bible, no book has changed my life as much as *Victorious Eschatology*. I remember in 2007 when Peter Wagner told me I must read this book, he said, "It's a game changer." This book has brought me so much joy and optimism about the future; I'm not afraid of the future. I've told my church and network they must read this book.

Dr. John M. Benefiel
Presiding Apostle, *Heartland Apostolic Prayer Network*
Founder and Senior Pastor, *Church on the Rock*
Oklahoma City, OK

My initial reading of *Victorious Eschatology* left an indelible imprint on my life. Finally, my spirit DNA that knew the "end" was bigger and better finally had a profoundly simple treatise to verify its hope. The years of fearful wondering melted away as I read the faith-filled perspective of a victorious King and Kingdom whose increase knows no end. Verses once oblique and shrouded in dread sprung to bold, clear and glorious life. I was free to trust in a bright future and had the theological explanation to support it.

Mark Durniak
Senior Pastor, *World Harvest Outreach*
Chambersburg, PA

Dr. Harold Eberle and Dr. Martin Trench have done the Body of Christ a great service by laying out with brilliance an eschatological perspective that is filled with victorious hope. This book "upsets the fruit basket" of a default eschatology that should have never existed.

Johnny Enlow
Co-Founder of *Restore7*
Speaker, Reformer, Author of
The Seven Mountain Prophecy and *Kingdom Come*

Harold Eberle is one of the greatest theological minds in the world today. He is the theologian's theologian. I have sat for hours sharing with Harold and dozens of his spiritual children discussing the details of theology. I am delighted that he is ever increasing the clarity of his eschatology and other points of theology. I am a better man because of the time that has been afforded me the privilege of being with Harold and Linda. The effect of your ministry is reaching to the uttermost parts of the earth. I am happy to have shared from the riches of Harold's work with thanksgiving.

Jack Taylor
President, *Dimensions Ministries*
Melbourne, FL

Credits and Thanks

We want to thank the thousands of Christians who listened to us teach these truths while we were still studying and developing our understanding of the Church rising in victory and power before the return of Jesus Christ.

We have drawn from the writings of numerous authors whose names and works are mentioned in the bibliography. They have done research from which we benefited and hope to bless you.

James Bryson is our most critical and gifted editor.

Linda Eberle, Harold's wife, spent several months meticulously combing through these pages, ensuring we present to you a well-written and well-documented work.

Many friends read through these pages and added their insights and suggestions.

Thanks to all of you.

Table of Contents

Foreword

It was 1965; I was 13 and had been born-again for about a year when I received a call to the ministry. From that moment on, I became keen to grow in the Lord, and I knew from my pastor that spiritual growth required a knowledge of the Word of God. Thus, I delved into the Bible with all my youthful exuberance, starting at Genesis 1 and setting my sights on Revelation 22.

Fortunately for me, the Book of Revelation comes last in the Bible, so I did not worry too much about the end of the world. It would take care of itself. My pastor, however, thought otherwise. Even though misguided tomes such as *The Late Great Planet Earth, The Left Behind Series*, and *Eighty-Eight Reasons Why the Rapture Will Be in 1988*, had not yet become the canon of modern eschatology, my pastor felt the need to indoctrinate me in all things end times.

Rolling out the current dispensational charts spanning Daniel to Revelation, with a brief detour into Thessalonians, he placed the American Church squarely at the intersection of the Church of Laodicea, the reign of the Antichrist, the decoding of 666, and the choreography of the post-rapture tribulation down to the minute. It was a thorough immersion into a pop-doctrine spiced with Hollywood drama and populated by a cast of sci-fi characters descending from heaven or spewing from hell itself.

From my pastor's well-intentioned teaching, I gleaned that the Church, in spite being inhabited by God and empowered by Holy Spirit, was destined to fail miserably in a sinful world. This necessitated Christ's return to rescue us from the gaping jaws of death, thus narrowly averting Satan's victory lap around our gilded altars. As the rapture whisked us away to the clouds, we would witness the wicked writhing in the wasted world while we worshiped God.

As convincing as this tapestry was—the illustrated charts were impressive—the fundamental logic of a doomsday scenario left me empty and questioning more than I understood. As I delved into the Old Testament prophets and New Testament letters—ignoring an eschatology to match the latest news events—it became clear to me that the biblical writers believed in a church that was not a failure, nor could it ever be. Rather, it was destined to be victorious, not in some future Hail-Mary rescue plan of the ages but in the here-and-now and eternally. The Bride of Christ, the Church, was called to be triumphant in Jesus.

And so, my views evolved counter to the modern dispensational beliefs saturating the Church at the time. I embraced the finished and triumphant work of Christ through His death, burial, ascension, and enthronement, all of which is brilliantly articulated in this Eberle / Trent book, *Victorious Eschatology*.

Today, their book is the primary textbook for our advanced course in eschatology at *Vision International University*. This text presents a robust view of the importance of biblical eschatology, and it does so with integrity and excellent research while providing profound insight into the wonderful work Christ has completed for us through His death and resurrection. It is one of a handful of books I read annually, always gaining new insight, uncovering the treasure of God's revelatory wisdom that He shares with people mature enough to receive it.

This is an excellent work, one that should be part of every leader's library.

Stan E. DeKoven, Ph.D., D.Litt
President, *Vision International University*
Ramona, CA

Introduction

Eschatology refers to the study of end times. The view of eschatology presented in this book reveals that the Kingdom of God will grow and advance until it fills Earth. The Church will rise in unity, maturity, and glory before the return of Jesus. We will present to you a victorious eschatology.

Most of the great leaders throughout Church history held to a victorious eschatology.

However, during the twentieth century, Christians became increasingly skeptical and pessimistic about the future. During World War I, Christians in Europe began to embrace a negative view of the world. Christians in North America followed suit during the Depression and World War II. As the world was thrust face-to-face with challenges and the wickedness of war, people embraced a more negative view of humanity and a pessimistic view of the future.

It was during those trying periods when many Christians embraced a defeatist eschatology. They came to believe that the world is gradually slipping under the influence of wicked leaders and eventually Satan will take control of the economic and religious systems of the world. Preachers who embraced that fatalistic view began to teach that an antichrist figure would soon rise to prominence and then deceive most of humanity. They also taught about a coming great tribulation during which God will pour out His wrath, judging and destroying much of the world.

The pessimistic view did not enter into Christianity in any significant way until the publication of the *Scofield Reference Bible* (1909), which proposed in its footnotes a very negative scenario of future end-time events. Since then, hundreds of frightening end-time books have been promoted within Christianity. The most widely read are the *Left Behind* series, written by Tim LaHaye and Jerry B. Jenkins. Such books and the associated teachings have become so commonly accepted in the modern Church that the negative eschatology has become the most popular view. However, it is important to note that this view has only been popular in Christianity since the 1960s. It reached its zenith of acceptance just before the close of the last millennium when Christians became fascinated with the possibility of the world ending in the year 2000.

Now that we are well into the new millennium, Christians are lifting their eyes to the future. Many leaders are discovering that the Scriptures give us a more optimistic view than they previously had believed. They are embracing a victorious eschatology that teaches that Jesus Christ and His Church are to reign over this world, not Satan.

The theological label used to refer to the victorious eschatology presented in this book is the *partial preterist view*. In contrast, today's popular view is called the *futurist view*.

Eschatological View	Theological Name
Victorious View	Partial Preterist View
Popular View	Futurist View

These theological labels, the partial preterist view and the futurist view, refer to when the prophecies in Matthew 24 and the book of Revelation are fulfilled.

The word "preterist" comes from the Latin *praeteritus*, meaning "that which has passed." So, the partial preterist view sees part of the prophecies in Matthew 24 and part of the book of Revelation as already fulfilled.

In contrast, adherents of the futurist view see virtually all the prophecies in Matthew 24 and the book of Revelation as waiting to be fulfilled in the future—hence, the label "futurist."

Eschatological View	Theological Name	Matt. 24 & Revelation
Victorious View	Partial Preterist View	Part Past, Part Future
Popular View	Futurist View	All Future

In the pages to follow, we will explain and contrast these views. Section One will go through the prophecies recorded in Matthew 24. Section Two will discuss some issues that are key in considering the partial preterist view. Section Three will study the prophecies in chapters 2 and 9 of the book of Daniel. Section Four will work through the book of Revelation. Then Sections Five, Six, and Seven will present the partial preterist views concerning the Jews, the antichrist, and the rapture. Finally, Section Eight will clarify what is meant by "the end times."

As pastors, we (Harold Eberle and Martin Trench) used to believe and teach the futurist view. However, even as we taught our church congregations the related ideas, we both realized that many Scriptures simply do not fit into the scenario of events proposed by the futurists. After several years of in-depth study, we came to believe that the partial preterist view is more faithful to the Scriptures. We will show you this in the following pages.

In addition to studying specific Bible passages, we will insert quotes from well-known preachers, teachers, and reformers that show how those fathers of the faith shared a victorious eschatology. Some of those fathers envisioned difficult times and challenges ahead. However, most believed the Church would overcome even in difficult times. They believed the Church will rise in victory and power before the return of Jesus Christ.[2]

2. For readers not familiar with the fathers of the faith who are quoted, a brief biography of each is given in Appendix A.

Origen of Alexandria

It is evident that . . . every form of worship will be destroyed except the religion of Christ, which will alone prevail. And indeed it will one day triumph, as its principles take possession of the minds of men more and more every day.

Origen Against Celsus, 1660, 8:68

John Wesley

All unprejudiced persons may see with their eyes, that he [God] is already renewing the face of the earth: And we have strong reason to hope that the work he hath begun he will carry on unto the day of the Lord Jesus; that he will never intermit this blessed work of his Spirit until he has fulfilled all his promises, until he hath put a period to sin and misery, and infirmity, and death; and re-established universal holiness and happiness, and caused all the inhabitants of the earth to sing together "Hallelujah."

The Works of John Wesley, 1985, 499

Jonathan Edwards

The visible kingdom of Satan shall be overthrown, and the kingdom of Christ set up on the ruins of it, everywhere throughout the whole habitable globe.

The Works of Jonathan Edwards, 1974, 488

Section One

Understanding Matthew 24

In this section, we will study Matthew 24, a passage known as the "Olivet Discourse" because Jesus gave this teaching to His disciples while they were gathered on the Mount of Olives just outside of Jerusalem.

We will begin in Matthew 24:3, where the disciples asked Jesus some key questions:

> *As He was sitting on the Mount of Olives, the disciples came to Him privately, saying, "Tell us, when will these things happen, and what will be the sign of Your coming, and of the end of the age?"*

In the verses that follow this one, our Lord gave answers to these questions. How you understand His answers determines what you believe about the end times, the tribulation, the antichrist, and the unfolding of all future events.

Introduction to Matthew 24

After the disciples asked Jesus their questions in Matthew 24:3, Jesus answered by talking about false leaders claiming to be Christ, wars, earthquakes, famines, persecutions, and people falling away from the faith. He also spoke about the gospel being preached worldwide, followed by destruction, tribulation, and people being taken away.

Christians who believe the futurist view study our Lord's answers and conclude that all the events listed will happen in the future, shortly before the end of the world.

Partial preterists come to very different conclusions when studying Matthew 24. We will go through Matthew 24, verse by verse, to explain, but first, we need to clearly identify the questions Jesus' disciples asked Him:

> *And as He was sitting on the Mount of Olives, the disciples came to Him privately, saying, "Tell us, when will these things happen, and what will be the sign of Your coming, and of the end of the age?"*
>
> —Matt. 24:3

Some translations, e.g., *King James Version*, end this verse with "end of the world" because the word *aion*, which is used in the original Greek, may be translated as "age" or "world." Using the term "world," futurist teachers summarize the questions asked by the disciples into an inquiry about the second coming of Jesus and the end of the world. Therefore, when Jesus gives His answers in the verses that follow, all His comments are thought to be about the short period leading up to the end of the world.

In contrast, partial preterist teachers begin by noting that in Matthew 24:3, the disciples asked Jesus three questions, not just one:

Question #1: *"When will these things happen?"*

Question #2: *"What will be the sign of Your coming?"*

Question #3: *"What about the end of the age?"*

Recognizing three distinct questions dramatically changes how we understand the answers Jesus gave in the verses that follow. We will see how our Lord answered question one in Matthew 24:4–28. Then He answered the second question in Matthew 24:29–35. Finally, He answered the question about the end of the age in Matthew 24:36–25:46.

Question #1: "When Will These Things Happen?"

The first question that the disciples asked Jesus was, *"When will these things happen?"* Before we look at Jesus' answer, we need to identify what are *"these things"* about which the disciples were asking.

Christians who have been taught the futurist view immediately think that *"these things"* refer to the events that will precede the second coming of Jesus and the end of the world. We will come to a different understanding if we read the context of this Bible passage.

To understand the context, we must back up and read Matthew 23. There we read about Jesus speaking in the Jewish Temple in Jerusalem. First, He warned the crowds and His disciples to watch out for the scribes and Pharisees (vv. 2–12). Then, beginning in Matthew 23:13, Jesus turned from the disciples and directed His words directly toward the Jewish religious leaders. We can sense the intensity of His message by glancing at the first few words of each verse that follows:

> *But woe to you, scribes and Pharisees, hypocrites.*
>
> —v. 13
>
> *Woe to you, scribes and Pharisees, hypocrites.*
>
> —v. 15
>
> *Woe to you, blind guides.*
>
> —v. 16
>
> *You fools and blind men!*
>
> —v. 17

Jesus was rebuking the religious leaders right there in their Temple. Glance down a few verses and pick up the intensity of His rebuke as He continued:

> *Woe to you, scribes and Pharisees, hypocrites!*
>
> —v. 23
>
> *You blind guides.*
>
> —v. 24

> *Woe to you, scribes and Pharisees, hypocrites!*
> —v. 25
>
> *You blind Pharisee.*
> —v. 26
>
> *Woe to you, scribes and Pharisees, hypocrites!*
> —v. 27
>
> *Woe to you, scribes and Pharisees, hypocrites!*
> —v. 29

Jesus built up to a climax in which He declared a severe judgment against those religious leaders:

> *You serpents, you brood of vipers, how will you escape the sentence of hell? . . . upon you may fall the guilt of all the righteous blood shed on earth, from the blood of righteous Abel to the blood of Zechariah, the son of Berechiah, whom you murdered between the temple and the altar. Truly I say to you, all these things will come upon this generation.*
> —Matt. 23:33–36

At that moment, you would not have wanted to be standing among the scribes and Pharisees.

Jesus declared a coming judgment. He referred to the blood of every righteous person, from Abel to Zechariah. That is significant because Abel is in the first book of the Hebrew Bible and Zechariah is in the last book. Jesus was saying to the religious leaders that the judgment for the blood of every righteous person—from the beginning of their Holy Book to the end—would come upon them and on their generation! Judgment had been decreed!

Typically, we understand a generation to be about 40 years long, e.g., the Hebrew people wandered in the wilderness for 40 years until a generation passed away.[3] So, if Jesus' words were to come true, then we should expect the judgment He

3. The word "generation" can mean different things in different contexts of the Bible. Some Bible teachers will argue that it can mean 30 or 35 years; or a generation may refer to the people living during that time, which means the judgment Jesus decreed in Matthew 23 and 24 would happen during the lifetime of the people to whom Jesus was speaking.

declared to have fallen upon some of those religious leaders who were listening to His words.

In Matthew 23, Jesus went on to tell more specifically how the judgment was to occur. In verses 37 and 38, He cried out:

> *Jerusalem, Jerusalem, who kills the prophets and stones those who are sent to her! How often I wanted to gather your children together, the way a hen gathers her chicks under her wings, and you were unwilling. Behold, your house is being left to you desolate!*

Jesus declared this while standing in the Temple in Jerusalem. He cried out to the scribes and Pharisees, saying that destruction would come upon them, their city, and their Temple.

John Chrysostom

So now a punishment is appointed, one that brings exceeding dread and implies the overthrow of the entire city.

The Gospel of Matthew, Homily 74.3

The Jewish Holocaust of AD 70

Did the words of Jesus come true? Historically, did anything happen? Yes, in AD 70, Jerusalem was destroyed. Within 40 years after Jesus declared judgment, 20,000 Roman soldiers surrounded the city and cut off all supplies of food so the people would starve. Then, the soldiers, under the command of General Titus, came into the city and mercilessly killed more than one million Jews. The soldiers set the Temple on fire and led away 97,000 Jews as captives.[4]

At that time, the Jewish population was decimated. It was not until AD 130–135 that they began reassembling with enough strength to attempt one last rebellion against Rome. Then, after three years of battling, the Romans were able to crush that rebellion by killing 580,000 Jews, and Israel was no longer recognized as a nation until 1948. It was also at that time that the Roman commander ordered the Temple in Jerusalem to be demolished so completely that each and every stone was carried away, and the land upon which the Temple had stood was plowed over. The Temple was destroyed, as Jesus said it would be.[5]

Historians have a good number of documents from that period that give us information about the destruction of the Temple and Jerusalem. However, most of our information comes from Josephus, a Jewish historian (not Christian) who was employed by the Roman government during that time to watch and record what took place. Concerning the war and destruction of Jerusalem, Josephus wrote many things, including the following:

> When they [the Roman soldiers] were come to the houses to plunder them, they found in them entire families of dead men . . . that is of such as died by the famine; they then stood in a horror at this sight, and went out without touching anything. But although they had this commiseration for such as were destroyed in that manner, yet had they not the same for those that were still alive, but they ran every one through whom they met with, and obstructed the very lanes with their dead bodies, and made the whole city run with blood, to such a degree indeed

4. Flavius Josephus, *Josephus: The Complete Works*. Translated by William Whiston (Nashville, TN: Thomas Nelson Publishers, 1998), *The Wars of the Jews*, VI.ix.iii.

5. Today's Western Wall (also called the Wailing Wall) in Jerusalem was never a part of the Temple that existed in Jesus' day. It was a part of the parapet that King Herod had built around the Temple.

that the fire of many of the houses was quenched with these men's blood.[6]

It is worth reading all of Josephus' writings about the fall of Jerusalem.[7] What is so astounding about them is how clearly—sometimes word for word—they fulfilled the prophecy of Jesus in Matthew 23 and 24.

Eusebius

All this occurred in this manner in the second year of the reign of Vespasian [A.D. 70], according to the predictions of our Lord and Saviour Jesus Christ.

Ecclesiastical History, III:7

John Wesley

This was most punctually fulfilled: for after the temple was burned, Titus, the Roman general, ordered the very foundations of it to be dug up; after which the ground on which it stood was ploughed by Turnus Rufus . . . this generation of men now living shall not pass till all these things be done—The expression implies that a great part of that generation would be passed away, but not the whole. Just so it was; for the city and temple were destroyed thirty-nine or forty years after.

The Works of John Wesley, 1985

6. Josephus, *Wars*, 1998, VI.viii.v.

7. The writings of Josephus are available in many places, including Google-Books: https://www.google.com/books/edition/The_New_Complete_Works_of_Josephus/kyaoIb6k2ccC?hl=en&gbpv=1&dq=Josephus:+The+Complete+Works&printsec=frontcover

The Context of Matthew 24

We will discuss the destruction of Jerusalem and the Temple more fully later, but here we are noting the context in which Matthew 24 begins. We know that there were no chapter breaks in the original Greek manuscripts of the New Testament (NT). Matthew 23 flowed right into Matthew 24 with no interruption. So, right after Jesus declared the coming destruction of Jerusalem and the Temple, Matthew tells us:

> *Jesus came out from the temple area and was going away when His disciples came up to point out the temple buildings to Him. And He said to them, "Do you not see all these things? Truly I say to you, not one stone here will be left upon another, which will not be torn down."*
>
> —Matt. 24:1–2

After repeating that the Temple would be completely demolished, Jesus walked away from the Temple, and His disciples followed Him. Then the next verse starts off saying:

> *And as He was sitting on the Mount of Olives . . .*
>
> —Matt. 24:3

The Mount of Olives is the mountain ridge just outside and east of Jerusalem. As Jesus sat down with His disciples, they were looking right at the Temple from which they had just exited.[8]

Put yourself in the disciples' shoes. What would you have asked if you had been sitting there with Jesus? The judgment that Jesus had just decreed over Jerusalem and the Temple was at the forefront of the disciples' minds. The disciples asked:

> *Tell us, when will these things happen . . . ?*
>
> —Matt. 24:3

8. This is confirmed in Mark 13, where the Olivet Discourse is also recorded, but there we are specifically told in verse 3 that Jesus and His disciples were facing the Temple when they asked their first question.

They were asking, "When will Jerusalem and the Temple be destroyed?"

As we mentioned earlier, futurist teachers assume that the disciples were asking about the end of the world. However, it was not until the third question that they asked Jesus about the end. The reason that they asked about the end at the same time that they asked about the Temple being destroyed was probably because, in their Jewish minds, what Jesus had just predicted was so cataclysmic that they must have wondered if it would be the end of the world. They were shocked at the thought of God's holy Temple being destroyed. How could life go on without it? Could it possibly coincide with the end of the world? If not, when would that occur?

We will examine our Lord's answers to the second and third questions later. Here, we need to realize that the first question the disciples asked Jesus was, "When will these things—Jerusalem and the Temple—be destroyed?"

Charles Spurgeon

The disciples enquired first about the time of the destruction of the temple . . .

The Gospel of the Kingdom, 1974, 212

Within a Generation

As we study our Lord's answers, keep in mind His time frame. Jesus said that Jerusalem and the Temple would be destroyed within a generation. He repeated that time frame in Matthew 24:34, saying:

> *Truly I say to you, this generation will not pass away until all these things take place.*

Can we accept these words of Jesus literally? Yes!

Futurist teachers see all the events that Jesus prophesied in Matthew 24 happening not by AD 70 but over 2,000 years later, sometime in our future. Therefore, they cannot accept the time frame of *"within a generation"* which Jesus declared in two separate passages (Matt. 23:36 and 24:34). Some futurist teachers will explain their position by redefining the word "generation" to mean "race." Hence, they can say that the race of Jewish people will not pass away before the end of the world. Others claim that the generation about which Jesus was talking was the generation that would see all the end-time events listed in Matthew 24:4–33—that generation will not pass away until Jesus returns.

We believe, as Charles Spurgeon did (as shown above in the quotation from Spurgeon), that everything Jesus prophesied between Matthew 23:36 and Matthew 24:34 took place precisely as He declared during the generation that was alive when Jesus declared those words. This is what we will explain in the following pages.

Origen of Alexandria

I challenge anyone to prove my statement untrue if I say that the entire Jewish nation was destroyed less than one whole generation later on account of these sufferings which they inflicted on Jesus. For it was, I believe, forty-two years from the time when they crucified Jesus to the destruction of Jerusalem.

Origen Against Celsus, IV:XXII

Jesus Answers the First Question

Jesus gave His answer to the first question in Matthew 24:4–28. We have not randomly chosen these verses as the verses in which Jesus answered the disciples' first question. As we proceed, we will show you the clear breaks given within the context of Matthew 24. Also, we will later examine Luke 21 and Mark 13, which also record the Olivet Discourse, but leave no doubt that the first question is being answered in these verses. Now let us examine, verse by verse, our Lord's answer to the question concerning when Jerusalem and the Temple will be destroyed.

Matthew 24:4 & 5: Many Claiming to Be Christ

Jesus began answering, saying:

> *See to it that no one misleads you. For many will come in My name, saying, 'I am the Christ,' and will mislead many.*
>
> —Matt. 24:4b–5

Christians who have heard only the futurist view immediately place these words of Jesus in the future, shortly before the end of the world. Futurists are looking for some evil leader or several leaders to start claiming that they are the Christ.

That is the first error we need to correct. Jesus was answering the question concerning when Jerusalem and the Temple would be destroyed. That event happened in AD 70, within the generation of the people to whom Jesus was speaking and within 40 years of the time Jesus prophesied it. Jesus told His disciples that soon many people would come claiming to be the Christ. For Jesus' words to be fulfilled, those imposters would have had to come in the first century.

Did that happen historically? Yes. Right after the death of Jesus, many leaders arose, capturing the hearts of the Jewish people. That may seem difficult for us to understand today, but we need to keep in mind the culture of that day. The Jewish people were desperately looking for a Messiah—someone to free them from Roman domination. Their hope and religious system were based on a coming Messiah.

When Jesus died, many of His followers gave up believing that He was the Messiah. Other leaders quickly arose, drawing large followings.

Eusebius

After the Lord was taken up into heaven the demons put forth a number of men who claimed to be gods.

The History of the Church, 1965, II:13

The Venerable Bede

For many came forward, when destruction was hanging over Jerusalem, saying that they were Christs.

Cited in *Thomas Aquinas' Golden Chain*, 1956

John Wesley

And, indeed, never did so many imposters appear in the world as a few years before the destruction of Jerusalem, undoubtedly because that was the time wherein the Jews in general expected the Messiah.

Wesley's Notes on the Bible–The New Testament, 2017, 40

Charles Spurgeon

A large number of imposters came forward before the destruction of Jerusalem, giving out that they were the anointed of God . . .

The Gospel of the Kingdom, 1974, 213

Matthew 24:6 & 7: Wars and Rumors of War

Jesus continued telling His disciples what signs would precede the destruction of Jerusalem and the Temple:

> *You will be hearing of wars and rumors of wars . . . For nation will rise against nation, and kingdom against kingdom . . .*
>
> —Matt. 24:6–7

Approximately 2,000 years ago when Jesus was sitting on the Mount of Olives, He prophesied of coming wars, even though there were no signs of *"wars and rumors of wars"* at that time. Rome's power seemed stable, strong, irresistible, and permanent. Historically, the period was referred to as *Pax Romana*, that is, "Roman Peace." Of course, the enemies of Rome would not have spoken of the time so graciously, but Rome was securely established in that region of the world. It was at that time that Jesus prophesied of coming wars.

Did the prophecy of Jesus come true within that generation? Indeed, wars broke out all over the Empire. Within 18 months, four emperors in Rome were violently murdered. Civil war broke out in the city of Rome. Then, in AD 66, 50,000 Jews were killed in Alexandria. Another 50,000 Jews were slain in Seleucia and 20,000 in Caesarea. It was a time of great turmoil, with constant rumors of new rebellions.

Matthew 24:7: Famines

Jesus then told His disciples the next sign to look for:

> *And in various places there will be famines and earthquakes.*
>
> —Matt. 24:7b

Did famines occur during the generation of the disciples? Acts 11 tells us about the *"great famine."*

> *One of them, named Agabus, stood up and indicated by the Spirit that there would definitely be a severe famine all over the world. And this took place in the reign of Claudius.*
>
> —Acts 11:28

As a result of that famine, we can read two places in the NT where Christians took offerings to collect money for believers suffering in the region of Judah (Acts 11:29–30; 1 Cor. 16:1–3).

The historian Josephus wrote about the devastation of that period:

> But the famine was too hard for all other passions, and it is destructive to nothing so much as to modesty . . . insomuch that children pulled the very morsels that their fathers were eating out of their very mouths, and what was still more to be pitied, so did the mothers do as to their infants; and when those that were most dear were perishing under their hands, they were not ashamed to take from them the very last drops that might preserve their lives . . . but the seditious everywhere came upon them immediately, and snatched away from them what they had gotten from others; for when they saw any house shut up, this was to them a signal that the people within had gotten some food; whereupon they broke open the doors, and ran in and took pieces of what they were eating, almost up out of their very throats, and

> this by force; the old men, who held their food fast, were beaten; and if the women hid what they had within their hands, their hair was torn for so doing; nor was there any commiseration shown either to the aged or to the infants, but they lifted up children from the ground as they hung upon the morsels they had gotten, and shook them down upon the floor.[9]

Knowing about this famine and the destruction of Jerusalem to follow, Jesus said to the women of Jerusalem:

> *Daughters of Jerusalem, stop weeping for Me, but weep for yourselves and for your children. For behold, the days are coming when they will say, "Blessed are those who cannot bare, and the wombs that have not given birth, and the breasts that have not nursed."*
>
> —Luke 23:28–29

Eusebius

In his [Claudius'] time famine descended on the whole world, a fact which writers whose point of view is very different from our own have recorded in their histories.

The History of the Church, 1965, II:8

Matthew 24:7: Earthquakes

Jesus then told His disciples about the coming earthquakes:

> *In various places there will be famines and earthquakes.*
>
> —Matt. 24:7b

Not only did the earth quake when Jesus died on the cross (Matt. 27:51–52) and again when He rose from the dead (Matt.

9. Josephus, *Wars,* 1998, V.x.iii.

28:2), but history also tells us that the few years just previous to the fall of Jerusalem was a time of unusually high seismic activity. The most well-known earthquake was the destruction of Pompeii in AD 62. The writers of the period also tell us about earthquakes at Colossae, Smyrna, Miletus, Chios, Laodicea, Samos, Hierapolis, Campania, Crete, Rome, and Judea.[10]

Matthew 24:8: Birth Pangs

But all these things are merely the beginning of birth pains.
—Matt. 24:8

It is common today for people trained in the futurist view to look at present-day natural disasters and claim that they are signs of the imminent return of Jesus, yet that is not what Jesus said. He was clear that these signs would happen within that generation; furthermore, they would *not* be signs of the end of the world but *"merely the beginning of birth pangs."* These birth pangs were to precede the destruction of Jerusalem and the Temple.

John Chrysostom

He speaks of the preludes to the troubles of the Jews. "All this is but the beginning of the birth pangs," that is, of the troubles that will befall them.

The Ancient Christian Commentary, 2002, Ib:190

10. J. Marcellus Kik, *An Eschatology of Victory*, (Phillipsburg, New Jersey: Presbyterian and Reformed Publishing Co., 1971), 93; David B. Currie, *Rapture*, (Manchester, NH: Sophis Institute Press, 2003), 159.

Matthew 24:9: Persecution

Still answering the disciples' first question about when Jerusalem and the Temple will be destroyed, Jesus said:

> *Then they will hand you over to tribulation, and will kill you, and you will be hated by all nations because of My name.*
>
> —Matt. 24:9

The Jewish religious leaders instigated the first persecution. Saul was among those leaders who oversaw the men who were putting Christians to death. The book of Acts describes that persecution, saying:

> *And on that day a great persecution began against the church in Jerusalem, and they were all scattered throughout the regions of Judea and Samaria, except for the apostles.*
>
> —Acts 8:1

That *"great persecution"* spread, and soon, government officials such as King Herod got involved (Acts 12:1).

The persecution became even more intense in AD 64. That was the year when more than one-third of the city of Rome burned to the ground. The significance of that event is difficult for modern people to grasp. If we compared it with the destruction of the Twin Towers in New York City in 2001, the fire in Rome was far more devastating.

Rome was considered the center of the civilized world, and more than one-third of the city was destroyed. Nero, who was the emperor at that time, blamed Christians for that terrible fire, and then he began what Church historians call "The Great Persecution." The historian Tacitus (c. AD 55–120) wrote how thousands of Christians were tortured, being covered in animal skins and then torn to death by dogs, or being nailed to crosses, or covered in tar and then lit on fire to illuminate Nero's gardens while he entertained guests in the evenings.[11]

Matthew 24:10–13: Apostasy and False Prophets

The next sign Jesus told the disciples to look for was described like this:

> *At that time many will fall away and will betray one another and hate one another. Many false prophets will arise and will mislead many. Because lawlessness is increased, most people's love will grow cold. But the one who endures to the end, he will be saved.*
>
> —Matt. 24:10–13

Soon after the death of our Lord, false prophets began appearing on the scene. Several times, Paul warned his followers to watch out for the false prophets. John explained that during his lifetime, *"many false prophets have gone out into the world"* (1 John 4:1). Similarly, Peter warned, *"But false prophets also appeared among the people, just as there will also be false teachers among you, who will secretly introduce destructive heresies . . ."* (2 Peter 2:1).

The first major group was the Judaizers, who taught that Gentiles had to become Jewish proselytes and adhere to the Law of Moses as well as have faith in Christ. Then came the Gnostics. They arose as soon as Christians brought the gospel to Greek-minded people, but by AD 150, about one-third of all Christians were involved in Gnosticism. To grasp the influence of this heresy, imagine how it would be today if a certain false teaching captured one-third of all Christians in your community. That is what happened during those early days when the Church was struggling to survive.

Since understanding Gnosticism is key to understanding

11. Cornelius Tacitus, *The Annals of Imperial Rome* (New York: Penguin Books, 1989), XV, 44.

the problems of the first and second-century Church, we will discuss it in more depth in Section Six.

Matthew 24:14: Preaching the Gospel

What about the sign Jesus told His disciples about in Matthew 24:14?

> *This gospel of the kingdom shall be preached in the whole world as a testimony to all the nations, and then the end will come.*

If you have been trained under the futurist view, you will think of this verse being fulfilled at some future time. This verse is often quoted among futurists to encourage Christians to help spread the gospel around the world so that Jesus can return.

Let us show you another way to understand this Scripture. Jesus said that all the events He spoke would happen in *that* generation. If we are going to believe the words of Jesus literally, then we must consider how this verse could have been fulfilled in the first century.

Any serious study of Scripture must apply the foundational principles of biblical study, one being that other Bible passages that talk about the same topics should be examined before drawing any conclusions about what a specific passage means. In this way, we allow the Bible to interpret itself with fewer misunderstandings due to our own biases and cultural influences.

For us to understand Matthew 24:14, it will be helpful to find out if other Bible passages talk about the gospel being preached to the whole world. If you do this in your study, you will discover five other passages that address this subject. Amazingly, all five passages reveal to us how the gospel was proclaimed to all nations within the generation of the apostles.

Let us look at those five passages.

Examine the words of Paul in Romans 1:8:

> *First, I thank my God through Jesus Christ for you all, because your faith is being proclaimed throughout the whole world.*

Did you catch that? Their faith *is being proclaimed*—in Paul's lifetime—throughout the whole world.

Paul makes this even more evident in Romans 10:18:

> *But I say, surely they have never heard, have they? On the contrary: "Their voice has gone out into all the earth, and their words to the ends of the world."*

Paul repeats this in Romans 16:25–26:

> *According to my gospel and the preaching of Jesus Christ . . . has been made known to all the nations . . .*

Paul tells us this again in Colossians 1:5–6:

> *The gospel which has come to you, just as in all the world also it is bearing fruit and increasing . . .*

There it is again. The gospel was bearing fruit in all the world—in Paul's lifetime.

Finally, let us look at the most explicit statement Paul made on this subject:

> *If indeed you continue in the faith firmly established and steadfast, and not shifting from the hope of the gospel that you have heard, which was proclaimed in all creation under heaven, and of which I, Paul, was made a minister.*
>
> —Col. 1:23

Could Paul have stated it any clearer? The gospel was proclaimed *"in all creation under heaven."*

As people read these passages, they may wonder if the words *"whole world," "ends of the world," "all the world,"* and *"all creation under heaven"* really mean the whole world in the way we understand today. Some may question if these words perhaps meant the world as far as the disciples knew it or just the Roman Empire.

In these passages, two different Greek words have been translated into the word "world." Paul used the Greek word *kosmos* in Romans 1:8 and Colossians 1:6. The word *kosmos* can be translated as "world" or "earth," but either way, it includes the entire world. The other Greek word for world is *oikoumene,* which can be translated "inhabited earth" or "civilized earth." In NT times, among Greek-speaking people, *oikoumene* was often used to refer to the Roman Empire because citizens of the Empire only considered the Empire civilized. Paul used this word in Romans 10:18 when he declared that the Word had gone out *"to the ends of the world."* Jesus also used this word, *oikoumene,* in Matthew 24:14. Hence, we understand that Jesus' original declaration was that the disciples would have time to preach the gospel of the Kingdom to the civilized world.

However we look at it, the words of Jesus were fulfilled within the generation of the first disciples. They did turn the world upside down.

John Chrysostom

You will preach everywhere . . . Then he added, "This gospel of the kingdom will be preached throughout the whole world, as a testimony to all nations; and the end will come." The sign of this final end time will be the downfall of Jerusalem.

The Ancient Christian Commentary, 2002, Ib:191

Eusebius

The teaching of the new covenant was borne to all nations, and at once the Romans besieged Jerusalem and destroyed it and the Temple.

The Ante-Nicene Fathers, 1989, *First Apology*, XXXIX

Justin Martyr

From Jerusalem there went out into the world, men, twelve in number . . . by the power of God they proclaimed to every race of men that they were sent by Christ to teach to all the word of God.

The Ante-Nicene Fathers, 1989, *First Apology*, XXXIX

Charles Spurgeon

There was a sufficient interval for the full proclamation of the gospel by the apostles and evangelists of the early Christian Church, and for the gathering out of those who recognized the crucified Christ as the true Messiah. Then came the awful end which the Saviour foresaw and foretold, and the prospect of which wrung from his lips and heart the sorrowful lament that followed his prophecy of the doom awaiting his guilty capital.

Spurgeon's Popular Exposition of Matthew, 1979, 211

After the disciples preached the gospel successfully, Jesus said, *"And then the end will come"* (Matt. 24:14). What end was He referring to? Remember, He was answering their question, "When will Jerusalem and the Temple be destroyed?" That is the "end" of which Jesus was speaking. Indeed, that destruction is what Jesus talked about in the following verses.

Matthew 24:15–20: Warning of Destruction

Jesus told the disciples that after they successfully preached the gospel, they needed to be ready to flee from Judea because destruction was about to occur:

> *Therefore when you see the abomination of desolation which was spoken of through Daniel the prophet, standing in the holy place (let the reader understand), then those who are in Judea must flee to the mountains. Whoever is on the housetop must not go down to get the things that are in his house. Whoever is in the field must not turn back to get his cloak. But woe to those women who are pregnant and to those who are nursing babies in those days! But pray that your flight will not be in the winter, or on a Sabbath.*
>
> —Matt. 24:15–20

Christians trained in the futurist view envision this passage being fulfilled in our future before the end of the world. Typically, they think of the abomination of desolation as the antichrist who will walk into the Temple (one that will be built in the near future) in Jerusalem, set up an idol of himself, and declare himself as God. That event is thought to begin a terrible worldwide tribulation.

To understand this passage from the view of the partial preterist, note that Jesus is talking about tragic events that will happen, not throughout the world, but right there in Jerusalem and the surrounding area of Judea. We know this because He is talking to His disciples and answering their question about when Jerusalem and the Temple will be destroyed. Jesus said that when the abomination of desolation (which we will define below) stands in the holy place, the people *"in Judea"* are to run to the mountains. He did not say that people all over the world should flee, but only those in Judea.

Further, we know that Jesus was addressing His warning to the Jews, for He warned people to pray that their flight may not be on the Sabbath—a warning that is particularly relevant to Jewish people, as they kept the Sabbath in a fashion that did not allow them to work or run—even in the event of a tragedy.

Also, He said that people on their housetops must not go into their houses to get their possessions; that, too, indicates that He was talking about people in that region of the world, for houses in Jerusalem often were constructed in a way in which people could gather on their rooftops. Jesus' warning tells us nothing about people living outside of Judea. Jesus was speaking of something terrible about to happen in Judea, and nothing in the passage indicates a worldwide event.

Parallel Passages in Mark 13 & Luke 21

To confirm that Jesus was speaking in Matthew 24:15–20 of events to happen around Jerusalem and Judea, it is helpful to glance at the Gospels of Mark and Luke, where the Olivet Discourse is also recorded. In looking at these parallel passages, it is worth noting how closely they correspond with Matthew 24.

1. Jesus exposed the wickedness of the Jewish religious leaders (Matt. 23:1–35; Mark 12: 38–40; Luke 20:45–47).
2. Jesus declared the Temple's destruction (Matt. 23:37–24:2; Mark 13:1–2; Luke 21:5–6).
3. The disciples questioned Jesus about the coming destruction (Matt. 24:3; Mark 13:3–4; Luke 21:7).

4. Jesus answered, talking about:
   - people claiming to be Christ (Matt. 24:5; Mark 13:5–6; Luke 21:8)
   - wars and rumors of war (Matt. 24:6–7; Mark 13:7–8; Luke 21:9–10)
   - earthquakes and famines (Matt. 24:7; Mark 13:8; Luke 21:11)
   - and the gospel being preached all over the world (Matt. 24:14; Mark 13:10)

These passages are amazingly similar, although each writer used slightly different terminology. This may have resulted from the different writers recording what they each remembered or considered most important. The differences also could be the result of different occasions on which Jesus talked about this subject. Several times, they were in the area of the Temple in Jerusalem, and Jesus would have had other opportunities to talk about the incredible destruction that was about to occur. Whatever the reasons for the slight differences, Jesus' answers were very similar in each of the three Gospel accounts.

After Jesus talked about the signs that would take place, He continued in each Gospel to warn that people would have to flee from Judea. Let us examine the accounts in the three parallel passages:

> *Therefore when you see the abomination of desolation which was spoken of through Daniel the prophet, standing in the holy place (let the reader understand), then those who are in Judea must flee to the mountains.*
>
> —Matt. 24:15–16

> *But when you see Jerusalem surrounded by armies, then recognize that her desolation is near. Then those who are in Judea must flee to the mountains . . .*
>
> —Luke 21:20–21

> *Now when you see the* <u>*abomination of desolation*</u> *standing where it should not be—let the reader understand—then those who are in Judea must flee to the mountains.*
>
> —Mark 13:14

Notice that in all three passages, Jesus clearly states that the people in Judea are to flee. Nowhere in any of the passages does He speak of or refer to any broader region.

The Abomination in the Holy Place

Now, we need to examine what Jesus was referring to when He warned the disciples about an *"abomination of desolation"* standing in the holy place.

As mentioned earlier, futurist teachers assume that the abomination is the antichrist who will set up an idol in a future temple or actually step into that temple and declare himself as God.

To see how unfounded that understanding is, note that the antichrist is never mentioned in Matthew 24 (or in any of the Gospels). Also, note that Jesus was talking to His disciples and telling them that they would witness this event. Jesus was not talking about an antichrist who would come hundreds or even thousands of years later, but rather some abomination that would be seen in their lifetime.

Next, we can identify where the abomination was to stand. Matthew refers to the *"holy place,"* and Luke refers to *"Jerusalem."* Which author is correct? Both! When Matthew mentions the holy place, he was referring to the same location as Luke when he referred to Jerusalem.

We can confirm this by examining the terminology *"holy place,"* which has been translated from the Greek words *hagios topos.* This terminology is never used anywhere in the Bible to refer to the Temple or the holy of holies in the Temple. As anyone with a Greek dictionary can learn, the word *hagios* means holy, and the word *topos* refers to a locality. It is used in expressions such as a "desert place" but never in reference to a building.

Since Luke referred to the holy place as *"Jerusalem,"* it follows that Jesus referred to Jerusalem in the parallel passage in Matthew 24.

Next, what is the abomination of desolation? When we speak of an abomination, we are referring to a horrible, detestable, unholy thing. Luke tells us that the abomination was the armies surrounding Jerusalem. What could be more detestable to Jewish people? The heathen armies would gather to make the holy city a desolation.

John Chrysostom

[T]he abomination of desolation means the army by which the holy city of Jerusalem was made desolate.

Cited in *Present Truth Lifestyle: Daniel in Babylon* by Scantelbury

Does this correspond with historical evidence? Perfectly! As we have noted, in the year AD 70, 20,000 Roman soldiers lined the mountains around Jerusalem, surrounding the holy city.

This description also matches the one we read in Daniel 9. Remember that Jesus referred in Matthew 24:15 to the abomination of desolation *"about which Daniel spoke."* We will examine the book of Daniel later (Section Three), but here note Daniel's reference to the abomination:

> *And the people of the prince who is to come will destroy the city and the sanctuary. And its end will come with a flood; even to the end there will be war; desolations are determined.*
>
> —Dan. 9:26

Indeed, the soldiers came to destroy Jerusalem. They starved the people; then they descended upon the city as a flood pouring into the valley.

Fleeing Jerusalem and Judea

When the abomination—that is, the Roman soldiers—began lining the mountains around Jerusalem, there was a short time during which people could flee. Hence, we can understand our Lord's exhortation for those on the housetops not to go down to get their possessions or those in the field to return to get their cloaks. Jesus was telling them that they must flee immediately. After those Christians in Jerusalem escaped, the Roman soldiers sealed off the city. No one else was allowed to go in or out. The Romans cut Jerusalem off so the people would starve. Josephus, who was there watching these events, wrote:

> So all hope of escaping was now cut off from the Jews, together with their liberty of going out of the city. Then did the famine widen its progress, and devoured the people by whole houses and families; the upper rooms were full of women and children that were dying by famine; and the lanes of the city were full of the dead bodies of the aged; the children also and the young men wandered about the marketplaces like shadows, all swelled with the famine, and fell down dead, wheresoever their misery seized them.[12]

Historically, we know that the early disciples fled Jerusalem before the destruction of the city. Why did they flee? Because they remembered the warning that Jesus gave them, that the city would be surrounded by armies and they must flee to escape the devastation to follow.

12. Josephus, *Wars*, 1998, V.xii.iii.

The Venerable Bede

[W]hen on the approach of the war with Rome and the extermination of the Jewish people, all the Christians who were in that province, warned by the prophecy, fled far away, as Church history relates, and retiring beyond Jordan, remained for a time in the city of Pella.

Cited in *Present Truth Lifestyle: Daniel in Babylon* by Scantelbury

Charles Spurgeon

The Christians in Jerusalem and the surrounding towns and villages, "in Judea", availed themselves of the first opportunity for eluding the Roman armies, and fled to the mountain city of Pella, in Perea, where they were preserved from the general destruction which overthrew the Jews. There was no time to spare before the final investment of the guilty city; the man "on the house-top" could "not come down to take anything out of his house", and the man "in the field" could not "return back, to take his clothes." They must flee to the mountains in the greatest haste the moment that they saw "Jerusalem compassed with armies."

The Gospel of the Kingdom, 1974, 215

Eusebius

The members of the Jerusalem church, by means of an oracle given by revelation to acceptable persons there, were ordered to leave the City before the war began and settle in a town in Peraea called Pella.

The History of the Church, 1965, III:5

John Chrysostom

"Then let those who are in Judea flee to the mountains." When does he mean by "then"? These things will take place, he says, "when you see the desolating sacrilege spoken of by the prophet Daniel, standing in the holy place." He seems to me to be speaking of the armies and wars. So flee. There is no hope of safety for you in the cities.

The Ancient Christian Commentary, 2002, Ib:193

Matthew 24:21 & 22: A Great Tribulation

Jesus warned the disciples to flee from Judea (Matt. 24:15–20). Then He prophesied the great destruction to follow:

> *For then there will be a great tribulation, such as has not occurred since the beginning of the world until now, nor ever will. Unless those days had not been cut short, no life would have been saved; but for the sake of the elect those days will be cut short.*
>
> —Matt. 24:21–22

Futurist teachers say that this great tribulation will come in our future, just before the end of the world. They believe it will spread over all the earth. This coming tribulation is talked about so much in some modern Christian circles that it has developed its own identity and is called "The Great Tribulation!"

In reality, Jesus was talking about the destruction of Jerusalem in AD 70. He was answering the disciples' question, "When will Jerusalem and the Temple be destroyed?"

If, indeed, Jesus was talking about the events of AD 70, then we have another question to answer. How could He have said that nothing so terrible has occurred since the beginning of the world until now, nor ever will? Have there not been more wicked things happen than the destruction of Jerusalem? What about the twentieth century Holocaust when six million Jews were murdered? What about other times of war and mass destruction?

The destruction of Jerusalem was not the greatest in magnitude, but Jesus was talking in terms of it being the greatest calamity in the sense of suffering and anguish.

Josephus describes what actually took place in AD 70. After the city was sealed off by the Roman soldiers, Josephus tells how the Jews committed terrible atrocities to each other, even horrific actions, such as cannibalism, which occurred during the famine. He narrates a vile, hopeless account of a woman murdering her small son, cooking him, and eating half of him, then arguing with thieves, who broke into her house looking for food, as to who would eat the other half.

While the Romans had Jerusalem sealed off so no one could escape, the famine got so severe that many tried to sneak out under cover of darkness. Those daring, but starving Jews sometimes swallowed diamonds and precious stones in hopes of escaping to a different region. Knowing this, the Roman soldiers would capture individuals coming out of the city and cut open their stomachs and entrails, searching for whatever they could find.

Eventually, General Titus put an end to those searches, but a new form of torture began. Josephus wrote that as men tried to escape the city or to crawl out to gather food, the Roman soldiers would cut off their hands and send them back inside the city. When the Roman soldiers finally were given the order to descend upon Jerusalem, Josephus tells us that more than 500 men were caught per day, then whipped, tortured, and crucified. Men were nailed to crosses in front of the city until there was no more space. Finally, the soldiers entered the city, and every person was killed except for 97,000, who were taken away to be slaves in the Egyptian mines or as gifts to various provinces so that they might be killed in the theaters.

The destruction of Jerusalem triggered a genocide of Jews throughout the surrounding regions. Josephus said:

> There was not any one Syrian city which did not slay their Jewish inhabitants, and were not more bitter enemies to us than were the Romans themselves.[13]

History provides many similar reports of what took place throughout the whole of the Roman Empire.

Eusebius

Thousands and thousands of men of every age who together with women and children perished by the sword, by starvation, and by countless other forms of death . . . all this anyone who wishes can gather in precise detail from the pages of Josephus's history. I must draw particular attention to his statement that the people who flocked together from all Judaea at the time of the Passover Feast and—to use his own words—were shut up in Jerusalem as if in a prison, totalled nearly three million.

The History of the Church, 1965, 69

13. Josephus, *Wars,* 1998, VII.viii.vii.

John Chrysostom

And this doubtless applies to the Jews at home and abroad. For the Romans were fighting not only against those in Judea but also against those Jews that were dispersed everywhere.

The Ancient Christian Commentary, 2002, Ib:197

Charles Spurgeon

The destruction of Jerusalem was more terrible than anything that the world has ever witnessed, either before or since. Even Titus seemed to see in his cruel work the hand of an avenging God. Truly, the blood of the martyrs slain in Jerusalem was amply avenged when the whole city became a veritable Aceldama, or field of blood.

Spurgeon's Popular Exposition of Matthew, 1979, 211

When we compare the genocide of AD 70 to the Jewish Holocaust of the twentieth century, we must admit that the more recent Holocaust was greater in number, with six million Jews killed over a six-year period. Living in labor camps and being killed with poisonous gas was horrific, but as far as we know, no one was crucified. In AD 70, more than one million Jews were starved, tortured, and killed in a four-month period. Despite the twentieth-century Holocaust's larger magnitude, the violence during the AD 70 tribulation ended the lives of a much greater percentage of the Jewish population and was far more extreme in the atrocities that were committed.

Matthew 24:23–27: False Christs Appear

As Jews were starved, then slaughtered throughout Judea, many held hopes of a Messiah appearing to deliver them at the last moment. Knowing the words of the prophets, the Jews would have most certainly cried out to God to send a deliverer. Several leaders took advantage of this. Josephus wrote how many false prophets and leaders arose, claiming to be the Christ. These were not the false Christs that Jesus prophesied about in Matthew 24:5. These were additional leaders who offered false hopes of being rescued as the city was being destroyed. Knowing that this would happen, Jesus gave a warning:

> *Then if anyone says to you, "Behold, here is the Christ," or "He is over here," do not believe him. For false christs and false prophets will arise and will provide great signs and wonders, so as to mislead, if possible, even the elect. Behold, I have told you in advance. So if they say to you, "Behold, He is in the wilderness," do not go out; or, "Behold, He is in the inner rooms," do not believe them. For just as the lightning comes from the east and flashes as far as the west, so will the coming of the Son of Man be.*
>
> —Matt. 24:23–27

Jerome

At the time of the Jewish captivity by Rome, many Jewish elders claimed to be the Christ. There were so many, in fact, that there were three distinct camps of them when the Romans besieged Jerusalem.

The Ancient Christian Commentary, 2002, Ib:197

Josephus gave one example of a false prophet who publicly declared to the desperate Jerusalem dwellers, that, on a certain day, God was going to deliver them supernaturally. Many Jews followed that leader and ended up losing their lives because of their false hope. Josephus also described how extraordinary signs appeared, including a star resembling a sword over Jerusalem and a light around the Temple for a half hour.[14] Just as Jesus had prophesied, the false christs demonstrated *"great signs and wonders."*

Jesus warned His disciples that when they hear about these false leaders rising, they should not listen to the rumors or declarations of christs or false prophets appearing here or there. Then Jesus made a declaration contrasting the false to the real. He said:

> *For just as the lightning comes from the east and flashes even to the west, so will the coming of the Son of Man be.*
> —Matt. 24:27

From this, the disciples were to know that Jesus' coming would not be made known through rumors or secret talk in the *"inner rooms."* When the Messiah indeed came, Jesus said, it would be as evident as lightning flashing across the sky.

Matthew 24:28: The Corpse and Vultures

Then Jesus said to His disciples:

> *Wherever the corpse is, there the vultures will gather.*
> —Matt. 24:28

Envision thousands of soldiers gathered on the mountains encircling Jerusalem. Now, add to that picture the banner under which they assembled—the banner of the vulture that

14. Josephus, *Wars*, 1998, VI.v.iii.

Roman soldiers carried on flags and often painted on their shields. Thousands of vultures waited on the hills surrounding Jerusalem; then they descended upon the city.

It is worth noting that some Bible translations refer here (Matt. 24:28) to eagles rather than vultures. During that time, eagles were not seen as separate from the family of vultures. All were recognized as carrion eaters that quickly descended upon corpses.

So, Jesus had declared that the vultures would gather and Jerusalem would be the corpse. This was, in fact, a warning God gave to the Jews through Moses, as recorded in Deuteronomy 28. In that chapter, God listed the blessings that would be upon them if they lived in obedience to Him and the curses that would come if they disobeyed Him. One of the curses was as follows:

> *The Lord will bring a nation against you from far away, from the end of the earth, as the eagle swoops down; a nation whose language you will not understand.*
>
> —Deut. 28:49

The Jews had rejected their Messiah. As Jesus said, "[The] *guilt of all the righteous blood shed on earth . . . will come upon this generation*" (Matt. 23:35–36).

Confirmation from the Parallel Gospels

Jesus finished answering the first question, having explained all the signs that would lead up to the destruction of Jerusalem and the Temple. Before we examine His answer to the second and third questions, it is worth pointing out the confirmation of two other Gospels.

We discussed how closely Mark 13 and Luke 21 parallel Matthew 24. There is, however, one key difference. In Matthew 24:3, the disciples asked Jesus three questions:

Question #1: *"When will these things happen?"*

Question #2: *"What will be the sign of Your coming?"*

Question #3: *"What about the end of the age?"*

In contrast, neither Mark nor Luke records the second or third questions. Luke 21:5–7 goes like this:

> *And while some were talking about the temple, that it was decorated with beautiful stones and vowed gifts, He said, "As for these things which you are observing, the days will come when there will not be left one stone upon another, which will not be torn down." They asked Him questions, saying, "Teacher, when therefore will these things happen? And what will be the sign when these things are about to take place?"*

Mark 13:1–4 reads very similarly to this passage, without asking anything about the signs of our Lord's coming or the end of the world.

This is significant because it gives us a clear framework to understand Matthew 24. Since Mark and Luke recorded only the question about when the Temple would be destroyed, we know that our Lord's answer addressed that question. And what signs did Jesus mention? People claiming to be Christ, wars, earthquakes, famines, persecutions, etc. The answers Jesus gave in Mark and Luke are almost identical to the answers Jesus gave in Matthew 24:4–22. Therefore, it is only reasonable to conclude that Matthew 24:4–22 records Jesus' answer to the first question.

We should expect Jesus' answers to the second and third questions to be in the rest of Matthew 24—the part that is not in Mark or Luke.

Acknowledging the parallels in the Gospels again shows how mistaken futurist teachers are when they try to combine all three questions recorded in Matthew 24:3, as if they all are asking about the Second Coming and the end of the world. We will look at the answers Jesus gave to the two remaining questions, and indeed, we will talk about His coming and the end of the world because those are the second and third questions. However, make no mistake that the first question was about the destruction of Jerusalem and the Temple. That happened in AD 70, within the generation of the disciples, precisely as Jesus prophesied.

Concluding Remarks About the First Question

We cannot emphasize enough how significant the destruction of Jerusalem and the Temple were for the Jews. Jerusalem was the "holy city." Mount Moriah, upon which the Temple stood, was the site where Abraham was willing to offer his son Isaac (Gen. 22:2). It also was the place where God appeared to David (2 Chron. 3:1). It was the site upon which Solomon had built the first Temple. There, the high priests offered sacrifices for the people's sins. It was the center of Jewish life, a deeply sacred site. When the Temple was destroyed, the Jewish heritage was destroyed. In one sense, they were cut off from God. They lost their identity.

The writer of Hebrews explained how the Jewish religious system was abolished and replaced with the new covenant established through Jesus:

> *When He said, "A new covenant," He has made the first obsolete. But whatever is becoming obsolete and growing old is about to disappear.*
>
> —Heb. 8:13

Today, we have a new covenant with better promises. We have a High Priest who has made the ultimate and final sacrifice.

The transition from the old to the new stands at the center of history and the Bible. It is a pivotal point in God's plan through the ages. When the Temple in Jerusalem was destroyed, it finalized the end of the old religious system.

Question #2: "What Will Be the Sign of Your Coming?"

Matthew recorded the second question that the disciples asked Jesus as follows:

> *What will be the sign of Your coming. . . ?*
>
> —Matt. 24:3b

Futurist teachers understand this question to be about the Second Coming. They say that Jesus will return to Earth after all the signs listed in Matthew 24:4–22 have occurred. In other words, at some point in our future, after wars, earthquakes, famines, and persecutions happen, then Jesus will return.

Partial preterists offer a different understanding of the disciples' second question. They will point out that Jesus' disciples could not have asked about the second coming of our Lord because, at that time, the disciples knew nothing about a Second Coming. When the disciples were sitting with Jesus on the Mount of Olives 2,000 years ago, they were not even convinced that Jesus would die (Matt. 16:21–23), let alone return to Earth someday.

Please do not misunderstand what we are saying. Partial preterists believe in a future Second Coming. However, they do not think the second question the disciples asked Jesus was about the Second Coming.

What, then, were the disciples asking Jesus? Look again at the question: *"What will be the sign of Your coming?"* What is meant by His "coming?"

Jesus used similar terminology earlier in Matthew:

> *Truly I say to you, there are some of those who are standing here who will not taste death until they see the Son of Man coming in His kingdom.*
>
> —Matt. 16:28

Notice the coming of Jesus was tied to His Kingdom. We can also see that this "coming" happened within the lifetime of some people who were listening to Jesus.

Some adherents of partial preterism equate this "coming of Jesus in His Kingdom" with Jesus coming in judgment of Jerusalem and the Temple. Hence, they see the first and second questions about the same event in AD 70. That view has some merit, but we will present an alternative partial preterist view here.

When the disciples asked Jesus, *"What will be the sign of Your coming?"* they were asking Jesus, "When will You step into Your Kingdom and reveal Yourself as King?" This understanding may be new to you, but please consider it seriously.

When the disciples asked Jesus, "What will be the sign of your coming?" the word "coming" was translated from the Greek word *parousia*. This Greek word may be accurately translated as "coming," "presence," or "arrival." *Parousia* was a common word used in NT times, but it was sometimes used to refer to the arrival of a noted individual, such as an important government official. The *parousia* of an emperor was typically accompanied by a grand ceremony.

Now, consider the events preceding Jesus' Olivet Discourse. Most historians place that discourse as happening on Tuesday, the last week of Jesus' life. Two days earlier, on Sunday, Jesus rode a donkey into Jerusalem in what is commonly called His "Triumphal Entry" (Matt. 21:1–10). As Jesus rode into Jerusalem, people spread their cloaks on the road, along with leafy branches. Then they shouted:

> *Hosanna!*
> *Blessed is <u>He who comes</u> in the name of the Lord;*
> *Blessed is the <u>coming kingdom</u> of our father David;*
> *Hosanna in the highest!*
>
> —Mark 11:9b–10

The people were honoring Jesus as the One sent by God to

rule over God's Kingdom on Earth. Their expectations were at their highest.

This idea of Jesus becoming King was in everyone's mind in Jerusalem. All the Jews knew Daniel's vision of the Messiah coming into His Kingdom:

> *One like a Son of Man was coming, and He came up to the Ancient of Days and was presented before Him. And to Him was given dominion, honor and a kingdom . . .*
>
> —Dan. 7:13b–14

The Jews knew God had promised to give authority to the Son of Man.

Even the thief who died on the cross next to Jesus said:

> *Jesus, remember me when You come into Your kingdom!*
>
> —Luke 23:42

The words of the thief are revealing. He was not referring to Jesus coming in judgment of Jerusalem in AD 70. That would have made no sense because the thief had no chance of being alive in AD 70. The thief was asking Jesus to remember him when Jesus came into His Kingdom in the sense of becoming King.

Knowing this, put yourself back in the shoes of Jesus' disciples. They were Jews. They were looking for God to send a Messiah / King to reign over God's Kingdom. They knew the words of the Old Testament (OT) prophets. Like every adult Jew, the disciples were looking to God to send a Redeemer and King to lead them to victory over their enemies!

Making these expectations even greater was the fact that the disciples had spent three years with Jesus preaching that the Kingdom of God was at hand. The disciples believed Jesus was the promised King.

The disciples were expecting to reign with Jesus. Remember when the mother of the sons of Zebedee asked Jesus, *"Say that in Your kingdom these two sons of mine shall sit, one at Your right, and one at Your left"* (Matt. 20:21b). After the other ten disciples heard about this request, they *"became indignant with the two brothers"* (Matt. 20:24b). That reveals what was in the disciples' hearts and minds.

In that context, the disciples asked Jesus, *"What will be the sign of Your coming?"* (Matt. 24:3b).

When did that "coming" happen? Jesus came into His Kingdom the moment He ascended into heaven and sat down next to the Father. All authority was given to Jesus, both in heaven and on Earth. It happened in AD 30.

A Bible passage that will lock in this understanding is in Luke 19, where Jesus compared Himself to a nobleman who had to go to a distant country to receive a kingdom:

> *So He said, "A nobleman went to a distant country to receive a kingdom for himself, and then to return."*
>
> —Luke 19:12

Jesus went on with this parable to explain that after the nobleman received his kingdom, he returned to judge his servants and his enemies. Concerning his enemies, the nobleman said:

> *But as for these enemies of mine who did not want me to reign over them, bring them here and slaughter them in my presence.*
>
> —Luke 19:27

Jesus told this parable to explain the events that were about to take place in His life. When did Jesus go away to receive His Kingdom? It was when He ascended in AD 30. When did Jesus come to judge His enemies? It was AD 70 when Jesus came in power to judge Jerusalem.

The first question that the disciples asked Jesus was, "When will Jerusalem and the Temple be destroyed." The disciples' second question was, "When will Jesus come into His Kingdom?"

Question #2: "What Will Be the Sign of Your Coming?"

Partial Preterists' View:
Jesus' Coming in AD 30; Jerusalem Judged in AD 70

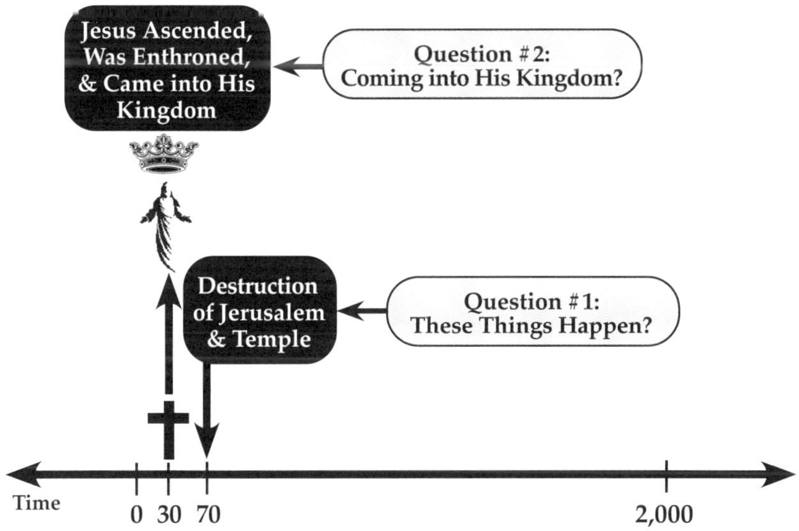

There is a way to prove that this is the correct way to understand the disciples' first two questions. All we need to do is look carefully at two time references that Jesus made. In Matthew 24:14, Jesus said:

> *This gospel of the kingdom shall be preached in the whole world as a testimony to all the nations, and then the end will come.*

Partial preterists see that *"the end"* referred to in this verse was referring to the destruction of Jerusalem in AD 70, but notice when this *"end"* was to happen—after they preached in the entire world.

Now consider a second time reference. In Matthew 10:23b, Jesus said to His disciples:

> *Truly I say to you, you will not finish going through the cities of Israel until the Son of Man comes.*

Jesus told His disciples that this event, referred to as *"the Son of Man comes,"* would take place before they finished *"going through the cities of Israel."*

Read carefully: the date when *"the Son of Man comes"* happened **before** they finished going through Israel. The judgment of Jerusalem happened **after** they finished preaching to the entire world.

The Partial Preterists' View: Jesus Came into His Kingdom in AD 30

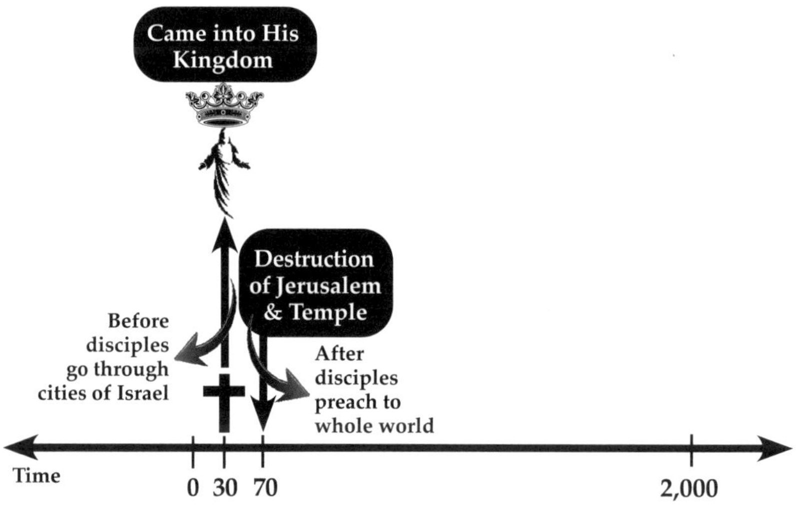

Certainly, the disciples finished *"going through the cities of Israel"* before they finished preaching *"in the entire world."* This proves that the reference, *"Son of Man comes,"* is not the same as the destruction of Jerusalem. The only way this distinction makes sense is to identify the disciples' second question as about Jesus coming into His Kingdom, which happened in AD 30.

With this understanding of *"coming in His Kingdom,"* we now can look at our Lord's answer.

Jesus Answers the Second Question

The coming of Jesus into His Kingdom is not the same as the destruction of Jerusalem. However, the destruction was proof that Jesus came into His Kingdom. Let us explain.

Jesus said:

> *But immediately after the tribulation of those days . . .*
> —Matt. 24:29

The context of this verse reveals that the "tribulation" referred to here was the destruction of Jerusalem. So, Jesus said that *"immediately"* after the destruction of Jerusalem, the disciples would know that He had come into His Kingdom. This will become clear as we continue.

Matthew 24:30a: The Sign of the Son of Man

> *And then the sign of the Son of Man will appear in the sky.*
> —Matt. 24:30a

Futurists look at these words and envision Jesus appearing in the sky at some future date. Still, remember, Jesus said this event would happen within the generation of His disciples. He also stated that some of those alive at that time would see Him come into His Kingdom (Matt. 16:28; Mark 9:1).

With those time references in mind, look at the verse quoted above. Does it say that Jesus will appear in the sky? No. It says that *"the sign"* will appear. A sign is similar to a modern-day billboard declaring something. What is the sign?

The *King James Version* of Matthew 24:30a reads like this:

> *And then shall appear the sign of the Son of man in heaven.*

This does *not* say Jesus will appear. It says the sign will appear. What will that sign indicate? That the Son of Man is in heaven. He has arrived. He has sat down on His throne. He made it!

The *King James Version* refers to the Son of Man in "heaven," while the *New American Standard Bible* (which we quoted earlier) refers to the Son of Man in the *"sky."* Either translation is correct because the Greek word *ourano* may be translated as either "heaven" or "sky." However, if we use the word "sky," the reader may envision Jesus above in the clouds. On the other hand, if we understand that Jesus is in "heaven," then we may envision Him with His Father sitting on His throne. This vision in heaven corresponds with Jesus' coming into His Kingdom.

Put yourself in the disciples' shoes 2,000 years ago, sitting on the Mount of Olives. They soon were going to lose the One whom they had been following. He would die. After His death, how were His disciples to know that He made it into heaven? How would they know that He was sitting on a throne, reigning over God's Kingdom?

That is precisely what Jesus was telling them. He was answering the question, "What will be the sign of Your coming into Your Kingdom?" And what is that sign?

Jesus just told them about all the signs that would end in the destruction of Jerusalem and the Temple. Those signs, followed by the destruction of Jerusalem, were the signs. They were the billboard. Once they saw the destruction of Jerusalem and the Temple, they were to know without a doubt that Jesus Christ was sitting on His throne in heaven.[15]

To gain an understanding of the impact that sign had on the first-century Jewish disciples, compare it with what happened to Japan in 1945 when two atomic bombs were

15. Some adherents of partial preterism will say that the sign of Jesus coming into His Kingdom was the outpouring of the Holy Spirit on Pentecost Day. That may be a valid understanding; however, it is difficult to reconcile with the time reference, *"But immediately after the tribulation . . . And then the sign . . ."* (Matt. 24:29–30).

dropped on Hiroshima and Nagasaki. When those bombs decimated the two cities, Japanese people watching from a distance realized that the war was over. They had lost; the United States had taken control. Now compare that with what happened when Jerusalem was destroyed in AD 70. *More people died in Jerusalem than when the two atomic bombs were dropped in Japan.* The Jewish nation fell. The Temple was destroyed. That was the sign.

The destruction of the Temple was catastrophic to the Jews. Their religious system ended (Heb. 8:13). No longer could people approach God through the Temple with animal sacrifices. There was a new High Priest (Heb. 7:26). The Stone that the builders had rejected had become the Chief Cornerstone (Matt. 21:42). Jesus was building a new Temple out of living stones (1 Peter 2:5). That was the sign that Jesus came into His Kingdom. The throne of David had been lifted to heaven. From there, Jesus Christ would rule over His eternal Kingdom.

Matthew 24:29: The Signs of Judgment

> *But immediately after the tribulation of those days the sun will be darkened, and the moon will not give its light, and the stars will fall from the sky, and the powers of the heavens will be shaken.*
>
> —Matt. 24:29

To understand this passage, first notice the time frame. Jesus said these things would happen *"immediately after the tribulation of those days."* Since the tribulation that Jesus described happened in AD 70, we should look for the fulfillment of this verse *"immediately"* after AD 70.

To see this fulfillment, we need to be familiar with certain Jewish idioms. The sun, moon, and stars frequently were used to refer to governing authorities. For example, Joseph had a dream in which the sun, moon, and stars all bowed down to him (Gen. 37:9); when Joseph relayed this dream to his family, they did not conclude that the sun, moon, and stars would literally bow, but that Joseph would be raised above governing authorities. Similarly, we can read in Revelation 12:1 that a woman appears with the sun and moon under her feet and a crown of stars on her head, meaning she has great authority. So, we can see how the Jewish people used stars symbolically to refer to governing authorities.

In modern times, we often use the word "star" symbolically, such as when we refer to a movie star, sports star, or superstar. Many countries put stars on their flags, representing various authorities. For example, the flag of the United States has 50 stars representing the authorities of the 50 states.

In biblical terminology, the fame and glory of large cities were said to shine as the sun, moon, or stars. When a certain city was destroyed, the sun, moon, or stars were said to darken.

In the book of Ezekiel, we can read about the judgment and coming destruction of Egypt:

> *"And when I extinguish you, I will <u>cover the heavens and darken their stars</u>; I will <u>cover the sun with a cloud</u> and <u>the moon will not give its light</u>. All the shining lights in the heavens I will darken over you and will set darkness on your land," declares the Lord God.*
>
> —Ezek. 32:7–8

Even though this judgment happened, there is no record of the sun, moon, and stars going dark.

Similarly, the Bible prophets used the phrase, *"the powers of the heavens will be shaken"* (Matt. 24:29), to mean the established authorities were being dethroned and new authorities put in their positions.

We can understand this when we realize that prophets sometimes spoke in this apocalyptic terminology. We can compare it with modern-day idioms that people may use when tragedy strikes: "Her life caved in around her!" "The rug got pulled out from under him!" "The sky is falling!" "Life threw a curve ball!" "The lights went out!" It may be difficult for modern-day Christians to think of Jesus using such terminology, but that is what He did. That is the only way we find this terminology used anywhere else in the Bible (as you will see in more examples listed below). Jesus used a Jewish idiom to refer to the coming destruction and the transfer of authority.

Consider how Isaiah decreed destruction upon a region south of Israel known as Edom:

> *And all the hosts of heaven will wear away, and the sky will be rolled up like a scroll; all their hosts will also wither away as a leaf withers from the vine, or as one withers from the fig tree. For My sword is satiated in heaven; behold it shall descend for judgment upon Edom, and upon the people whom I have devoted to destruction.*
>
> —Is. 34:4–5

At that time, the sky was not literally *"rolled up like a scroll."* The hosts of heaven did not fall to the ground as leaves from a fig tree. Yet Edom was destroyed.

Finally, consider God's declaration of judgment through Isaiah upon Babylon:

> *For the stars of heaven and their constellations will not flash their light; the sun will be dark when it rises and the moon will not shed its light.*
>
> —Is. 13:10

When Babylon was judged, there was no record of stars and constellations ceasing from shining. The sun was not dark when it came up. The moon did not dim. Yet destruction came.

If we are going to allow the Bible to interpret itself, we will conclude that Jesus was using apocalyptic language to declare destruction. Just as the prophets Isaiah and Ezekiel spoke judgments against Egypt, Edom, and Babylon, Jesus declared destruction upon Jerusalem. The disciples of Jesus would have recognized that phraseology. They knew the OT. Such terminology was part of their cultural expressions.

This fits perfectly with what occurred after Jesus died, was resurrected, and ascended into heaven. Jesus sat at the right hand of the Father. He was given all authority over heaven and Earth. The evidence on Earth of Jesus ruling in heaven was that the old Temple was destroyed. A new High Priest sitting in heaven. There was a new Ruler: the King of kings and the Lord of lords:

> *Who is at the right hand of God, having gone into heaven, after angels and authorities and powers had been subjected to Him.*
>
> —1 Peter 3:22

Heaven was shaken because Jesus Christ came into His Kingdom.

Matthew 24:30: The Son of Man in Glory

We have already examined the first part of Matthew 24:30; now let us consider the rest of the verse:

> *And then the sign of the Son of Man will appear in the sky, and then all the tribes of the earth will mourn, and they will see the Son of Man coming on the clouds of the sky with power and great glory.*
>
> —Matt. 24:30

What is the meaning of *"all the tribes of the earth will mourn?"*

To answer this, we need to examine the Greek word *ge*, translated in this verse to "earth." When the word *ge* is translated in other passages of the NT, it is most often translated as "land." This word is often used when referring to the Promised Land of the Jews. This is what we believe is more faithful to the context of this passage. Hence, we are told that all the tribes of the land shall mourn. Who are the tribes of the land? The land that is spoken of in this passage is the Promised Land. Therefore, all the tribes of Israel will mourn.

When news of the destruction of the Temple and the whole of Jerusalem reached the tribes of Israel scattered throughout the Roman Empire, great mourning took place in their synagogues and homes. The *"sign"* (the destruction of Jerusalem) caused the *"tribes"* (of Israel) to mourn greatly, yet they still missed the significance of the sign. It was the sign that *"the Son of Man"* was *"in heaven,"* that He had ascended to His Father.

When Jesus referred to *"the Son of Man coming on the clouds of the sky with power and great glory,"* He did not say that the Son was coming back to Earth. This event was to happen in the sky (or in heaven, according to the *King James Version*). In heaven, Jesus was clothed with power and glory.

This is exactly what Daniel saw in a vision—Jesus Christ taking His position at the right hand of the Father:

> *I kept looking in the night visions, and behold, with the clouds of heaven one like a Son of Man was coming, and He came up to the Ancient of Days and was presented before Him. And to Him was given dominion, glory, and a kingdom, that all the peoples, nations and men of every language might serve Him.*
>
> —Dan. 7:13–14a

Daniel prophesied it. Then Jesus fulfilled it when He received the right to rule from His Father.

Matthew 24:31: Angels Gather the Elect

> *And He will send forth His angels with a great trumpet and they will gather together His elect from the four winds, from one end of the sky to the other.*
>
> —Matt. 24:31

To many people, this can speak only of the second coming of Christ at the end of history. However, that is not what Jesus said it meant. Only three verses after this, He stated that *"this generation will not pass away until all these things take place."* Jesus said that this verse was descriptive of one of the things that would happen within the span of one generation.

How can we understand this? As Jesus sat down on His throne, all authority was given to Him in heaven and on Earth. Everything changed the moment Jesus came into His Kingdom. The blowing of a trumpet meant to the Jews that a royal decree was announced. And what was that decree? It was time to release the angels of God to go and gather His people from every nation. At the same time, the disciples of Jesus were commissioned to go and preach the gospel, making disciples of every nation. No longer was the Jewish nation the only people allowed within a covenant relationship with God. Jesus had become the Good Shepherd who was gathering His sheep from across the world.

Matthew 24:32 & 33: Know That He Is Near

> *Now learn the parable from the fig tree: when its branch has become tender and puts forth its leaves, you know that summer is near; so you too, when you see all these things, recognize that He is near, right at the door.*
>
> —Matt. 24:32–33

To understand this, see yourself with the disciples sitting with Jesus. You are on the Mount of Olives, overlooking Jerusalem and the Temple. Our Lord could have easily taken a tender branch from a nearby fig tree and reminded the disciples how they can know summer is near when the branch becomes tender and puts forth its leaves. The important lesson is that one thing follows another. So, too, Jesus was assuring His disciples that all the signs He had so far listed would be followed by the destruction of Jerusalem.

Futurists have a very different understanding. Most futurists claim that the fig tree symbolizes Israel and that when Israel is reborn as a nation, the generation that sees it happen will also see the second coming of Christ.

That interpretation reveals how much the futurists will stretch the meaning of Scripture to try to make it fit their understanding of future events. In the Bible, Israel typically is pictured as an olive tree rather than a fig tree, e.g., Jer. 11:16; Rom. 11:17. Furthermore, there is no mention of a rebirth of Israel in the context of Matthew 24. Jesus already listed all the signs for which they were to watch, and none of them imply anything about Israel being reborn.

We can also know that the fig tree illustration was not about the future rebirth of Israel and that generation seeing the second coming of Jesus because it simply is not true! Israel became a nation in 1948, and one generation from that was 1988. Jesus did not return! Several decades have passed since then and still Jesus has not come back.

The obvious, simple lesson of the fig tree was to watch for all the signs listed in Matthew 24:4–28. When those signs were fulfilled, the disciples were to know that Jesus had come into His Kingdom and judged Jerusalem.

Matthew 24:34: In This Generation

Jesus ended His answer to the disciples' second question by saying:

> *Truly I say to you, this generation will not pass away until all these things take place.*
>
> —Matt. 24:34

If we take this verse literally, we will believe everything Jesus prophesied in Matthew 24:5–34 was fulfilled by AD 70.

Of course, futurist teachers cannot accept the words of Jesus literally. Sometimes, they redefine the word "generation" (Greek, *genesis*) to be "race," and hence, they claim that all the events listed in Matthew 24 will happen before the race of the Jews passes away. However, that reinterpretation is inconsistent with the rest of the NT. The Greek word *genesis* is used 34 times in the NT, and it is never translated as "race" in any commonly used translation of the Bible.

Suppose we accept the natural and literal meaning of Jesus' statement. In that case, we will conclude that all the events recorded, including the coming of the Lord, happened within the lifetime of the disciples who were listening to Jesus at that time.

Charles Spurgeon

The King left his followers in no doubt as to when these things should happen: "Verily I say unto you, this generation shall not pass till all these things be fulfilled." It was just about the ordinary limit of a generation when the Roman armies compassed Jerusalem, whose measure of iniquity was then full, and overflowed in misery, agony, distress, and bloodshed such as the world never saw before or since. Jesus was a true Prophet; everything that he foretold was literally fulfilled.

The Gospel of the Kingdom, 1974, 218

John Calvin

Christ informs them, that before a single generation shall have been completed, they will learn by experience the truth of what he has said. For within fifty years the city was destroyed and the temple was razed, the whole country was reduced to a hideous desert.

Commentary on a Harmony of the Evangelists, Matthew, Mark, and Luke, 1949, vol. 3, 151

Question #3: "What About the End of the Age?"

The third question the disciples asked pertains to the end of the age (Matt. 24:3). As we mentioned earlier, the Greek word for age, *aion,* is translated in some Bible versions as "world." Some Bible readers may equate the "end of the age" with the "end of the world as we know it," but the astute Bible teacher will stick with what the disciples actually asked about the end of the age.

Jesus Answers the Third Question

In Matthew 24:35–25:46, Jesus answered the third question. Christians who have a red-letter edition of the Bible (that is, an edition in which all the words of Jesus are printed in red) will notice that Matthew 24:35–25:46 are all the words of Jesus. It is one long discourse in which Jesus answers the question about the end of the age.

We will go through this discourse passage by passage, but first, it is essential to identify how we know that Matthew 24:35 is the verse where Jesus begins answering the third question. We did not arbitrarily choose this as the verse in which He began. A quick examination of the Scriptures reveals that this is, indeed, where Jesus started talking about the end of the age. Allow us to explain.

We already studied Matthew 24:34, where Jesus said everything preceding that verse would happen in that generation. He was giving a notable break and a reasonable place for us to see how the events after Matthew 24:34 could happen later, in a later generation.

Further, we can note the next verse, where Jesus began answering the third question:

> *Heaven and earth will pass away, but My words will not pass away.*
>
> —Matt. 24:35

Jesus was emphasizing how His words certainly would come true, but He was also making a statement about the end of things—heaven and earth passing away.[16] That is what the disciples asked in their third question: *"What about the end of the age?"*

We can know that this is where Jesus began answering the third question because He started talking about the *"day and hour"*:

> *But about that day and hour no one knows, not even the angels of heaven, nor the Son, but the Father alone.*
>
> —Matt. 24:36

When the Bible uses the terminology "the day and hour," "the Great Day," or "the last day," or in some contexts, "the day," it refers to judgment day, and not just any judgment day, but the final great judgment day when God will call all people to account at the end of the world, e.g., Matt. 7:22; Luke 10:12; John 6:39–40; 12:48; Rom. 2:16; 1 Cor. 1:8; 3:13; 5:5; Phil. 1:6; 1:10; 2 Thess. 1:10; 2 Tim. 1:18; 4:8; Heb. 10:25.

That final great judgment day is the topic of the rest of Matthew 24 and all of Matthew 25. Jesus compared the great judgment day with the judgment of Noah's flood (Matt. 24:37–39), two men in a field (24:40–41), a thief coming in the night (24:42–44), a master returning to demand that his servants give an accounting (24:45–51), a groom returning for his bride (25:1–13), and a master returning to see how his servants have used their talents (25:14–30). Jesus ended this great teaching by talking about the Son of Man coming in glory

16. Some eschatology teachers equate "heaven and earth passing away" with the Temple and Jerusalem being destroyed in AD 70. Dr. Eberle explains why that understanding is incorrect in his book entitled *The Comings of Christ*. In Matthew 24, heaven and earth passing away is an event associated with the final great judgment that will happen in the future.

with all the angels and the nations being gathered before Him (Matt. 25:31–46).

We will examine these passages briefly but notice that each one talks about the coming judgment and the returning Judge. Hence, we understand that Jesus is answering the third question concerning the end of the age (or world).

> **Charles Spurgeon**
>
> There is a manifest change in our Lord's words here, which clearly indicate that they refer to His last great coming to judgment.
>
> *The Gospel of the Kingdom*, 1974, 218

Matthew 24:36: No One Knows When

> *But about that day and hour no one knows, not even the angels of heaven, nor the Son, but the Father alone.*
>
> —Matt. 24:36

The key point of this passage is that the day of the Lord will be a surprise. Jesus does not know when it will come. The angels do not know. Only the Father knows. Jesus went on to explain that it would come with no warning.

Notice how different our Lord's answer is to this question than to the other two questions. Concerning the destruction of Jerusalem, Jesus said that there would first be wars, famines, earthquakes, a falling away, time to preach the gospel, and then armies surrounding Jerusalem. Concerning our Lord's coming into His Kingdom, Jesus said that the primary visible sign would be the destruction of Jerusalem and the Temple. However, concerning the end of the age, Jesus said, *"No one knows, not even the angels of heaven, nor the Son."*

This surprise element of the end of the age is a fundamental theme of each parable that Jesus gave in the rest of Matthew 24 and all of Matthew 25. Let us look at them.

Matthew 24:37–39: As the Days of Noah

> *For the coming of the Son of Man will be just like the days of Noah. For as in those days before the flood they were eating and drinking, marrying and giving in marriage, until the day that Noah entered the ark, and they did not understand until the flood came and took them all away; so will the coming of the Son of Man be.*
>
> —Matt. 24:37–39

Jesus wanted to impress upon the disciples' minds (and our minds) that the final day of judgment will come as a surprise. Just as in Noah's day, people will be eating and drinking, marrying and giving in marriage; then suddenly, Jesus will appear and judgment day will have arrived.

Matthew 24:40–42: As Two Men in a Field

> *Then there will be two men in the field; one will be taken and one will be left. Two women will be grinding at the mill; one will be taken and one will be left. Therefore be on the alert, for you do not know which day your Lord is coming.*
>
> —Matt. 24:40–42

The primary point of this passage is that the great judgment day will come suddenly, and therefore, people should always be alert.

Matthew 24:43–44: As a Thief in the Night

Next, Jesus taught the surprise element with a parable of a thief coming in the night.

> *But be sure of this, that if the head of the house had known at what time of the night the thief was coming, he would have been on the alert and would not have allowed his house to be broken into. For this reason you must be ready; for the Son of Man is coming at an hour when you do not think He will.*
>
> —Matt. 24:43–44

Not only will the great judgment day arrive without warning, but it will come when we do not expect it. Therefore, be ready at all times.

Matthew 24:45–51: As a Master Returning

> *Who then is the faithful and sensible slave whom his master put in charge of his household to give them their food at the proper time? Blessed is that slave whom his master finds so doing when he comes. Truly I say to you that he will put him in charge of all his possessions. But if that evil slave says in his heart, "My master is not coming for a long time," and he begins to beat his fellow slaves and eat and drink with drunkards; the master of that slave will come on a day when he does not expect him, and at an hour that he does not know, and will cut him in pieces and assign him a place with the hypocrites; in that place there will be weeping and gnashing of teeth.*
>
> —Matt. 24:45–51

Many lessons can be taken from this passage, but the most fundamental truth is that judgment day will arrive as a surprise with no warning. Therefore, Jesus tells the listener to continue being diligent in service and living righteously.

Matthew 25:1–13: As Ten Virgins Waiting

In the next passage, Jesus told a parable of ten virgins who were waiting for the groom to come and take them. Five of the virgins were foolish, not ready for the return of the groom, while the other five were wise, staying prepared for the groom.

The obvious lesson, again, is that God's people must be ready because Jesus could return at any time without warning.

Matthew 25:14–30: As Servants with Talents

Jesus then offered a parable about a man entrusting his possessions to three servants. To one, he gave five talents, to another two, and to the last servant one talent. When the master returned, he demanded that each servant give an account of how he had used the talents. Then, he rewarded them each accordingly.

The primary lesson here is that the Master will return without warning.

A secondary lesson is that there would be a great delay before the return of Christ. We see that delay in verse 19, which says:

> *Now after a <u>long time</u> the master of those slaves came . . .*

Notice the timing of this event will be separated and distant (*"a long time"*) from the first two events. When the disciples asked Jesus Questions 1 and 2, He said the corresponding events would take place within their generation. When the disciples asked Question 3, Jesus said there would be a long time before the Great Day came.

MATTHEW 25:31–46: THE GREAT DAY OF JUDGMENT

In the final passage of Matthew 25, Jesus gave a description and summary of the coming great Day of Judgment.

> *But when the Son of Man comes in His glory, and all the angels with Him, then He will sit on His glorious throne. All the nations will be gathered before Him; and He will separate them from one another, as the shepherd separates the sheep from the goats; and He will put the sheep on His right, and the goats on the left. Then the King will say to those on His right, "Come, you who are blessed of My Father, inherit the kingdom . . ." Then He will also say to those on His left, "Depart from Me, accursed ones, into the eternal fire . . ." These will go away into eternal punishment, but the righteous into eternal life.*
>
> —Matt. 25:31–46

The lesson is clear: Jesus will return to judge the righteous and the unrighteous. On that Great Day, Jesus will come in glory with all His angels. Then, He will judge all the nations.

JESUS ANSWERED THE DISCIPLES' THREE QUESTIONS

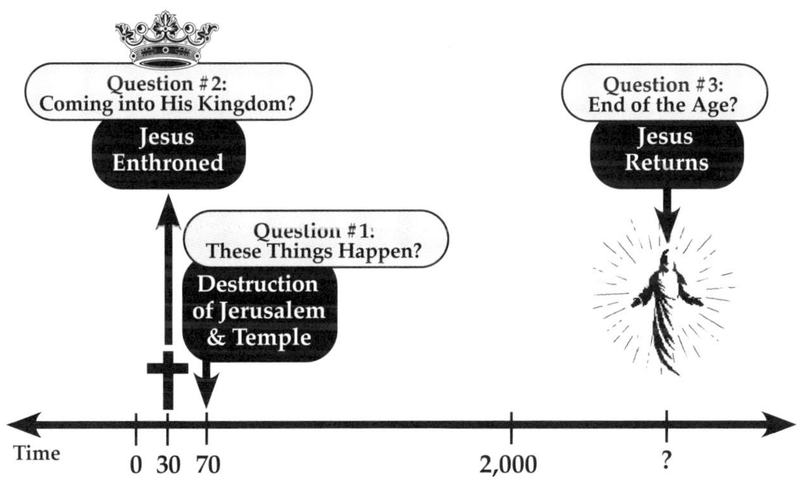

Summary

The partial preterist understanding of Matthew 24, which we have just presented to you, is held by a significant portion of the Body of Christ worldwide. We mention this to clarify that we have not presented some bizarre doctrine that no one else believes. Thousands of Bible teachers would explain Matthew 24 similarly to how we have just explained it.

If you come to accept the partial preterist view of Matthew 24, then you will embrace many ideas that may be new to you, the most critical point being that there will be *no signs* preceding the second coming of Jesus or the end of the world. Jesus did not know of any signs, and no one else will be able to figure it out either. Jesus was emphatic about this point, giving no less than six different parables to make sure His followers would understand that it will be a total surprise to everyone except the Father.

This is contradictory to what is spoken of by futurist teachers, who love to create in their listeners' anticipation of the Second Coming by talking about increasing wars, famines, earthquakes, false religious leaders, and people falling away from the faith. In reality, all of those signs preceded the destruction of Jerusalem in AD 70. When Jesus returns at some point in the future, you will be eating and drinking, driving your car, sleeping in bed, or working at your job. Then suddenly, Jesus Christ will appear in the sky! No warning, no signs.

Section Two

Understanding the Partial Preterist View

In this section, we will discuss issues that are important for any individual to consider before embracing the partial preterist view. This is the only section in this book where we will not focus on specific Bible passages. Instead, we will address issues related to eschatology that, unless discussed, may become stumbling blocks to people considering the partial preterist view.

The Partial Preterist View Is the Victorious View

Partial preterists sometimes refer to their view as "the victorious view." This is objectionable to some futurists because they consider their view victorious. After all, Jesus will return, conquer all evil, and win in the end. Indeed, futurists see victory in the end but compare the unfolding of events in the two views.

The futurists teach that in the near future there will be great earthquakes, famines, and wars. Then, an antichrist will take over the world by establishing one world government, one economic system, and a false religion. That antichrist will then deceive the mass of humanity into following him and cut off the heads of Christians who will not receive his mark. Then God will release His wrath upon the world, burning up one-third of the earth and inflicting great pain upon humanity during a seven-year tribulation. Even more discouraging is the futurist's belief that the Church will experience a great falling away before the tribulation, with masses abandoning the true Church. Indeed, God will win in the end, but the road between now and then is devastating, according to the futurist view.

Compare this with the partial preterist view that sees the tragedies and destruction reported in Matthew 24 as already fulfilled. As we study the book of Daniel in Section Three, we will see that the Kingdom of God is here, and it will continue to grow until it fills the whole earth. In Section Four, we will study the book of Revelation and learn how all the enemies of Jesus are progressively being placed under His feet until the end, when all the kingdoms of this earth become the Kingdom of our God. Throughout the coming pages, we will see how the Church rises in victory, maturity, unity, and power before the return of Jesus Christ.

When the two views are placed side-by-side, there is no doubt which one is victorious.

STRENGTHS OF THE PARTIAL PRETERIST VIEW

In addition to the futurist view and the partial preterist view, there is a third view called the full preterist view (sometimes referred to simply as the preterist view). Christians holding to the full preterist view see all the prophecies of Matthew 24 and the book of Revelation as already fulfilled.

Other than identifying the full preterist view, we will not say much about it. We believe it is an unbiblical view that Christians should be exhorted to avoid. Most disturbing, adherents of full preterism believe that the second coming of Jesus took place before or in AD 70 when the Romans destroyed Jerusalem. Therefore, adherents do not believe in the future return of Jesus.[17]

Eschatological View	Matt. 24 & Revelation
Futurist View	All Fulfilled in the Future
Partial Preterist View	Part Future, Part Past
Full Preterist View	All Fulfilled in the Past

Another negative about full preterism is that adherents come to the Scriptures with the supposition that all the end-time prophecies have been fulfilled. Therefore, they must try to figure out how each and every prophecy was fulfilled in the past.

Adherents of the futurist view approach Scripture with the opposite supposition that all the pertinent prophecies will be fulfilled in the future. Both of these views have the same problem; they have to make every passage fit their presupposition.

In contrast, teachers who hold to the partial preterist view are not obligated to fit any specific passage into the future

17. For those interested in further studying the differences between partial preterism and full preterism, see Harold Eberle's book, *The Comings of Christ: Why I Am a Partial Preterist, Not a Full Preterist.*

or the past. They are free to understand each passage in its context and historical setting. Partial preterists look for indications within the text whether a prophetic passage is about to be fulfilled "very soon," "within that generation," or "a long time off." Then, partial preterists consider the historical record to see if any historic events correspond to the prophetic passage. In this way, partial preterists let Scripture and history speak for themselves. This pattern allows for an understanding of Scripture without having to force passages into predetermined expectations.

Multiple Fulfillments of Prophecy?

When futurist Christians first hear about the historical fulfillment of Matthew 24 and other related Scriptures, they often try to hold to their futurist view by saying that there must be more than one fulfillment of the pertinent Bible prophecies.

To support their view of multiple fulfillments, futurists often give the example of God's promise to King David that one of his descendants would build a Temple and establish a Kingdom (1 Chron. 17:11–12). Solomon built the Temple in Jerusalem and reigned over a large region in the Middle East. However, we also know that Jesus, another descendant of David (born of God and born of man), is building a house and establishing a Kingdom. Futurists sometimes take examples like this of a twofold fulfillment and then say that God may have a twofold fulfillment of passages such as Matthew 24:4–34.

Please consider more closely this twofold fulfillment theory. The 1 Chronicles 17 passage that records the promise of God to David says that the Kingdom will endure forever. This is a clear indicator that Solomon did not fulfill the promise. Since his Temple and kingdom were destroyed, we immediately know that we must look for another descendent of David to fulfill that promise. To be accurate, we must recognize Solomon not as the first fulfillment but as a foreshadowing of the true fulfillment. Jesus was the only fulfillment. He is the King of the Eternal Kingdom!

Unlike the promise to King David, we can find no clear indicator in Matthew 24:4–34 that there will be a later fulfillment. Two times, Jesus clearly said all those events would occur within a generation (Matt. 23:36; 24:34).

As mentioned in the previous chapter, we must look for time indicators within the passage being discussed. If there are no indicators of a future fulfillment, then there is no reason to look for a future fulfillment.

We should also consider that people tend to see what they believe, both because they are looking for it and because faith has power to influence certain events. We do not mean to imply that every careless thought that we have changes the world around us, but in some cases, our faith can move mountains. Therefore, when futurist teachers tell their followers that there will be famines, earthquakes, wars, and a great falling away, the people's faith has some power to open their eyes to see negative things and activate that for which they believe.

Is it wise to create faith in such negative possibilities? We think not.

CHALLENGES TO OUR PRESENT BELIEFS

Most Christians will claim they base their beliefs on the Bible. Still, every one of us—no matter how sincere we may be—brings to the Bible a mind full of presuppositions, beliefs, views of reality, and experiences that influence how we see things and interpret Scripture. Because we look at the Bible through the lens of our culture and our view of reality, anyone can misinterpret the Bible.

Test yourself: Have you ever changed your beliefs about something? Everyone who has been a Christian for very long has to answer in the affirmative. The truth is that we (Eberle and Trench) used to believe the futurist view. As pastors, we used to teach that view, but we became convinced that we had been incorrectly swayed, leading us to misunderstand key biblical prophecies.

Now, we are hoping that you will lay aside—to the best of your ability—your presumptions and preconceived beliefs about the end times—presumptions that you may have picked up, not from the Bible itself, but from novels, movies, televangelists, and your favorite teachers. See the Scriptures through new eyes. Only if you approach this subject with a willingness to change can we show you end-time truths from another perspective.

Through many years of presenting biblical truths to various Christian groups, we have observed how people react and struggle when challenged. Christians say they believe the Bible, but most Christians cannot tell you from where in the Bible their own beliefs originated. We dare say that most Christians believe what they believe, not because they can support those beliefs with Scripture, but *because they believe what they were taught by their favorite pastor, Sunday School teacher, Bible teacher, denomination, or television preacher*. Of course, we all need teachers to help us see things we have missed in the Bible. Jesus is the One who gives us teachers. However, we should be concerned when Christians are so loyal to one teacher or denomination that they cannot seriously consider the views of other teachers who are also trying their best to serve the Lord.

Most Christians will struggle to hold to their present beliefs no matter how compelling the historical and biblical evidence is to the contrary. *They will hold to those beliefs not because they can defend them biblically but because of their loyalty to a spiritual leader they love and admire.*

For them, to question their own beliefs is to be disloyal to the leaders who taught them. It is easier not to question. It is easier to let things remain as they are. It is difficult to consider other ways of thinking because you must entertain the possibility that you have been misguided and that teachers whom you love and admire have been incorrect.

It is unsettling to have your present beliefs challenged because you may not know with what to replace your present beliefs if they crumble. We want to reassure you that if you embrace the partial preterist view, you will soon have a victorious, optimistic view that will give you confidence and energy to plan for the future and live today.

Things Are Getting Better

The futurist view is deeply intertwined with the belief that this world is worsening. A popular futurist teacher, Jack Van Impe warned, "All hell will break loose on planet earth—a furious time of pain, mayhem, and agony for millions," and "the signs of global economic chaos are on the horizon."[18] Hal Lindsey started his tremendously popular book, *The Late Great Planet Earth*, by telling the reader about the "World in a Mess."[19] John Hagee, one of the strongest radio and television personalities promoting the futurist view, wrote that the world is "standing on the brink of nuclear Armageddon" and "teetering on the brink of World War III."[20] Such phrases and ideas permeate futurists' teachings because their view is entirely interdependent with the belief that things are getting worse and the world is about to self-destruct.

Therefore, it is difficult to let go of the futurist view without releasing the pessimistic view of the world and the future.

Indeed, things can look dismal if we focus on what the news media brings before us each day. Terrible events are occurring in the world, and evil is very evident. However, let us lift ourselves higher and look at history more broadly. Compare our world today with what the world was like in the past.

Start by taking a snapshot of what life was like in the United States 200 years ago. In the early 1800s, there were about five million immigrants in the United States, but 20 percent of them were slaves. Those statistics reveal a great evil but consider what else was happening. The age of sexual consent in many states was 9 or 10 years old.[21] Abortion was legal throughout

18. Jack Van Impe, *Millennium: Beginning or End?* (Nashville, TN: Word Publishing, 1999), 5, xvi, 1.

19. Hal Linsey, *The Late Great Planet Earth* (Grand Rapids, MI: Zondervan Publishing, 1975), 7.

20. John Hagee, *Jerusalem Countdown* (Lake Mary, FL: Frontline, 2006), 6, 17.

21. Stephanie Coontz, *The Way We Never Were: American Families and the Nostalgia Trap* (New York: Basic Books, 1992), 184.

most of the nineteenth century, and records tell us that more than one-fifth of all pregnancies were aborted, with Michigan having the highest rate at 34 percent.[22] Alcoholism was much higher than it is today. Prostitution was also higher, with New York City having approximately one prostitute for every 64 men; the mayor of Savannah estimated that his city had one for every 39 men.[23] The percentage of Americans attending church was about equal to what it is today: 30 to 45 percent.[24] Thousands of people were moving West, and most had no churches to attend until years after they had settled and communities had been developed. Native Americans were being forced off of their lands and, in some cases, murdered. Thousands of Chinese people were being brought to the West Coast of the United States to serve as forced laborers. When gold was discovered in various regions of the West, gold rushes occurred, producing some of the world's vilest and most dangerous communities. Many people in the West carried guns for protection because murder was commonplace. Throughout the United States, women could not vote, and men could legally beat their wives so long as they did not maim or kill them. Things in the United States were not better morally, ethically, or spiritually.

Of course, some godly individuals laid the foundations of the United States government, but America's moral and ethical climate was much worse than it is today. The "good ole days" were not so good.

Let us go back further in time and take a snapshot of the whole world around the time Jesus was born. The Roman Empire dominated civilization around the Mediterranean Sea. In Italy, approximately 40 percent of the population consisted of slaves. Throughout the Empire, homosexuality

22. Ronald A. Wells, *History Through the Eyes of Faith* (New York: HarperCollins Publishers, 1989), 179.

23. John D'Emilio and Estelle Freedman, *Intimate Matters: A History of Sexuality in America* (New York: Harper and Row, 1988), 65, 133–134.

24. Dean Merrill, *Sinners in the Hands of an Angry Church* (Grand Rapids, MI: Zondervan Publishing, 1997), 96–97.

between a master and slave was commonplace. Most Roman and Greek people worshiped many gods, such as Jupiter, Juno, and Neptune.

Outside the Roman Empire, people in Africa, Asia, and Australia worshiped nature, demons, and their dead ancestors. In North America, people had no revelation of the Messiah. In South America, millions worshiped a bloodthirsty god, and they offered human sacrifices, often numbering in the thousands in one ceremony.

When Jesus came to Earth, only one tiny nation in the Middle East had a revelation of the one true God, and even its citizens were living in a time of great doubt. All the rest of the world was lost in darkness. As the apostle Paul wrote:

> *Therefore remember that formerly you, the Gentiles . . . were at that time separate from Christ . . . having no hope and without God in the world.*
>
> —Eph. 2:11–12

That was the condition of the world 2,000 years ago. As Ernest Hampden Cook wrote:

> The fact is that bad as the world still is, yet morally it is vastly better than it was when Jesus was born in Bethlehem of Judea. . . . Few people in these days have an adequate conception of the misery and degradation which were then the common lot of almost all mankind, owing to the monstrous wickedness of the times, to continual war, to the cruelties of political despotism, and of everywhere-prevailing slavery.[25]

Now, think how blessed the world is today. The gospel is being preached in every corner of the earth. Christianity is exploding in growth worldwide, with more than 200,000 people becoming born-again Christians every day. In China, there are more than 29,000 per day becoming Christians, and in South America, there are more than 35,000 per day. All

25. Earnest Hampton Cook, *The Christ Has Come,* 1895, xvi.

total, there are more than a million people per week becoming Christians. The tiny seed that came to Earth in that little Jewish nation has grown to permeate the world. With more than 2.4 billion people claiming to be Christians today, Christianity is the world's largest, most influential block of humanity.

Are things getting better? Yes, they are. Of course, many tragic things are still happening, and we have a long way to go before we can say everything is wonderful. But things are much better today than they were when Jesus came into the world 2,000 years ago.

This optimistic view can be challenging to accept for Christians who have been submerged in a pessimistic worldview. Indeed, many Christian preachers regularly rally the troops and motivate people to action by emphasizing the dire conditions of the world around us. Of course, Christians must stay vigilant—we have much work ahead of us—but we must not lose sight of the fact that we are gaining ground. Jesus Christ is Lord, and the Kingdom of God is advancing.

SUMMARY

As you continue studying the partial preterist view with us, you will learn what millions of your brothers and sisters in Christ believe. We hope you will embrace a victorious view similar to that held by most of the noted leaders throughout Church history.[26] You will learn truths that will give you an optimistic view of life and the future.

26. Again, we want to mention that not every partial preterist teacher would explain every verse the same way we are, but the fundamental idea that the Church will rise in unity, maturity, and glory before the return of Jesus was the common belief of the historical Church before the mid-twentieth century.

Section Three

Prophetic Messages Given to Daniel

Living several hundred years before Jesus came into the world, Daniel recorded visions, dreams, and prophecies concerning the coming of the Messiah, the end times, the future of the Jews, and the coming of the Kingdom of God. Here we will examine the divine messages recorded first in Daniel 2 and then in Daniel 9.

THE MESSAGE OF DANIEL 2

Nebuchadnezzar, the king of Babylon, had a dream in which God revealed the future. Daniel was able to tell the king his dream and give its interpretation. Daniel told King Nebuchadnezzar that he saw in his dream a tremendous statue with a head of fine gold, a breast and arms of silver, a belly and thighs of bronze, legs of iron, and feet partly of iron and partly of clay. Daniel then told the king that in his dream a rock appeared and hit the feet of the statue, causing the statue to collapse. The statue was then blown away as dust in the wind. Finally, the stone became a great mountain and filled the whole earth (Dan. 2:31–35).

Daniel then revealed to the king what the dream meant:

> *You, O king . . . are the head of gold. After you there will arise another kingdom inferior to you, then another third kingdom of bronze. . . . Then there will be a fourth kingdom as strong as iron . . .*
>
> —Dan. 2:37–40

Here, Daniel told the king that the four parts of the statue represented four kingdoms, one following after the other.

Daniel told King Nebuchadnezzar that his kingdom—the Babylonian kingdom—was the first kingdom. Other passages in the book of Daniel talk further about these four kingdoms. They identify the Medo-Persian kingdom as the second kingdom (Dan. 5:28; 8:20) and the Greek Empire as the third kingdom (Dan. 8:21). Finally, the fourth kingdom was the Roman Empire. Indeed, we know from history that there were four consecutive kingdoms in that region of the world: the Babylonian Empire, the Medo-Persian Empire, the Greek Empire, and the Roman Empire.

Timeline Showing the Revelation of Daniel 2

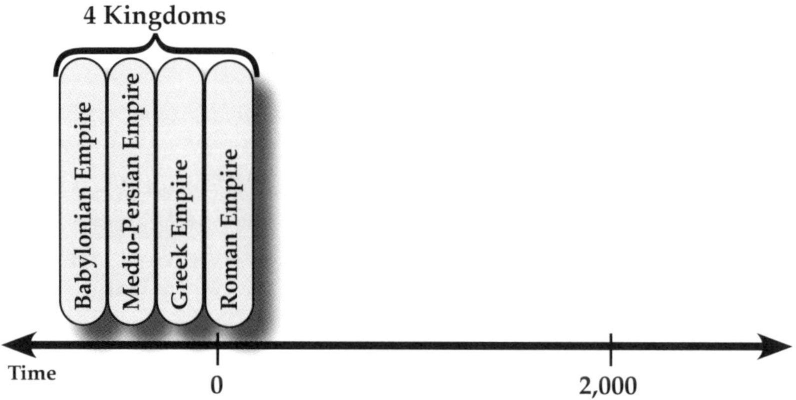

Whether readers believe the futurist or partial preterist view, they will agree that God revealed to Daniel that there would be these four earthly kingdoms.

Daniel then explained the rock in Nebuchadnezzar's dream:

> *In the days of those kings the God of heaven will set up a kingdom which will never be destroyed, and that kingdom will not be left for another people; it will crush and put an end to all these kingdoms, but it will itself endure forever.*
>
> —Dan. 2:44

Daniel explained that a rock will come into the earth and establish the Kingdom of God. That rock will crush all other kingdoms. Then the rock will grow as a mountain, and that mountain will fill the whole earth (Dan. 2:35, 44).

Whether readers believe the futurist or partial preterist view, they will agree that the Rock is Jesus Christ because He is the One who comes into the world to establish God's eternal Kingdom.

The two views *disagree* concerning *when* the Rock comes to Earth and *when* the Kingdom of God gets established. Allow us to explain.

Futurist Understanding of God's Kingdom

The futurist teachers say that the Rock (Jesus) will come to the Earth at some future date. That will be the second coming of Jesus Christ. After a seven-year tribulation, Jesus will bring the Kingdom from heaven down to Earth. Then, the Kingdom of God will remain upon Earth for 1,000 years.

Timeline of Daniel 2 According to the Futurist View: Jesus, the Rock, Comes to Earth to Establish God's Kingdom

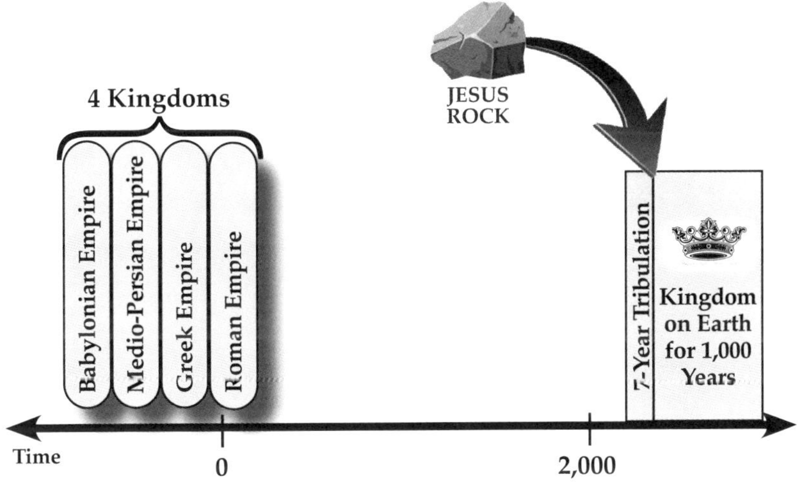

Partial Preterist Understanding of God's Kingdom

Those who hold to the partial preterist view say that the Rock (Jesus) came to Earth 2,000 years ago. Hence, Jesus is the stone that the builders (the Jewish religious leaders) rejected (Ps. 118:22; Matt. 21:42).

When Jesus came 2,000 years ago, He established God's Kingdom. The Kingdom has been growing on Earth and will continue to grow until it fills the earth, as did the mountain in Nebuchadnezzar's dream grew until it filled the earth.

Timeline of Daniel 2 According to the Partial Preterist View: Jesus, the Rock, Came to Earth 2,000 Years Ago

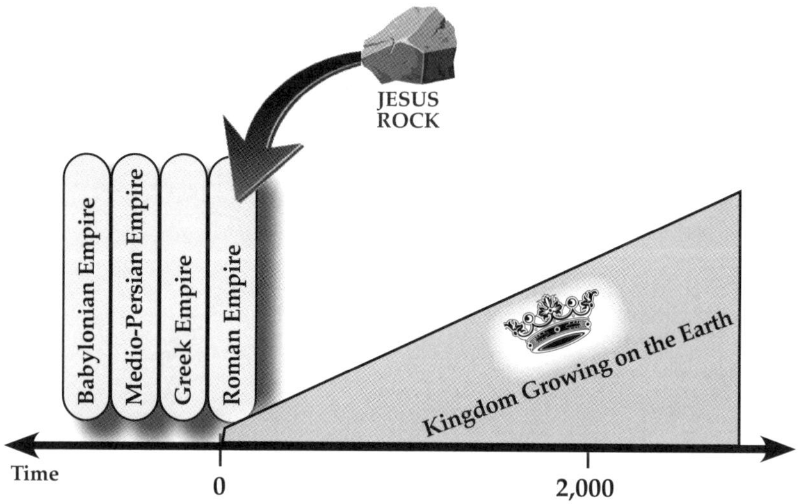

The partial preterist view teaches that the Kingdom of God eventually will fill Earth; however, evil will remain on Earth until the second coming of Jesus. We can see this by examining our Lord's parable in which He compared the Kingdom of God to seeds sown in a field. Those seeds grew to maturity, but an enemy sowed tares in the same field, and those tares also grew. Jesus' explanation of this parable makes it clear that both good and evil are growing on Earth, and they will both continue growing together until the day Jesus returns and separates good from evil (Matt. 13:24–43).

In another parable, Jesus compared the Kingdom with a mustard seed growing into the biggest tree in a garden. Comparatively, the Kingdom of God has been growing on Earth and one day will be the biggest, most influential entity on Earth (Matt. 13:31–32).

This is what we see happening historically since Jesus sat down on His throne. Christianity started in one small region in the Middle East with one Leader and 12 followers. Today, 2,000 years later, it is the largest religion covering the face of the earth. With about eight billion people in the world, more than 2.4 billion claim to be Christians today.

God's Kingdom Destroys the Roman Empire

Daniel's interpretation of King Nebuchadnezzar's dream reveals that the Rock comes to Earth at the time of the fourth kingdom, which is the Roman Empire. The Rock grows into God's Kingdom and destroys the Roman Empire.

Since the futurist view says that the Kingdom of God will come to Earth at the second coming of Jesus, they must identify some Roman Empire that will be in a ruling position at the time Jesus returns. Some futurist teachers say there must be a revived Roman Empire on Earth at that time. Some teachers are looking at the United Nations, the European Union, or some confederation of Muslim nations as that revived Roman Empire. Others say that the Roman Catholic Church is the Roman Empire that the Rock soon will come and crush.

Since futurist teachers envision the antichrist playing a central role in the end times, they typically place that evil ruler as head or in a place of great influence in the Roman kingdom that will be destroyed by the Rock. That belief leaves adherents very critical and suspicious of the Roman Catholic Church or any Roman governmental entity that they think may be in power at the time of our Lord's return.

In contrast, partial preterists are not looking for a revived Roman Empire. Adherents believe that the Rock came to Earth 2,000 years ago. Jesus came and established the Kingdom of God during the first century when the Roman Empire was in power. God's Kingdom has already destroyed the Empire, and there will be no future revived Roman Empire.

Summary of Daniel 2

If you embrace the partial preterist understanding of Daniel 2, you will believe that the Kingdom of God was established when Jesus came to Earth 2,000 years ago. You will not be looking for a revived Roman Empire. You will not be suspiciously watching various governments associated with that area of the world where Rome once ruled, nor will you be suspicious of the Roman Catholic Church becoming that Roman Empire. The Rock that came to Earth 2,000 years ago caused the Roman Empire to crumble exactly as the words of Daniel revealed.

If you embrace the partial preterist view, you will also realize that it is possible to experience and walk in God's Kingdom today. That Kingdom consists of *"righteousness and peace and joy in the Holy Spirit"* (Rom. 14:17). As you seek first God's Kingdom, you will experience the blessings of God through which *"all these things* [food, clothing, and other provisions] *will be added to you"* (Matt. 6:33).

Many Christians who believe the futurist view claim these benefits but then, a moment later, teach that the Kingdom of God will not be available until the second coming of Jesus. Hence, they try to hold two contradictory views at the same time, or they vacillate between the two views.

If you embrace the partial preterist view, you will be convinced that the Kingdom is already here. It is growing and advancing every day. When Jesus Christ returns, He will subdue all remaining evil and establish His perfect will throughout the world. Since God's Kingdom is advancing progressively on Earth, you can confidently say that God's Kingdom is here, and it is growing.

The Message of Daniel 9

In Daniel 9, we read about Daniel praying for his people, the Jews. At that time in history, the Jews were in captivity in Babylon. Their holy city, Jerusalem, was in ruins. Daniel knew that God would free His people from their bondage, for it had been promised through earlier prophets (Dan. 9:2). Daniel confessed the sins of his people and asked for mercy (Dan. 9:3–19). Then God sent the angel Gabriel to Daniel, and Gabriel told Daniel what would happen in the future (Dan. 9:21–27).

The words that Gabriel declared revealed the future of the Jews and Jerusalem, along with some significant facts about the future of the whole world. However, some of Gabriel's words are understood differently by those who believe the futurist view than those who believe the partial preterist view.

Seventy Weeks for the Jews and Jerusalem

Gabriel's declaration about the future began as follows:

> *Seventy weeks have been decreed for your people and your holy city, to finish the transgression, to make an end of sin, to make atonement for iniquity, to bring in everlasting righteousness, to seal up vision and prophecy, and to anoint the Most Holy Place.*
>
> —Dan. 9:24

Whether Christians hold to the futurist view or the partial preterist view, they will agree that the Jews and their holy city, Jerusalem, were to experience 70 weeks of God's favor, during which time God would fulfill the prophecies and promises that He had previously made to them.

Both futurist and partial preterist teachers hold that God's promise of *"seventy weeks"* equals 490 years. This is because there are seven days in a week, and 70 times seven equals 490. A study of the prophetic language of that period leads us to understand these as years (see Gen. 29:27; Lev. 25:8; Num. 14:34; Ezek. 4:4–6); hence, God promised the Jews 490 years of favor. Indeed, as we apply this period to the historical events, it reveals some remarkable—divine—predictions worth our attention.

As Gabriel went on speaking to Daniel, he divided the 490 years into three periods. First, he talked about seven weeks (seven times seven, or 49 years), and then 62 weeks (62 times seven, or 434 years). Finally, he talked about the last week (seven years). Together, these three periods total 490 years. Generally, futurists and partial preterists agree upon this.

The First 69 Weeks

Consider Gabriel's decree concerning the first 69 weeks (7 weeks plus 62 weeks):

> *So you are to know and discern that from the issuing of a decree to restore and rebuild Jerusalem, until Messiah the Prince, there will be seven weeks and sixty-two weeks; it will be built again, with plaza and moat, even in times of distress.*
>
> —Dan. 9:25

Gabriel gave a precise time for the coming of the Messiah. He said that from the decree to rebuild Jerusalem until the Messiah, there would be seven weeks and 62 weeks, that is, 69 weeks or 483 years.

In 457 BC, Artaxerxes, the king of Persia, decreed that the Jews were free to return to their homeland and rebuild Jerusalem and the Temple (Ezra 7:12–26). If we add 483 years to that date, we come to the year AD 27.[27] That was the year

27. The accuracy of this prediction is so remarkable that scholars questioning the trustworthiness of Scripture used to argue that the book of Daniel must

Jesus was water-baptized and began His public ministry. To accurately calculate this, it is necessary to know that Jesus was born in 4 BC,[28] which means that He was 30 years old in AD 27.

Timeline Showing the 483 Years Between the Decree for Freedom and the Messiah Revealed

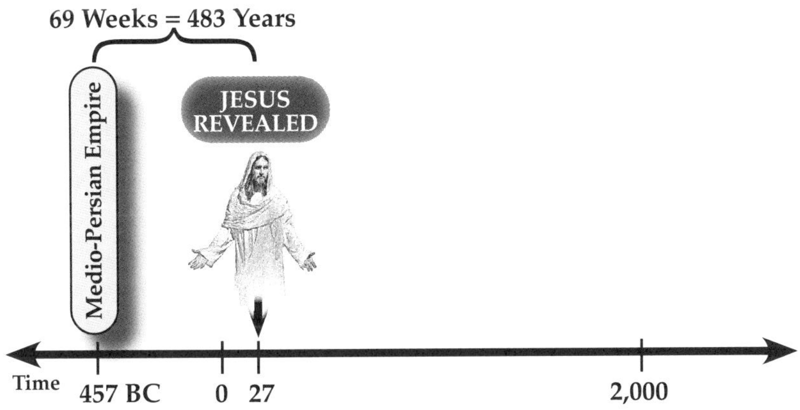

Indeed, there were 483 years between the decree to rebuild Jerusalem and the revealing of the Messiah. Gabriel's prophecy was remarkably accurate and must have been inspired by God, seeing as how it was given five and a half centuries before Jesus came into the world.

Gabriel went on to declare what would happen after the Messiah came:

> *Then after the sixty-two weeks the Messiah will be cut off and have nothing, and the people of the prince who is to*

have been written after the prophesied events were fulfilled. The discovery of the Dead Sea Scrolls between 1946 and 1956 proved that Daniel was written before the prophesied events were fulfilled.

28. Historians know that Jesus was not born in the year 0 because Matthew 2 reveals that Jesus was born while Herod was alive and Herod died in 4 BC. The confusion about dates is due to miscalculations made in the 6th century by Dionysius Exeguus, a monk who was commissioned by the pope to reform the Western calendar to center around the birth of Jesus.

> *come will destroy the city and the sanctuary. And its end will come with a flood; even to the end there will be war; desolations are determined.*
>
> —Dan. 9:26

As this verse tells us, Jesus was *"cut off."* He was put to death.

Then Gabriel said that the people of the prince would come and destroy the city and the sanctuary. Notice how similar Gabriel's wording is to the wording that Jesus used in Matthew 24 and Luke 21: desolations, the end, and destruction as a flood. As we explained earlier, Jerusalem and the Temple were destroyed in AD 70.

Some observant readers may question the timing of the Messiah being *"cut off"* and the destruction of Jerusalem. Gabriel reported these two events, but only said, *"Then after the sixty-two weeks."* The word *"then"* does not indicate any specific time, but refers to sometime after the Messiah was revealed.

Daniel's Seventieth Week

Generally, both the futurist and partial preterist teachers agree on how to understand the first 69 weeks (483 years) of God's favor. It is the remaining one week (seven years) about which they disagree. They have different ways of understanding what has become known as "Daniel's Seventieth Week."

Those who hold to the futurist view believe that God has not yet given the Jews their last seven years of favor, and, therefore, Daniel's seventieth week will come in the future. In contrast, partial preterists teach that Daniel's seventieth week has already occurred; therefore, we are not still waiting for it to be fulfilled. Allow us to further explain these different understandings.

The Futurist View of Daniel's Seventieth Week

Futurists see a considerable gap—at least 2,000 years—between the 69 weeks of God's favor and the seventieth week of God's favor upon the Jews. They explain that in between those two periods, God has been focusing on and dealing with the Gentiles, but at some point in the future, He will turn His attention back to the Jews and fulfill His promises to them.

Futurist teachers say that before the end of the world, God will turn His favor to the Jews and allow them to return to the Promised Land. Then, they will be given seven years of favor, during which time God will fulfill His promises to them, including elevating them as a nation to great authority in the world. During that time, the Jews will rebuild the Temple and restore their ancient religious system of offering sacrifices.

Timeline Showing Futurist View of Daniel's Seventieth Week

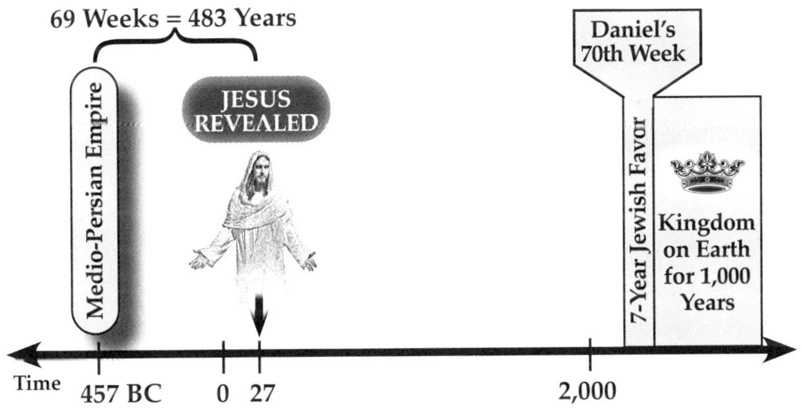

Futurist teachers also believe there will be a tribulation upon the whole world during the same seven years of Jewish favor. However, we will not describe that Great Tribulation until Section Four, when we study the book of Revelation.

As futurists envision the seven years of Jewish favor, they insert the last verse of Daniel 9:

> *And he will confirm a covenant with the many for one week, but in the middle of the week he will put a stop to sacrifice and grain offering.*
>
> —Dan. 9:27a

Futurists understand that the pronoun "he" mentioned in this verse refers to the antichrist who, at some point in the future, will make a covenant with the Jews, promising them peace and safety. That covenant will mark the beginning of Daniel's seventieth week. In the middle of those seven years—that is, three and a half years into it—the antichrist will break his covenant, turn against the Jews, and put an end to their religious practice of offering sacrifices to God. Most futurist teachers understand that God will then begin pouring out His wrath upon the earth, destroying much of it, but most of all, destroying the antichrist and all who follow him.

Partial Preterist View of Daniel's Seventieth Week

Teachers of partial preterism have a very different understanding of Daniel's seventieth week. Instead of inserting 2,000 years between the 69 weeks and the seventieth week, partial preterists see no gap. Teachers will explain that in Daniel 9, no gap is stated or implied. The natural reading of Daniel 9 leads us to believe that the seventieth week follows immediately after the sixty-ninth week.

This understanding has been the understanding of the historical Church. Most of our forefathers saw no gap between the 69 weeks and Daniel's seventieth week.

Augustine

For let us not suppose that the computation of Daniel's weeks was interfered with . . . or that they were not complete, but had to be completed afterward in the end of all things, for Luke most plainly testifies that the prophecy of Daniel was accomplished at the time when Jerusalem was overthrown.

Epistle of Augustine, 199:31, cited in Thomas Aquinas' *Golden Chain,* 1956

If there was no gap, then the last seven years of God's favor upon the Jews began immediately after the 69 weeks. It started in AD 27, the year Jesus was water-baptized and began His public ministry.

PARTIAL PRETERIST VIEW OF DANIEL'S SEVENTIETH WEEK

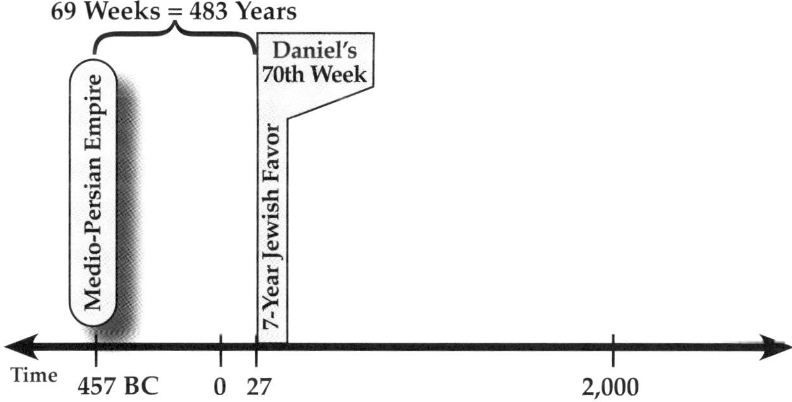

If we accept this idea that AD 27 is the beginning of Daniel's seventieth week, then we must explain how God fulfilled the words of Gabriel when he said, *"In the middle of the week he will put a stop to sacrifice and grain offering."* Partial preterist teachers say the *"he"* spoken of in this verse is Jesus Christ, not the antichrist. In the preceding two verses (Dan. 9:25–26), the Messiah was the main subject, and therefore, it is natural to conclude that the *"he"* referred to in the next verse is the Messiah.

To see the fulfillment of this, first, note that Jesus' public ministry was three and one-half years in length.

Eusebius

Now the whole period of our Saviour's teaching and working of miracles is said to have been three and a half years, which is half a week. John the evangelist, in his Gospel makes this clear to the attentive.

The Proof of the Gospel, 1920, VIII:I

At the end of those three and one-half years, Jesus shared the Last Supper with His disciples, during which time He took bread and said, *"This is My body,"* and then He took the cup and said, *"This cup is the new covenant in My blood"* (1 Cor. 11:24–25). After sharing that meal, Jesus fulfilled His words by dying on the cross. At that time, He put an end to sacrifice and grain offerings. As the writer of Hebrews explained, Jesus made the Jewish religious system obsolete (Heb. 8:7–13). A new covenant was established, and the old system was abolished. Once the ultimate sacrifice had been made, there was no longer any need for further sacrifices.

That explains the first three and one-half years of Daniel's seventieth week, but what about the last three and one-half years? The Jews were supposed to experience God's favor and the fulfillment of His promises for seven years. Indeed, they had the Messiah in their midst for the first three and one-half years, but what about the three and one-half years following the death of Jesus?

If we add three and one-half years to the time when Jesus was crucified, we come to another historic event. Although the exact date cannot be proven, most partial preterists believe that the last three and one-half years bring us to the time when Stephen was stoned to death (Acts 7:59–60). After Stephen gave a clear presentation concerning who Jesus was, the religious leaders rejected the Messiah. This event was especially significant because the high priest, who represented the Jews before God, was among those who rejected our Lord (Acts 7:1).

Shortly thereafter, Jesus revealed Himself in a blinding light to Saul (later to be called Paul) (Acts 9:1–6). Jesus told Paul to go and preach to the Gentiles (Acts 26:15–18). After that appearance, God spoke to Peter and gave him a vision in which all types of animals were presented to him. *"A voice came to him, 'Get up, Peter, kill and eat!'"* (Acts 10:13). At first, Peter refused to obey the voice because he was faithful to the Jewish laws concerning abstaining from unclean animals. After meditating on the vision and witnessing a Gentile group receive God's favor, Peter realized that God was declaring that no longer were any people—including Gentiles—to be considered unclean (Acts 10:28). All were welcome to come to God through Jesus Christ (Acts 10:34, 35).

What did all this mean? In the beginning of the book of Acts, the disciples presented the truths of Jesus Christ only to the Jews, for as Paul said to the Jews, *"It was necessary that the word of God be spoken to you first"* (Acts 13:46). However, after three and one-half years, God spoke to both Paul and Peter, telling them that now they were to present the gospel to all the world.

With this understanding, we see that Daniel's seventieth week was fulfilled. Beginning the day Jesus revealed Himself as the Messiah in AD 27, the Jews were given seven years of favor: three and one-half years during which Jesus walked among them, and then another three and one-half years during which the disciples preached the good news to them. The Jews received God's favor in that Jesus was first revealed to them. Also, God chose them to be the people from whom the Messiah came into the world, and they were the most privileged among all people because God first offered salvation to them.

Summary of Daniel 9

If you accept the understanding of Daniel 9 that we have just explained, you will realize that all 70 weeks of God's favor upon the Jews were fulfilled almost 2,000 years ago. Look again at Gabriel's initial words of prophecy and see how beautifully they were fulfilled. Gabriel said:

> *Seventy weeks have been decreed for your people and your holy city, to finish the wrongdoing, to make an end of sin, to make atonement for guilt, to bring in everlasting righteousness, to seal up vision and prophecy, and to anoint the Most Holy Place.*
>
> —Dan. 9:24

The most significant and wonderful prophecies ever given to the Jews were those about the coming Messiah. When Jesus came, the Jews could accept or reject Him. They were given the opportunity *"to finish the transgression, to make an end of sin, to make atonement for iniquity,* [and] *to bring in everlasting righteousness."*

Hence, the Jewish 70 weeks of God's favor were completed in the first century. This includes Daniel's seventieth week. Those final seven years of God's favor began when Jesus started His public ministry, and they ended when the high priest rejected the message preached by Stephen.

SUMMARY

If you come to believe the partial preterist view of Daniel 2 and 9, then you will embrace many ideas that may be new to you, but there are two key points.

First, you will understand that Christians may experience the Kingdom of God now. Furthermore, the Kingdom is growing on Earth and will come upon Earth in full power at the second coming of Jesus.

Second, you will realize that there will be no seven-year period of Jewish favor in the future. In Section Five, we will discuss how the Jews still have God's promise for a future spiritual awakening; however, Daniel's seventy weeks have already passed.

Section Four

Understanding the Book of Revelation

In this section, we will study the book of Revelation.

Many Christians shy away from Revelation because John, the writer, described spiritual images that may be difficult for the Western mind to understand. Revelation does not need to be difficult. Jesus instructed John to write what he saw (Rev. 1:19). John wrote to reveal, not conceal.

The reader simply needs to keep in mind that John was *"in the Spirit"* (Rev. 1:10; 4:2). He was in heaven, seeing into the spiritual realm. Compare John's perspective to that of a person watching what is going on behind a stage while a play is being performed on the stage. The area behind the stage is the spiritual realm. The area on the stage is the natural realm. The spiritual dynamics happening behind the stage influence what happens on stage.

John Saw into the Spiritual Realm, which Influenced the Natural Realm

John actually "saw" the visions he recorded in Revelation. Thirty-nine times, John said, *"I saw . . ."* (e.g., Rev. 5:1, 2, 6). Jesus instructed John to write down what he *saw* (Rev. 1:11, 19).

This is important to note because some eschatology teachers assume and imply that John made up figures and symbols to help him communicate what he wanted to communicate. That error sees John's imagination as the origin of the figures and symbols. Revelation clearly shows us that the figures and symbols originated in the spiritual realm, and John was an observer.

As John watched what was happening in the spiritual realm, he did not understand everything he saw. He was familiar with some spiritual figures and images because the OT prophets saw similar figures and images in their visions. John also had angels appear to him at key moments to explain what the figures and images meant.

Fortunately, as readers, we have access to the writings of the OT prophets and the explanations the angels gave John. We have everything we need to understand what Jesus wanted to communicate.

All we need to do is listen. Jesus said, *"The one who has an ear, let him hear . . ."* (Rev. 2:7). With slight variations, this is stated eight times in Revelation. This means we can understand if we are willing to understand.

Readers who only desire a cursory understanding of the futurist and partial preterist views may be content by reading the introduction which gives a brief overview. Readers desiring a thorough understanding will want to read through this entire section.[29]

29. Readers desiring even more in-depth teaching may read an additional book by Dr. Harold Eberle entitled *The Comings of Christ, Why I Am a Partial Preterist, Not a Full Preterist.*

Futurists and partial preterists generally agree about the meaning of the first three chapters of the book of Revelation. They recognize chapter 1 as a record of John's encounter with Jesus. Chapters 2 and 3 are seven letters written to seven churches.

Futurists and partial preterists also agree that 2,000 years ago, Jesus ascended into heaven and sat down at the right hand of God. Since then, Jesus has been seated at the right hand of God, reigning over God's Kingdom in heaven.

FUTURISTS AND PARTIAL PRETERISTS AGREE

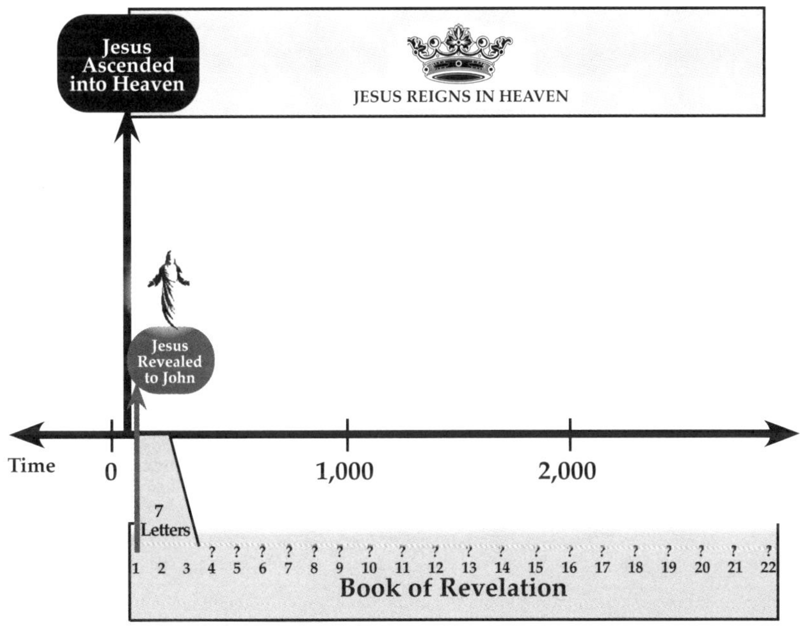

Futurists and partial preterists disagree about the rest of the book of Revelation. They have different understandings of chapters 4–22.

Overview of the Futurist Understanding

Futurists believe that Revelation 4–22 will be fulfilled in the future. In particular, the judgments described in Revelation 4–18 will be fulfilled during a future seven-year period of tribulation. After that, futurists envision the return of Jesus (Rev. 19), followed by a 1,000-year reign of Jesus on Earth (Rev. 20). Then futurists envision the creation of a new heaven and Earth (Rev. 21–22).

The Futurist Understanding of the Book of Revelation[30]

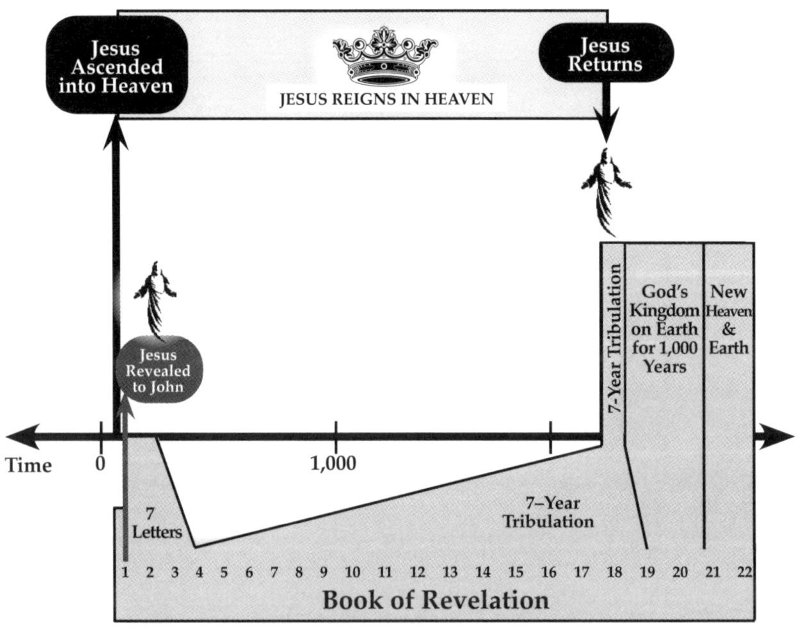

Different futurist teachers make some modifications to this view. For example, some futurists vary as to when they place a rapture of the Church: at the start, middle, or end

30. This diagram shows Rev. 1–3 happening in the past, but this view is not a partial preterist view because Rev. 1–3 are not considered prophecies.

of the seven-year tribulation. Other minor modifications are numerous, but the main point is that futurists see that almost all the book of Revelation (chapters 4 to the end) will be fulfilled in our future.

John Is the Reference Point

The first important distinctive of the partial preterist view is how adherents understand Revelation 4:1. After John recorded the seven letters to the seven churches (Rev. 2–3), he wrote that a voice from heaven said to him, *"Come up here . . .* (Rev. 4:1).

John was taken up into heaven. That happened in the first century while John was alive.

Then, John was told that he would see what would take place in the future.

> *I will show you what must take place after these things.*
>
> —Rev. 4:1b

This gives us a framework in which we should understand the whole book of Revelation. John saw from heaven's perspective how events would unfold from his lifetime forward.

In contrast, most futurists place a future rapture of the Church to heaven at Revelation 4:1.[31] They may admit that John was taken to heaven during his lifetime, but most will also say the words, *"Come up here,"* mark the future date when the Church will be raptured to heaven. Futurist teachers claim that Revelation 4:1 marks the future rapture of the Church because it fits with their view that the Church will not be on Earth during the judgments described in chapters 4–18 of Revelation.

In reality, there is no mention of the Church in Revelation 4:1, let alone of it being raptured to heaven. We are specifically

31. Jack Van Impe, *Millennium: Beginning or End?* (Nashville, TN: Word Publishing, 1999), 43.

shown that *John was taken to heaven*. Furthermore, the literal timing of this "taking up" was during John's lifetime in the first century.

The partial preterist's understanding that Revelation 4:1 took place in John's lifetime leads one to conclude that the events John saw began to unfold in his lifetime. To confirm this understanding, consider the other time references within the text. Revelation begins with Jesus saying that He was going to reveal *"things which must soon take place"* (Rev. 1:1).

Lest people rationalize that *"soon"* does not really mean soon, we can note that Jesus re-emphasized this by saying, *"the time is near"* (Rev. 1:3). Christians with a partial preterist view of the book of Revelation take these words literally. They understand that what John saw and reported began to unfold during his lifetime in the first century.

Jesus instructed John:

> *Therefore write the <u>things which you have seen</u>, and the <u>things which are</u>, and the <u>things which will take place after</u> these things.*
>
> —Rev. 1:19

It is important to notice the sequence of events. We are told that what John saw started soon, but John also saw events that would unfold from his lifetime forward. This is what we will see as we study through Revelation.

Overview of the Partial Preterist Understanding

Different partial preterist teachers have variations on how they teach Revelation. They agree that John was taken to heaven in Revelation 4:1 and Jesus will return in the future. We will see how they also agree that Revelation 7–11 is about the judgment of the early Jews and Jerusalem that happened by AD 70.

PARTIAL PRETERIST UNDERSTANDING OF THE BOOK OF REVELATION[32]

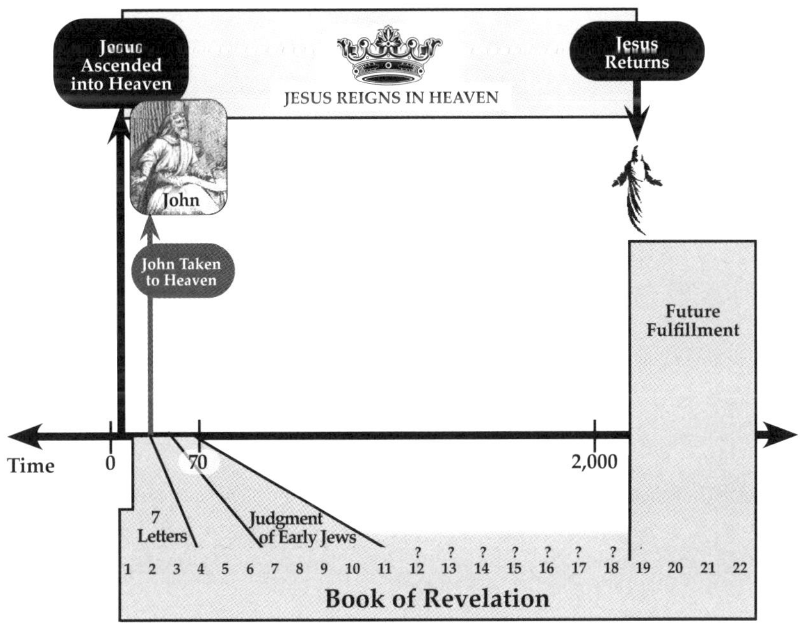

Beyond these basics, there is some variety in what partial preterists believe will happen. We will explain those differences as we continue in this section.

32. This diagram is an oversimplified version of the partial preterist view primarily because some partial preterists see some or all of Revelation 20–22 as being fulfilled in the present.

When Did John Write Revelation?

Before we delve into the text of Revelation, we should discuss *when* John wrote the book. Futurist teachers usually say John wrote it around AD 96. If, indeed, it was not written until the end of the first century, how can partial preterists say that any part of the book speaks prophetically of the coming destruction of Jerusalem in AD 70?

There is historical documentation indicating that John wrote Revelation at an earlier date.

In Revelation 1:9, John wrote that he was on the island of Patmos when he received what he wrote in Revelation. There is some evidence that John was exiled to Patmos under the reign of Domitian between AD 81 and 96, but there are also historical documents telling us John was exiled to Patmos at an earlier date.

For example, the writings of Epiphanius (c. 315–403) state that John was first imprisoned under Claudius, who reigned from AD 41 to 54.[33]

We also have the *Syriac Version* of the NT, which says the following on the title page of the book of Revelation:

> The Revelation which was made by God to John the Evangelist in the island Patmos, into which he was thrown by Nero Caesar.[34]

Nero Caesar ruled over the Roman Empire from AD 54–68. So, according to the quotation above, John had to have been on the island of Patmos during this earlier period.

Tertullian similarly placed John on the island of Patmos during the reign of Nero, saying that John survived after being boiled in oil in Rome. After that, John was sent to Patmos.

33. Epiphanius, *The Panarion of St. Epiphanius of Salamis*, Frank Williams, trans. (New York: E. J. Brill, 1987), 11.

34 .The following sources provide this information: Moses Stuart, *Commentary on the Apocalypse*,1845, Vol. I, 267; Kurt Simmons, *The Consummation of the Ages* (Carlsbad, NM: Bimillennial Preterist Association, 2003), 17–18.

Tertullian

Rome . . . where Peter had a like Passion with the Lord; where Paul hath for his crown the same death with John; where the Apostle John was plunged into boiling oil, and suffered nothing, and was afterwards banished to an island.

Apologetic and Practical Treatises, 1842, 470–471

It is possible that all these historical documents are true. John could have been sent to the island of Patmos more than once.[35] Reports of multiple imprisonments should not surprise us any more than hearing of modern-day criminals being sent to prison several times. We know that Paul was imprisoned several times (2 Cor. 11:23).

Advocates of the futurist view do not want Christians to consider any authorship date other than AD 96 because that date supports their view that the events reported in Revelation will be fulfilled in the future, long after the destruction of the Jewish Temple in AD 70.

Yet, Revelation itself indicates an authorship date before AD 70. In Revelation 11:1, John was given instructions to measure the Temple in Jerusalem. Since John had to measure the Temple, the book must have been written before the Temple was destroyed.

Another reason to believe Revelation was written at an earlier date is that Jerome (c. 340–420) noted in his writings that John was seen in AD 96, and he was so old and infirm that "he was with difficulty carried to the church, and could speak only a few words to the people."[36] We must put this fact

35. Prisoners were sometimes released at the death of the government leader who sent them to prison. Since John outlived several emperors, it is reasonable to think he served more than one sentence on Patmos.

36. Cited in Kurt Simmons, *The Consummation of the Ages* (Carlsbad, NM: Bimillennial Preterist Association, 2003), 13.

together with what Revelation 10:11 says: John must *"prophesy again concerning many peoples and nations and tongues and kings."* It is difficult to imagine that John would be able to speak to many nations and kings at any date after AD 96, since he was already elderly and feeble.

There are additional reasons to believe that John wrote the book of Revelation before AD 70. In his excellent book *Rapture,* David Currie offers a more thorough discussion of this topic. So also does Kurt Simmons, in his book, *The Consummation of the Ages*.

Revelation 2 & 3: Seven Letters to Seven Churches

In chapters 2 and 3 of Revelation, John recorded seven letters to seven churches as instructed by Jesus. Our Lord started each letter by declaring who He is and His awareness of what they each were experiencing: *"I know your deeds," "I know your tribulation and your poverty,"* and *"I know where you dwell."* Jesus knows, and He cares.

These letters were written to real churches that existed in Asia Minor during John's lifetime. Indeed, we have historical evidence that each of those churches existed in the first century. Of course, we can learn from those messages and apply them to our lives today. Jesus even encouraged us to do so by ending each letter by saying, *"He who has an ear, let him hear what the Spirit says to the churches."* We should pay close attention to what Jesus said to those churches. We should also keep them in their historical context, realizing that they were written to real churches that existed during John's life.

Many futurists have taught that the seven churches represent seven time periods spreading over the last 2,000 years, the first church being the Church of the first century, the second church being the Church of the second and third centuries, and so on, with the last church being our modern-day Church. That would make us the Laodicean church, which is called lukewarm and harshly rebuked by Jesus. Such a negative view of the present Church fits well with the futurist view that there will be a great falling away during the last days and the Church will grow cold.

We hope you immediately reject that way of interpreting Revelation 2 and 3. There is no indication in the text that the churches represent time periods. They are literal churches that existed in the first century. Furthermore, we are not the lukewarm church. The Church today is alive and healthy. Perhaps your corner of Christianity is struggling, but worldwide, the Church is exploding in growth. Today, more zealous Christians, evangelists, missionaries, and others are giving their lives for the gospel than at any other time in history. Please do not accept any inferences from the pessimistic crowd that we are the Laodicean church.

Of course, tragic things are going on in the world today, and more Christians are being martyred now than at any time in history, but the Church is also marching ahead, and the gates of hades will never prevail against it. As we will see in the following pages, Jesus is raising His Church to a position of unity, power, and glory.

Revelation 4 & 5: Heavenly Scene of Christ's Reign

In Revelation 4:1, John was lifted into heaven and saw the throne of God:

> *Immediately I was in the Spirit; and behold, a throne was standing in heaven, and One sitting on the throne.*
>
> —Rev. 4:2

John saw God sitting on His throne.

Also, 24 elders were sitting around the throne of God, each on their own throne. John was overwhelmed as he saw flashes of light and heard peals of thunder. He saw four living creatures around the throne, and he heard them saying:

> *Holy, holy, holy is the Lord God, the Almighty, who was and who is and who is to come.*
>
> —Rev. 4:8b

The majesty of the moment cannot be adequately conveyed with words, but John does a better job than we can, as you can see if you read the entire chapter.

For our purposes here, we can see how the stage was set for the rest of the book of Revelation. John was in heaven. From that perspective, he got to see everything that would take place from his life forward: *"I will show you what must take place after these things"* (Rev. 4:1). John got to watch events unfold as God acted from His throne in heaven.

Revelation 5: Jesus Is Worthy to Open the Book

In chapter 5 of Revelation, John watched what happened before the throne:

> *I saw in the right hand of Him who sat on the throne a book written inside and on the back, sealed up with seven seals.*
>
> —Rev. 5:1

The seals on this book signify that the book had not yet been opened. This brings to remembrance the words Daniel wrote as he recorded the visions that were to be fulfilled in the future. Daniel was told to *"conceal these words and seal up the book until the end of time"* (Dan. 12:4). As those words of Daniel were sealed until the time of their fulfillment, so also the book held in the hand of God in Revelation 5 was sealed until the day its contents should be fulfilled.

In John's lifetime, the day of fulfillment had come. As we continue in our study, we will see how the judgments of God were executed after the seals were broken.

When we think of those judgments, we should not think of a judge declaring punishments for criminals. Instead, think of a king rendering judgments to extend his government. These are kingly decrees to establish the will of the King.[37]

In Revelation 5, we see that all God had decreed concerning His Kingdom was about to be executed. The day of fulfillment had come, but first, there had to be found one who was worthy to break the seals and open the book. Emphasizing this truth, Revelation 5 is the record of searching for Him who is worthy to open the seals, and of course, it was the Lamb who was slain, the Lion of the tribe of Judah. He is the One who took the book from the Father while the elders, angels, and living creatures cried out in worship.

37. Some partial preterists believe the primary message of Revelation is about God abolishing the old covenant that He had with His OT covenant people and replacing it with the new covenant that God established through Jesus with His NT covenant people. Corresponding to that view, those partial preterists see the sealed book as a scroll that was God's certificate of divorce being given to the Jews. That view is taken by Kenneth Gentry Jr., in his book, *The Book of Revelation Made Easy*, pages 48, 88. The major errors of Gentry's view are explained in *Section Five: The Jews, Israel, and the Temple*, subtitled, *The Jews Were Judged but Not Rejected*. See pages 247–256.

Revelation 6:
God's Army Is Arrayed for Battle

Beginning in chapter 6 of Revelation, we read about Jesus breaking the seals of God's book one at a time. With the breaking of the first four seals, four warhorses were commanded to come before God, and each was given power to destroy. The first horse was white, having the power to conquer. The second horse was red, having the power to take peace from Earth. The third horse was black, having the power to make supplies and sustenance difficult to obtain. The fourth horse was ashen, with the power to kill with the sword, famine, pestilence, and wild beasts.

The First Four Seals Were Broken and Four Warhorses Came Before God in Heaven

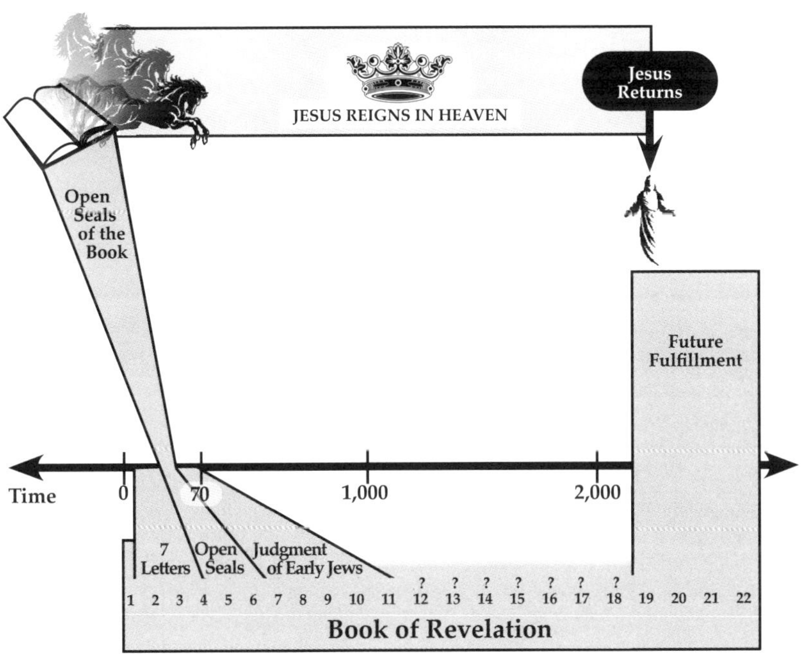

Futurist teachers see those warhorses coming down to Earth to judge humanity during a future seven-year tribulation. In reality, none of those horses are shown coming to Earth. They are each told to "come" in the sense of presenting themselves to God in heaven. Each horse was given power to destroy and then released—not to go to Earth, but to take their positions in heaven where they could exercise authority over Earth.

Compare that image to how a natural king at that time in history would position his forces at the battlefront before the battle begins. The commanders of the army would take their positions on their horses overlooking the battlefield. In like manner, God was setting the stage for the ensuing battles. This happened in John's lifetime in the first century. The warriors were arrayed for battle and waited for the call to action.

The waiting period is confirmed when we read about the fifth seal being broken and John seeing the souls of people who had been previously slain for their faith. They were watching and crying out to God:

> *How long, O Lord, holy and true, will You refrain from judging and avenging our blood on those who dwell on the earth?*
>
> —Rev. 6:10

Put yourself in John's position in heaven. The first five seals of God's book of judgments were broken. The four warhorses took their positions and waited for the command to start the battle. God's people who had been martyred for their faith saw this, and they immediately wondered if it was the time that their blood would be avenged. God would be answering the prayers of His saints when He released His judgments. In anticipation, the saints cried out but they were told to wait a little longer, even though the battle was impending.

Revelation 6: Breaking of the Sixth Seal

With the breaking of the sixth seal, John watched signs indicating catastrophic events:

> *And there was a great earthquake; and the sun became as black as sackcloth made of hair, and the whole moon became like blood; and the stars of the sky fell to the earth, as a fig tree casts its unripe figs when shaken by a great wind. The sky was split apart like a scroll when it is rolled up.*
>
> —Rev. 6:12–14a

As we explained earlier,[38] the sun, moon, and stars were frequently used to refer to governing authorities. When governing authorities were removed or diminished, the sun, moon, or stars were said to fall or darken. In this passage, we see these authorities being shaken by the presence of God. The apocalyptic reference to earthquakes meant that God was intervening and acting in judgment to remove established authorities and replace them with His authority.

To see this in another passage, we can read Hebrews 12:26–28:

> *And His voice shook the earth then, but now He has promised, saying, "Yet, once more I will shake not only the earth, but also the heaven." This expression, "Yet once more," denotes the removing of those things which can be shaken, as of created things, so that those things which cannot be shaken may remain. Therefore, since we receive a kingdom which cannot be shaken, let's show gratitude . . .*

This is another example of God shaking authorities and establishing His authority.

Once the sixth seal was broken, we are told:

38. This was explained in Section One, under *Question #2: "What Will Be the Sign of Your Coming?"* when discussing Matthew 24:29 on pages 53–56.

> *Then the kings of the earth and the great people, and the commanders and the rich and the strong, and every slave and free man hid themselves in the caves . . . "Fall on us . . . for the great day of their wrath has come, and who is able to stand?"*
>
> —Rev. 6:15–17

John was seeing a vision of what *"must soon take place."* God had arrayed His warhorses, which represented His authority and power. In God's glorious presence and the presence of His power, the authorities of Earth were struck with terror. They could see that judgment and war were about to begin.

The War Begins

Now, we are ready to study God's war through which the kingdoms of this world become the Kingdom of our Lord Jesus Christ.

There are three sets of judgments in Revelation 7–18:

1. First set of judgments: Revelation 7–11
2. Second set of judgments: Revelation 12–14
3. Third set of judgments: Revelation 15–18

In the following pages, we will examine each set of judgments one at a time.

Revelation 7–11: The First Set of Judgments

The first set of judgments was directed against the early Jews and Jerusalem. As Paul warned in Romans 2:9:

> *There will be tribulation and distress for every soul of mankind who does evil, for the Jew first and also for the Greek.*

It is the way of God to first judge His people before judging the world (1 Peter 4:17).

Many Christians today have difficulty conceiving of God harshly judging His OT covenant people. Yet, a fundamental declaration of God's covenant with the Jews was that if they obeyed Him, He would bless them; if they forsook Him, they would be judged (Deut. 28). The OT tells us about how the Jews forsook God, and hence, suffered judgment. During the sixth century BC, the Jews were driven from their land, Jerusalem was destroyed, and those who were not killed were taken away as slaves. It was because of their disobedience and hardness of heart that their enemies were able to defeat them.

Similarly, in the NT, we read declarations of the coming judgment of the Jews. John the Baptist called the Jews to repent, but most of the religious leaders would not. So, John declared that the axe was laid to the root, meaning that judgment was falling upon them (Luke 3:7–9).

Jesus bemoaned the fact that God had sent many prophets to the Jews, but the Jews had persecuted and even killed the prophets (Matt. 23:29–35). Of much greater offense was the Jewish rejection of Jesus as the Messiah, the Son of God.

Several times, Jesus declared the destruction about to come upon Jerusalem and the Jewish Temple:

> *So that upon you will fall the guilt of all the righteous blood shed on earth . . . Behold, your house is being left*

> *to you desolate!*
>
> —Matt. 23:35–38

> *But when you see Jerusalem surrounded by armies, then recognize that her desolation is near.*
>
> —Luke 21:20

> *And they will fall by the edge of the sword, and will be led captive into all the nations; and Jerusalem will be trampled underfoot by the Gentiles until the times of the Gentiles are fulfilled.*
>
> —Luke 21:24

Jesus decreed destruction.

In Section One, we discussed the Jewish holocaust of AD 70. We do not need to repeat that discussion, but some readers may be jumping ahead to this section on the study of Revelation instead of reading from the beginning. If readers are not aware of the first-century Jewish holocaust, they will be unable to grasp how clearly it was the fulfillment of the judgment described in Revelation 7–11. If you have not already, please take a moment to read the brief description of the Jewish holocaust in Section One.[39] More than one million Jews were killed—thousands of them were crucified.

Of course, not all the Jews rejected Jesus, and in fact, much of the early Church was made up of Jews who believed in Jesus. However, the vast majority rejected Him. The apostle Paul wrote how he yearned for his people, the Jews, to recognize Jesus as the Messiah, but only a remnant had accepted Him (Rom. 11:5). Paul wrote how the great majority of Jews had become enemies of the gospel (Rom. 11:28).

Jesus declared to the Jews that He was the Stone that the builders rejected (Matt. 21:42). He then went on to say that the Kingdom of God would be taken away from them and given to a people producing the fruit of the Kingdom (Matt. 21:43). In that context, Jesus declared that the Stone—He, Himself—would crush and scatter like dust whoever rejects Him (Matt.

39. See pages 11–13.

21:44). That is what John described in Revelation 7–11. It was the judgment of the Jews and Jerusalem in AD 70.

Arethas of Caesarea

Here, then, were manifestly shown to the Evangelist what things were to befall the Jews in their war against the Romans, in the way of avenging the sufferings inflicted upon Christ.

Cited in *A Commentary on The Apocalypse* by Stuart, 1845, 268

Revelation 7: Sealing 144,000 Sons of Israel

Before the Jewish judgment began, God sealed a number of the Jews so a remnant would remain alive after the AD 70 holocaust.

> *Do not harm the earth or the sea or the trees until we have sealed the bond-servants of our God on their foreheads . . . and forty-four thousand sealed from every tribe of the sons of Israel.*
>
> —Rev. 7:3–4

This marking would have been understood by the Jewish readers of that period as God's mark of protection. As blood was placed on the doorpost of the homes of the Hebrews to protect them from the death angel at the first Passover in Egypt (Ex. 12), a number of the Israelites[40] were marked by God so that a remnant would be spared from the slaughter to come. This seal is not to be understood as a physically visible mark, but instead as God knowing those who were His.

There may have been precisely 144,000 sons of Israel

40. "Israelites" refers to the descendants of Abraham, Isaac, and Jacob. God changed Jacob's name to Israel; his descendants were called Israelites.

protected from the destruction, but the Jews in Bible days often used certain numbers in a symbolic sense. The Jews understood the number 144,000 as a chosen multitude.

In Revelation 7:5–8, we are further told that 12,000 were marked from each of the 12 tribes.[41] There may have been a literal 12,000 from each tribe marked, but the Jewish readers of that time would have understood this number in a less strict sense. They would have concluded that God was favoring each tribe equally, and He was marking a plentiful, sufficient number to be spared from the coming judgment.

Some Western readers may hear us using these numbers in a non-literal sense and accuse us of "spiritualizing" Scripture. We would respond by saying they are "westernizing" Scripture. The Western mind insists on taking such numbers in their strictest sense. If we are going to understand Scripture from the framework in which the authors wrote it, we must acknowledge the symbolic and apocalyptic language they used. Indeed, God marked a significant number from each of the 12 tribes of Israel. They were marked so as not to be destroyed in the impending war.

Revelation 8:1–7: Trumpets Blow and the War Begins

In chapter 8 of Revelation, the judgment of Jerusalem began. Jesus was holding the book of the decrees of God. He broke the seventh and final seal of the book. Then, *"there was silence in heaven for about half an hour"* (Rev. 8:1). It was the calm before the storm. The stage was set; the war was about to begin. The strategy of God to take over this world was about

41. Originally, the 12 tribes were the descendants of the 12 sons of Jacob (Israel). However, by the time of Christ, the Jews in Palestine were mostly made up of the tribes of Judah and Benjamin, along with some Levites. The other tribes had been scattered throughout the surrounding regions, due to migrations, persecutions, and the exile into Assyria around 720 BC. By the first century, the 12 tribes were mixed and not actually the descendants of all of the 12 sons of Israel.

to be executed.

The blowing of trumpets started the war:

> *And I saw the seven angels who stand before God, and seven trumpets were given to them.*
>
> —Rev. 8:2

To grasp the dramatic event that followed, envision a war in ancient times. A king would have his soldiers take their positions and form a tremendous battlefront. Then, a series of trumpets would be blown for all to hear, and with each trumpet blown some force among the king's army would be released.

When the first trumpet was blown, it was customary to have the archers release their arrows. Corresponding to that, we read in Revelation 8:7 that when the first angel sounded the first trumpet:

> *There came hail and fire, mixed with blood, and they were thrown to the earth; and a third of the earth was burned up . . .*

As arrows being launched from thousands of archers, destruction was launched from heaven.

Revelation 7–11: Judgment of the Jews and Jerusalem

Before we go on to see what happened as the second to seventh trumpets were blown, it will be helpful to identify who was on the receiving end of the judgment and destruction. As already mentioned, judgment began with God's people, the Jews, during the first century.

Making this difficult for some readers to accept is the fact that some translations of the book of Revelation offer a confusing translation of the Greek word *ge*. This word may be translated as "earth," "ground," or "land," and each Bible translator decided which word to use according to their understanding of the context. When we study the rest of the NT, we learn that in most versions, the word *ge* is usually translated as "land."

Further leading us to translate *ge* as "land" is the *Septuagint*, the Greek translation of the OT and the primary version used by the early Church. In the *Septuagint*, there are many references to the Gentiles being driven out of the *ge* or land, and the land being referred to was the land God promised to the Jews, e.g., Num. 32:17; 33:52, 55; Josh. 7:9; 9:24; Judges 1:32; 2 Sam. 5:6; 1 Chron. 11:4; 22:18; Neh. 9:24. This same term, "land," was frequently used by the OT prophets when they spoke of the Jews being driven from their land in the fifth and sixth centuries BC, e.g., Jer. 1:14; 10:18; Ezek. 7:7; Hosea 4:1; Joel 1:2, 14.

To be consistent, we should translate the term *ge* as "land" in Revelation 7–11. John was referring to the land once promised to the Jews rather than to the whole earth. Therefore, in Revelation 8:7, when John described one-third of the *ge* being burned up, he was saying that one-third of the land was burned, and that land was the land of Israel.

Revelation 8:8–13: The Second to Fourth Trumpets

Next, the second angel sounded the second trumpet:

> *Something like a great mountain burning with fire was thrown into the sea; and a third of the sea became blood, and a third of the creatures which were in the sea and had life, died; and a third of the ships were destroyed.*
>
> —Rev. 8:8–9

When the third angel sounded the third trumpet:

> *A great star fell from heaven, burning like a torch, and it fell on a third of the rivers and on the springs of waters*

> *. . . and many men died from the waters . . .*
>
> —Rev. 8:10–11

When the fourth angel sounded the fourth trumpet:

> *A third of the sun and a third of the moon and a third of the stars were struck . . .*
>
> —Rev. 8:12

As already explained,[42] the darkening or falling of lights, such as the sun, moon, or stars, was the language that the OT prophets used to announce the judgment and fall of authorities.

John was watching these dynamics in the spiritual realm, but they had consequences in the natural realm. God's enemies were being defeated.

Revelation 9:1–12: The Fifth Trumpet Is Blown

When the fifth angel sounded the fifth trumpet (Rev. 9:1), a bottomless pit (called an abyss in some translations) opened and out came locusts with power like scorpions to harm the people who did not have the seal of God on their foreheads (Rev. 9:1–4). We are told that the locusts had faces like the faces of men, hair like that of a woman, and teeth like a lion. In their tails was the power to sting people and inflict great pain for five months.

Some of the most well-known futurist teachers say that these locusts are futuristic helicopters that swarm out of the sky and shoot out of their tails a poison that inflicts great pain. Other noted futurists have observed the recent uprising of Islamic terrorists and concluded that the locusts must be the Muslim extremists who will someday attack God's people.

These interpretations of the futurists are interesting because futurists often claim to take the Bible literally. If we take those

42. See pages 53–56, under the title, *Matthew 24:29: The Signs of Judgment.*

verses literally, we have to believe that actual locusts with gold crowns, faces like men, hair like women, teeth like lions, and tails like scorpions will swarm across the earth. Furthermore, if the futurist teachers were taking the Scriptures literally, they would have to say that their helicopters or their Muslim terrorists were coming out of a bottomless pit. Of course, no futurist could reasonably say that. The idea that futurists take the book of Revelation literally is a myth.

Partial preterists attempt to see the context in which images and symbols are referred to in other passages of Scripture. For example, the sight of beings coming from the abyss was contrasted to beings coming from men who dwell on Earth. That contrast separated spiritual beings from human beings. Coming from the abyss also identified those beings as evil, unlike those from heaven.

Swarming locusts were mentioned in Exodus 10 when Moses released God's judgment upon the Egyptians. After that time, locusts were thought of as a symbol of judgment. The prophet Joel used this symbol:

> *What the gnawing locust has left, the swarming locust has eaten; and what the swarming locust has left, the creeping locust has eaten; and what the creeping locust has left, the stripping locust has eaten.*
>
> —Joel 1:4

In this passage, Joel was speaking about the destruction that came upon the Jews in OT times.

Similarly, John saw visions of locusts swarming upon the land (*ge*). John understood those locusts as the judgments that were about to come upon the early Jews and Jerusalem.

Communication of Spiritual Realities

Next, the sixth and seventh angels blew their trumpets, but

before we examine the relevant verses, it will be beneficial to check our perspective. We must see from John's perspective to accurately understand what John wrote.

What we read in the book of Revelation is information that John received through revelation. John was in the spiritual realm. He watched spiritual dynamics happening in the spiritual realm.

John Saw Millions of Locusts in the Spiritual Realm

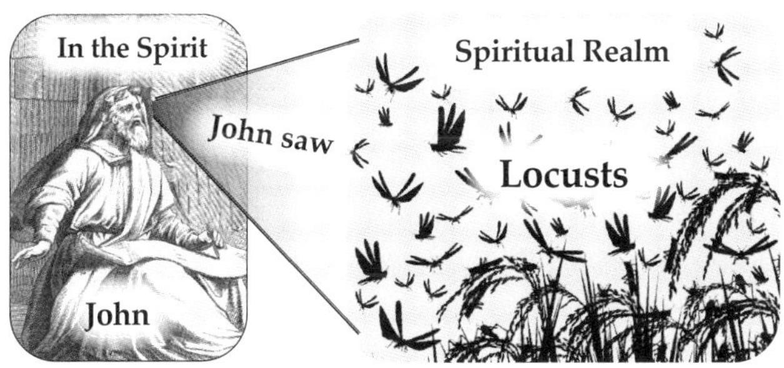

John did not understand everything he saw in the spiritual realm because many spiritual dynamics can only be communicated through visions, with images, symbols, and metaphors. This is similar to how Jesus used parables to explain realities of the Kingdom of God.

Other individuals in the Bible saw into the spiritual realm, and they also saw visions that used images, symbols, and metaphors. For example, the prophet Elisha prayed for his servant's eyes to be opened to the spiritual world, and as a result, *"he saw; and behold, the mountain was full of horses and chariots of fire all around Elisha"* (2 Kings 6:17). Seeing those horses and chariots, Elisha and his servant knew God's power was present to protect them.

Think more deeply about what Elisha and his servant saw. It is difficult to say whether horses and chariots were literally present in the spiritual realm or whether those horses and chariots represented the power of God that was available to defend Elisha and his servant. For us today, horses and chariots would not effectively represent God's power because one modern military machine such as a tank could defeat thousands of horses and chariots. Perhaps, if God wanted to reveal His power to us, He would show visions of armies with the most advanced and deadly equipment.

That reveals how realities in the spiritual realm are communicated. It is similar to the images one sees in dreams. There may be spiritual realities behind spiritual images, but the images are a form of communication. It is with this understanding that we must examine the visions recorded throughout the book of Revelation.

For another example, consider Revelation 1:18, where Jesus said He has the keys of death and hades. From this, we do not need to conclude that death and hades have doors requiring keys to open, but rather, this is symbolic language representing how Jesus has the authority over both death and hades.

So also, Jesus said to the Laodicean church that He is standing at the door and knocking (Rev. 3:20), but we do not need to conclude that there is a literal door that must be opened; instead, we understand this terminology as symbolic.

With this perspective, we must understand all the visions John recorded in the book of Revelation. John did "see" what he said he saw. However, we must understand that he was *"in the Spirit"* (Rev. 1:10). He was receiving images that communicated spiritual realities. Fortunately, angels came alongside John to explain the visions to him.

Spiritual Dynamics Have Natural Consequences

John's visions revealed spiritual realities. However, that was only half of the revelation. The second half was knowing what consequences the spiritual realities had upon the natural realm.

For example, John saw into the spiritual realm and received revelation when he saw swarms of locusts. The other half of the revelation was knowing that locusts in the spiritual realm correlated with a huge army bringing destruction in the natural realm.

Dynamics in the Spiritual Realm Influence the Natural Realm

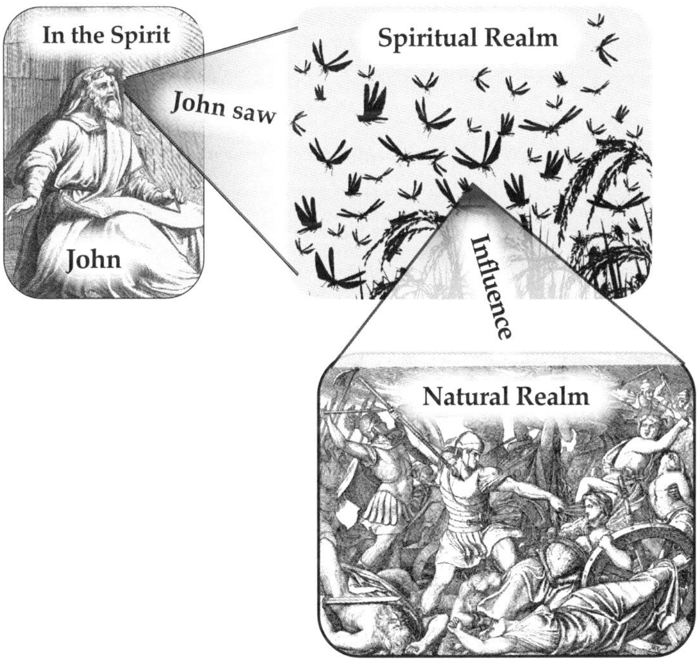

Notice that what is seen in the spiritual realm (locusts) may correlate with something that looks very different (an army bringing destruction) in the natural realm.

Comparative correlations can be seen in other Bible passages, as well. Consider the death of Herod as recorded in Acts 12:23:

> *And immediately an angel of the Lord struck him because he did not give God the glory, and he was eaten by worms and died.*

In the spiritual realm, an angel struck Herod. In the natural realm, Herod died and was eaten by worms.

Consider how a dream gave King Nebuchadnezzar sight into the spiritual realm. The king did not understand the dream, but Daniel was able to see in the spiritual realm and tell the king that he had dreamed about a four-part statue being crushed by a rock (Dan. 2:31–35). Part two of the revelation came when Daniel explained that the four-part statue being crushed correlated with four kingdoms that would be destroyed by the Kingdom of God (Dan. 2:36–45).

This is the common pattern we see in Scripture when someone sees in the spiritual realm: first, a vision with images, symbols, and metaphors reveals what is in the spiritual realm; second, it becomes evident that what is seen in the spiritual realm correlates with some event in the natural realm.

Revelation 9:13–15: The Sixth Trumpet Is Blown

In Revelation 9:13, John saw in the spiritual realm the sixth angel blowing the sixth trumpet. Then, in the spiritual realm, four angels who had been bound at the great river Euphrates were released to kill a third of the people of the land (Rev. 9:14–15).

Knowing what happened in the spiritual realm, it should not surprise us to learn that four legions of the Roman army had been quartered in the region of the Euphrates before they traveled to Jerusalem to destroy the city in AD 70.[43]

43. Kurt Simmons, *The Consummation of the Ages* (Carlsbad, NM: Bimillennial Preterist Association, 2003), 198; Josephus, *Wars,* V.i.vi; III.iv.ii; Tacitus, *Annals,* V; Cassius Dio, *Roman History*, IV, xxxiii.

Revelation 9:16: Calvary of 200 Million

John saw more about the army that came to destroy Jerusalem. He wrote that the number in the cavalry was 200 million. It would be wrong to take this literally for several reasons.

First, the Greek word translated "cavalry" specifically tells us that this cavalry was made of men riding horses. The verses which follow speak more of these horses, but modern armies no longer depend upon men on horses or even upon great numbers of soldiers. Instead, modern armies are organized around intelligence, airpower, and technology. A cavalry of 200 million would be ineffective against a modern, well-organized military machine of even 50,000 soldiers. In light of this, we must think more deeply about the historical setting.

To the Jewish people, the 200 million number would have had special significance because it is, as some translations word it, *"twice ten thousand times ten thousand."* The number 10,000 had special meaning to every Jew because their greatest military hero, King David, was said to have conquered 10,000. The Jews even had a song in which they honored David for being able to kill 10,000 (1 Sam. 18:7; 21:11). The Jews under threat of war encouraged themselves, claiming that God was with them, and hence, they could defeat their Goliath, but when John declared that *"twice ten thousand times ten thousand"* were coming against them, they would have been overwhelmed by the vision of an army so large that they had no hope of resistance.

At the hands of that army, John said one-third of all people were killed. From this, we need not conclude that one-third of the whole world was killed. We are talking in these chapters about the land of Israel and the war against the Jews. The armies that came from the great river Euphrates slaughtered one-third of the Jews.

This, however, was not the end of the war. John noted how the rest of the people still alive did not repent of their sins (Rev. 9:20–21). Hence, judgment continued as he recorded in the chapters that follow.

Revelation 10: John Eats the Book

In chapter 10 of Revelation, John recorded how he watched another angel bringing further judgments. This was a strong angel with a rainbow on his head, a face like the sun, and feet like pillars of fire. This angel held in his hand a little book that was open. He placed his right foot on the sea and his left on the land. Then he cried out with a voice like a lion's roar. Seven peals of thunder sounded, and John was about to record what had been thundered, but a voice told him not to, but rather to seal up those things.

John was then told to take the book of God's decrees and eat the book. This brings to remembrance how Ezekiel was told to eat a book upon which were written: *"lamentations, mourning and woe"* (Ezek. 2:10). Just as Ezekiel did, John found the book as sweet as honey, which is fitting, for we know that the words of God are sweet and wonderful (Ezek. 3:1–3; Rev. 10:10). However, the words written in this book were decrees of coming judgment, and hence, they caused bitterness in John's stomach. Both Ezekiel and John were told that they would have to go speak the words of the prophecy to the people (Ezek. 3:4; Rev. 10:11). They were both sent to declare coming judgments.

Revelation 11: Jerusalem Is Destroyed

Revelation 11 makes it most evident that the battles up to this point occurred in the spiritual realm, with destruction manifesting in natural Israel and especially Jerusalem.

Revelation 11:1–2 talk about the Temple and the altar that were located in Jerusalem. Revelation 11:2 refers to Jerusalem as the *"holy city."* Then, the most direct decree against Jerusalem is made in Revelation 11:8:

> *The great city which spiritually is called Sodom and Egypt, where also their Lord was crucified.*

We know Jesus was crucified in Jerusalem. That was the great city about which John was writing. Hence, we know that these judgments were against Jerusalem and the early Jews.

REVELATION 7–11: JUDGMENT OF THE JEWS

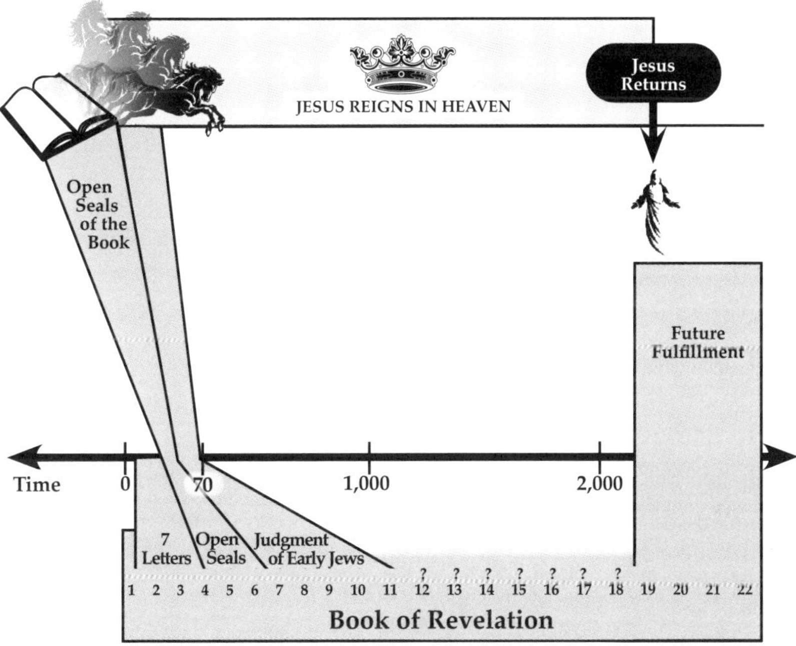

Jerusalem was identified by the fact that Jesus was crucified there but also by referring to the city as Sodom and Egypt. When the Jews were living in rebellion against God in OT times, the prophets accused them of being like the sinful cities of Sodom (Deut. 32:32; Is. 1:9–10; Jer. 23:14; Ezek. 16:48–49, 53) and Egypt (Is. 20:5, 31:1, 36:6; Jer. 42:14; Ezek. 29:16). So, when John called Jerusalem Sodom and Egypt, it was similar to telling the Jews that they were committing the same sins that their forefathers had. God was disappointed with the Jews because they rejected the prophets. Jesus expressed His disappointment when He cried out, *"Jerusalem, Jerusalem, who kills the prophets and stones those who are sent to her!"* (Matt. 23:37).

Revelation 11:2 tells about Jerusalem being destroyed:

> *It has been given to the nations; and they will tread under foot the holy city for forty-two months.*

It is no coincidence that the war against the Jews in Jerusalem lasted precisely 42 months. Vespasian was commissioned by Nero in February of AD 67, and the city fell in August of AD 70.[44] Along with directly telling us that this war destroyed the holy city, the time references confirm that Revelation 11 is about the war that destroyed Jerusalem in AD 70.

Revelation 11: Jewish Temple Replaced by New Temple

Before Jerusalem was destroyed in AD 70, John was given a measuring rod and told to measure the Temple in Jerusalem (Rev. 11:1). We know this was the actual Temple in Jerusalem because he was told to measure it before it was trampled underfoot by the Gentiles (Rev. 11:2). This confirms an earlier point we made: that the Temple in Jerusalem must have still been in existence when John wrote the book of Revelation. This leads the reader to believe the book of Revelation was written before AD 70.

Teachers holding the futurist view have a different explanation. Thinking that chapters 7–18 must be fulfilled during a

44. Josephus, *Wars*, VI.ii.i, fn; David Currie, *Rapture* (Manchester, NH: Sophia Institute Press, 2003), 225.

seven-year tribulation in the future, they have to believe that the Temple in Jerusalem will be rebuilt before the unfolding of the events of Revelation. Therefore, even today, the futurist teachers are hoping for and wanting to help the Jews rebuild the Temple in Jerusalem.

In contrast, partial preterists recognize that the Temple was still standing when John wrote the book of Revelation. It was destroyed by God's decree in AD 70, and God wants it to remain in ruins. Jesus declared:

> *Behold, your house is left unto you desolate.*
>
> —Matt. 23:38

Again, we can point out that the desolation was significant in the fact that we no longer need the Temple, nor the Jewish high priest, or the animal sacrifices that were carried out in that Temple. Jesus had made the ultimate sacrifice that put an end to all other sacrifices (Heb. 9:26; 10:8–18).

Revelation 11:3–12: Two Witnesses in Jerusalem

Chapter 11 of Revelation tells us about God's two witnesses who were present in Jerusalem during her judgment:

> *And I will grant authority to my two witnesses, and they shall prophesy for twelve hundred and sixty days, clothed in sackcloth.*
>
> —Rev. 11:3

Who are these two witnesses? Futurist teachers usually envision two men walking through the streets of Jerusalem during part of a future seven-year tribulation.

In contrast, partial preterists identify the context as the destruction of Jerusalem in AD 70. We are told that two witnesses prophesied for 1,260 days, which is three and one-half years, the same length of time the war in Jerusalem lasted.[45] The two witnesses were clothed in sackcloth, signifying they were in mourning. They had a tragic message to bring. Under Mosaic Law, two witnesses were required before a person could be put to death. These two witnesses were present in Jerusalem, witnessing to the impending destruction.

John told us more about these two witnesses:

> *These have the power to shut up the sky, so that rain will not fall during the days of their prophesying; and they have power over the waters to turn them into blood, and to strike the earth with every plague, as often as they desire.*
>
> —Rev. 11:6

To any Jewish person reading this, there would have been an immediate association with Elijah and Moses. Elijah was the one who shut up the skies so it would not rain. Moses is the one who struck the waters and turned them into blood. Moses is also the one who released plagues.

Even though we recognize this association of the two witnesses of Revelation 11 with Moses and Elijah, we must broaden our understanding. John also told us the following:

> *These are the two olive trees and the two lampstands that stand before the Lord of the earth.*
>
> —Rev. 11:4

Olive trees represent the source whence oil comes, that is, from where the anointing of God flows. The lampstands represent the source of light.

Now ask yourself: Who were the two witnesses who gave witness to the Jewish people throughout their history? They were not only Moses and Elijah but also the Law and the prophets. Moses is the one who gave the Law, and Elijah was

45. This period varies slightly from the 42 months referred to earlier, only because the Jewish calendar is based on lunar months, which have 30 days per month.

the greatest of the OT prophets.[46] So, we see the Law and the prophets, but also Moses and Elijah as the personification of the Law and the prophets.

Therefore, when we read about the two witnesses in Jerusalem, we must see the voice of God, which Moses and Elijah brought into the world. It was that voice—the Law and the prophets—that sounded throughout the streets of Jerusalem before destruction came. The Law and the prophets witnessed against the Jewish people. The Jews had been unfaithful in their covenant with God, and therefore, judgment was coming upon them.

However, the Law and the prophets were also the authoritative witnesses of the early Church. As Christians witnessed to the Jews about Jesus Christ, they did not have the NT from which to preach. They spoke from the Law and the prophets, convincing many that Jesus was the Christ. Again, we see how the Law and the prophets sounded throughout the streets of Jerusalem, testifying against the rebellious people.

John explained how a beast (who we will later show is a spiritual power behind a Roman emperor) made war with the witnesses and killed them (Rev. 11:7).[47] Their bodies were left on the streets of Jerusalem (Rev. 11:8). In what way were the Law and prophets put to death? When Jerusalem was destroyed by the Roman army, it appeared that everything in which the Jews had put their trust had failed. So also, the Jews were no longer God's unique mouthpiece to reveal His will to the world.

While the two prophets lay in the street dead, the world rejoiced and celebrated. Why? Because the Law and the prophets had proclaimed the testimony against them and

46. More precisely, John the Baptist was the greatest prophet functioning under the old covenant (Matt. 11:11), but the same passage refers to John the Baptist being under the influence of the spirit of Elijah (Matt. 11:13–14). Therefore, we do not need to separate them when talking about how God used them in the world.

47. Some teachers equate the roles of Peter and Paul to the two witnesses of the Law and the prophets, for they both preached throughout Jerusalem and both were put to death around AD 68, by Nero, the emperor of the Roman Empire.

their sinfulness. So, while the Law and prophets were dead, the world rejoiced in their sins.

After three and one-half days, *"the breath of life from God"* came back into the two witnesses (Rev. 11:11). The voice of the Law and the prophets rose again. The two witnesses were called back into heaven (Rev. 11:12). Still, at that same time, *"there was a great earthquake"* (Rev. 11:13). As we have discussed before, in apocalyptic language, earthquakes represented a demolition or transfer of authority. Indeed, two witnesses were taken to heaven, but the Law and the prophets continued to sound through the Church. The voices of two witnesses were transferred from the Jews to the Church. Hence, the Law and prophets continued sounding forth the voice of God!

Revelation 11:15–18: Rejoicing in Heaven

When the destruction of Jerusalem was completed in AD 70, a celebration broke out in heaven with loud voices declaring:

> *The kingdom of the world has become the kingdom of our Lord and of His Christ; and He will reign forever and ever.*
>
> —Rev. 11:15b

The Temple had been destroyed and the Kingdom was taken away from the Jews just as Jesus said it would be (Matt. 21:43).

Following this, the 24 elders in heaven fell on their faces and worshiped God, saying:

> *We give You thanks, O Lord God, the Almighty, who are and who were, because You have taken Your great power and have begun to reign.*
>
> —Rev. 11:17

The judgment of the Jews was completed, but notice how God was praised that He had *"begun to reign."* This meant that this was only the beginning and there would be greater advancements of His Kingdom to follow.

John then described how *"the nations were enraged"* (Rev. 11:18). We can see how this happened in both the spiritual and natural realms. The spiritual powers and authorities that governed the nations had seen God take the Kingdom away from the Jews, and they knew that God would soon come to expand His Kingdom over their regions.

Revelation 11:19: The New Temple Was Opened

At the end of chapter 11, we see that God replaced the Temple on Earth with a new Temple in heaven:

> *And the temple of God which is in heaven was opened; and the ark of His covenant appeared in His temple, and there were flashes of lightning and sounds and peals of thunder and an earthquake and a great hailstorm.*
>
> —Rev. 11:19

The significance of this event can be realized when we recognize that earlier in Revelation 11, the Temple in Jerusalem was destroyed. The old Temple was gone. A new Temple was opened in heaven. The lightning, thunder, earthquake, and hailstorm mark the changing of authorities. There was a new High Priest in the new Temple.

REVELATION 12–14: THE SECOND SET OF JUDGMENTS

The two authors of this book, Harold Eberle and Martin Trench, agree that Revelation 7–11, which we studied in the preceding pages, describes the judgment of the Jews and Jerusalem that happened in AD 70. However, Harold and Martin hold different views about the judgments described in Revelation 12–18.

There are three primary views that partial preterists hold about the book of Revelation. We will start the following discussion by explaining those three views. We will also tell you which view Eberle favors and which view Trench favors.

VARIATIONS ON THE PARTIAL PRETERIST VIEW

There are three sets of judgments in Revelation 7–18:

1. First set of judgments: Revelation 7–11
2. Second set of judgments: Revelation 12–14
3. Third set of judgments: Revelation 15–18

Some partial preterists see all three sets of judgments as directed toward the early Jews and Jerusalem. Corresponding to this, they see all those judgments fulfilled around AD 70 when Jerusalem was destroyed. This is the first view held by partial preterists.

Other partial preterists see the first set of judgments directed toward the early Jews and Jerusalem (AD 70) and the rest of the judgments directed toward the Roman Empire, which was destroyed by AD 476. This is the second view held by partial preterists.

Other partial preterists see the first set of judgments as directed toward the early Jews and Jerusalem (AD 70), the second set toward the Roman Empire (AD 476), and the third set toward the whole world, which is still under judgment today. This is the third view held by partial preterists.

	Three Partial Preterist Views of Revelation	Judgment against:
View #1	All three sets of judgments against:	Jews & Old Jerusalem
View #2	First set of judgments against: Second & third set of judgments against:	Jews & Old Jerusalem Roman Empire
View #3	First set of judgments against: Second set of judgments against: Third set of judgments against:	Jews & Old Jerusalem Roman Empire World

Of these three primary partial preterist views, Eberle favors view number three. Trench favors view number one.

Some readers may be puzzled as we, Eberle and Trench, espouse differing views. We see this as a strength rather than a weakness. You can be partial preterists and still have different views. You can even hold different views and be good friends.

None of these three views originated with Eberle or Trench. Although each author has unique insights, the general teachings offered here are held by significant portions of the Body of Christ, which we will explain as we continue.

Now, as we study the second set of judgments (Rev. 12–14), you will see that as coauthors, we still agree on many points, but about halfway through this discussion of Revelation 12–14, our views will diverge.

Revelation 12:2: Jesus Is the Male Child

In Revelation 12:1–2, John recorded another vision:

> *A great sign appeared in heaven: a woman clothed with the sun, and the moon under her feet, and on her head a crown of twelve stars; and she was with child; and she cried out, being in labor and in pain to give birth.*

Who is the woman in this vision? We can see this by first determining who the child is to whom she gave birth. Revelation 12:5a says:

> *And she gave birth to a son, a male child, who is to rule all the nations with a rod of iron.*

More than once in the book of Revelation, Jesus is described as the One who is to rule the nations with a rod of iron. Glance ahead to Revelation 19:13–15, where heaven opens and Jesus rides out on a white horse:

> *His name is called The Word of God. . . . From His mouth comes a sharp sword, so that with it He may strike down the nations, and He will rule them with a rod of iron . . .*

From verses like this (see also Rev. 2:27), we know that Jesus is the Male Child who was destined to rule the nations with a rod of iron.

Revelation 12 goes on to tell us that the Male Child was in this world for only a short time: *"her child was caught up to God and to His throne"* (Rev. 12:5). Indeed, Jesus did His work on Earth during a short period and then ascended into heaven where He was seated at the right hand of God.

Revelation 12:1: Who Is the Mother of the Male Child?

Jesus is the Male Child. Then, who is the woman who gave birth to Jesus? Some teachers have taught that it is Mary, the literal mother of Jesus. Some teachers have declared that it is the Jewish people. Still, others have taught that it is the Church.

We are thinking too small if we settle for any one of these explanations. We must think in spiritual terms. John was seeing these visions while in heaven, receiving spiritual communication of spiritual dynamics.

To identify the concept of spiritual mother or father, consider how Jesus talked critically about the Jewish religious leaders: *"You are of your father the devil, and you want to do the desires of your father"* (John 8:44). Jesus said that the devil was their father, but He did not mean that the devil had sexual relations with their human mothers. Jesus was speaking of how their thoughts, motivations, and desires were being birthed and nurtured by the devil.

In another passage, Jesus explained:

> *That which has been born of the flesh is flesh, and that which has been born of the Spirit is spirit.*
>
> —John 3:6

It is in this sense of being born that we must understand the spiritual dynamics of a mother or father.

When we read of a mother giving birth to the Male Child, Jesus, we see this mother throughout the ages. Beginning way back in the Garden of Eden, God promised Eve that she would be the mother of the Seed that would crush Satan's head (Gen. 3:15). He promised to Abraham that his Seed—that is, Jesus—would become a blessing to all the earth (Gal. 3:16). To David, God promised that one of his descendants would establish a Kingdom that would endure forever (1 Chron. 17:11–12). To the Jewish people, He repeatedly promised that a Messiah would come forth from them. Finally, Mary gave birth to the Son.

Who then is the mother of Jesus? It is Eve. It is Abraham. It is David. It is the Jewish people. It is Mary. It is God's heart and His promises being received by God's people. It is God's Spirit mothering His own Son so that the Son could be ushered into the world. It is the womb that nurtured the promises of God. It is all who said by faith, *"Be it done to me according to your word"* (Luke 1:38). We can include in this mothering role each of the prophets to whom God spoke of the coming Messiah. All who received God's promise by faith played a role in bringing forth the fullness of times when Jesus came into the world.

Because this woman bore the promises of God through the ages, she carried the authority to conquer all, represented by the crown of stars on her head and the moon under her feet.

Towards the end of Revelation 12, we are told that the woman bore other children (Rev. 12:17). Indeed, the heart of God has always been to raise many children. Jesus was the firstborn, but the Spirit of God came upon the Church on Pentecost Day, and now the Church carries the Word and Spirit of God. The Holy Spirit in the Church is now the woman who enters into the hearts of believers and births them into the family of God. So, the Church is also the Mother who has authority through Her Seed.

Thinking in Hebraic and Spiritual Terms

Some readers may have difficulty accepting the explanation we just offered of the Mother of the Male Child. It may be especially difficult for individuals trained in the Western world because Western thought leads people to look for concrete objects, people, or ideas to which each word may be attached. Hebrew thought upon which the Bible is built is more fluid, pictorial, and relational. Rather than connecting a word with a concrete object, person, or idea, it is more common to associate words with ideas that have several layers or implications. Ideas form images and words may have several meanings.

To help Western readers understand Jewish thought, consider how the Jews honored the Sabbath. Each Sabbath day, they thought of themselves as connected to all the Jews throughout the past and into the future who honored or will honor the Sabbath. They saw themselves connected throughout time with everyone who had ever or would ever celebrate the Sabbath.

Similarly, when the Jews celebrated the feasts at a set time each year, they saw themselves celebrating with all others who had or would celebrate those feasts.

For the Jewish people in Bible times, thoughts were not always associated with one concrete object, person, time, or idea. This is especially important to know when talking about the Jewish understanding of spiritual realities.

We saw this earlier when we discussed the two witnesses who lay in the streets of Jerusalem. Revelation 11 shows us how the two witnesses were like Moses and Elijah. Then, we are told that the witnesses are *"two olive trees and the two lampstands"* (Rev. 11:4). We also saw how the two witnesses are associated with the Law and the Prophets. Notice how Hebraic thought about the spiritual realm makes associations.

For this reason, the mother of the Male Child talked about in Revelation 12:5 need not be tied to one individual. Hebraic thought would have associated that mother with all who were part of the process of birthing the Male Child into the world throughout time.

Thinking in these terms may be uncomfortable for the Western mind, but it is necessary for a clear understanding of the book of Revelation. We must think like the Jews of that period did. We must hold our definitions of words and symbols loosely.

Revelation 12:3 & 9: What Is the Great Red Dragon?

Next, Revelation 12 tells us about a great red dragon (Rev. 12:3). Who is this dragon? The great dragon *"is called the devil and Satan"* (Rev. 12:9).

This is another example of how the Bible's communication about the spiritual realm is fluid and relational. To the Western mind, saying that the dragon is Satan is very concrete, leading the Western reader to conclude that the dragon is the same as Satan. However, we should remember how the Bible communicates about the spiritual realm in layers. It is wise to ask, "In what way was the dragon Satan?"

Compare this to the time Peter tried to correct Jesus (Matt. 16:22), and in response, Jesus said, *"Get behind Me, Satan!"* (Matt. 16:23). Our Lord's rebuke did not mean Peter was Satan. It is better to think that Satan, at that moment, was inspiring Peter to think and say what he did. At that moment, Satan was present and relating to Peter in a way that allowed Satan to speak through Peter. Therefore, when Jesus told Peter, *"Get behind Me, Satan!"* Jesus was speaking to the spiritual being associated with Peter at that time.

For another example, think of Elijah, an OT prophet. As Elijah was being taken up to heaven, his spirit came upon his servant Elisha (2 Kings 2:15). As a consequence, Elisha began having a ministry like Elijah's. Similarly, Elijah's spirit came upon John the Baptist, who did not live until 900 years later. In one passage, we are told that John the Baptist is Elijah (Matt. 11:14; see also Matt. 17:11–13 and Mark 9:13). In another passage, John the Baptist denied that he was Elijah (John 1:21). In a third passage, we are told that the spirit of Elijah was upon John the Baptist (Luke 1:17).

To the Western mind, these verses sound like they contradict each other. To the Hebraic mind, communication about the spiritual realm is often like this. If we think of the spirit of Elijah in relational terms, we can understand that the spirit of Elijah was at work in John the Baptist in a way that it is correct to say John the Baptist is Elijah and he is not Elijah at the same time.

We can also say that at the moment Peter was trying to correct Jesus as recorded in Matthew 16:22–23, Peter was Satan and he was not Satan. Peter was thinking and acting as Satan because Satan was present and working through Peter at that moment.

Similarly, we must consider the spiritual dynamics going on with every person or being mentioned in the book of Revelation. Revelation 12:9 tells us that the great dragon *"is called the devil and Satan."* From this, we do not know if the great dragon was Satan in the Western sense of equating the two or if Satan was present in the dragon, relating to the dragon in a way that controlled the dragon. Keep this in mind as we continue to talk about the dragon and Satan.

Revelation 12: Great Red Dragon and Roman Empire

Revelation tells us more about the great red dragon:

> *And the dragon stood before the woman who was about to give birth, so that when she gave birth he might devour her child.*
>
> —Rev. 12:4b

From this, we know that the dragon (Satan) tried to kill Jesus as His mother was about to give birth.

Let us consider the historic events that may correspond to this. Think of Herod, a king within the Roman Empire, who tried to kill Jesus by murdering all the male children in Bethlehem (Matt. 2:16). Although Satan failed at killing Jesus as a baby, it was the Roman government that ultimately crucified Jesus.

Revelation 12 reveals more about the relationship between the dragon (Satan) and the Roman Empire. Revelation 12:17 tells us that the great dragon became enraged and turned his anger toward the rest of the woman's children *"who keep the commandments of God and hold to the testimony of Jesus"* (Rev. 12:17). Historically, we know it was the Roman government that killed hundreds of thousands of Christians during the great persecutions of the first two centuries.

Considering the relationship between the dragon and the Roman Empire, it is worth noting that the Roman calvary carried an image of "Draco," which means dragon, on a standard-length pole, with a windsock banner trailing behind.[48] The Draco symbol also appeared on many Roman coins.

Draco Windsock

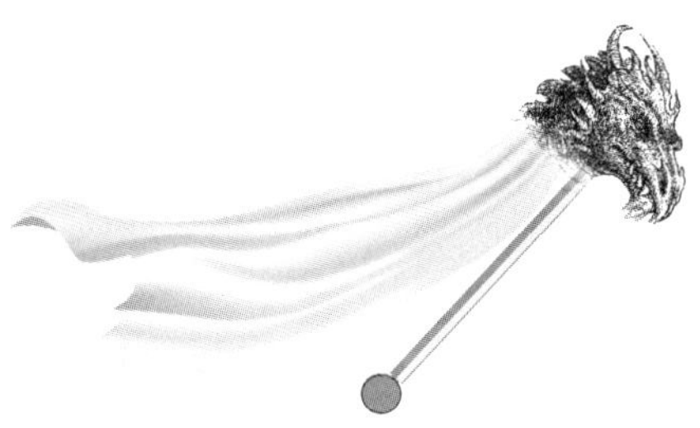

Another indicator that the dragon was associated with the Roman Empire is given to us in Revelation 12:3. We are told that the dragon had *"seven heads and ten horns"* (Rev. 12:3). In the book of Daniel, we are shown that heads and horns represent various authority figures within governments. For example, Daniel 7:24 tells us, *"As for the ten horns, out of this kingdom ten kings will arise."* Later in Revelation, we are told that *"the ten horns which you saw are ten kings"* (Rev. 17:12). So then, the seven heads and ten horns of the dragon correlate with seven and ten ruling authorities within the Roman Empire.

48. Although the symbol of the dragon was carried by the Roman calvary, the eagle or vulture was the image carried by the Roman legions.

We can see a correspondence between the seven heads and the first seven Caesars.[49] In Revelation 17:9–10, an angel said:

> *The seven heads . . . are seven kings; five have fallen, one is, the other has not yet come; and when he comes, he must remain a little while.*

The phrase *"five have fallen"* implies that the first five Caesars had died. When John wrote *"one is,"* we can equate this with Nero, the sixth Caesar, who was in power at the time of John's writing. Finally, John told us about one who had yet to come and remain a little while. This fits with Galba, who reigned for only seven months.

GREAT RED DRAGON (SATAN) INFLUENCING THE SEVEN CAESARS

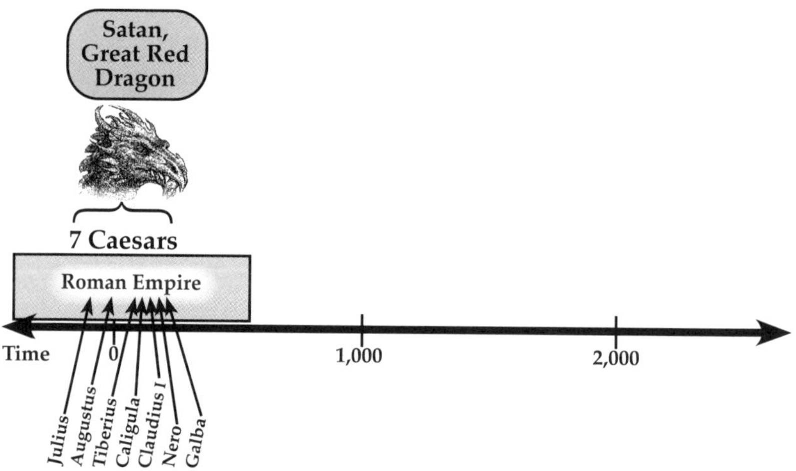

Under the authority of the Roman emperors, ten senior leaders governed over ten regions into which the Empire was divided. These were the ten kings that corresponded with the ten horns of the dragon.[50]

49. There were 12 Caesars over the Roman Empire, but John only saw a vision of the first seven.

50. During some periods of the Roman Empire, the number of regions varied.

The Ten Provinces of the Roman Empire

Achaia	Gaul
Africa	Germany
Asia	Italy
Britain	Spain
Egypt	Syria

These are not the only reasonable ways to understand the seven heads and ten horns of Revelation. As pointed out, communication about spiritual realities may have more than one valid explanation.

However, we can be pretty sure that the great red dragon is associated with Rome and the Roman Empire.

This is so evident that even futurists commonly make this association. However, futurists envision Revelation 7–18 as being fulfilled during a seven-year tribulation in the future. Therefore, they usually believe that there will be a revived Roman Empire that will emerge between now and the second coming of Jesus.

In contrast, partial preterists see the great red dragon associated with Rome and the Roman Empire that existed in ancient times.

Revelation 12:7–9: The War in Heaven

Once we have seen the association of the dragon (Satan) with the Roman Empire, we can understand a war that John watched from heaven:

> *And there was war in heaven, Michael and his angels waging war with the dragon. The dragon and his angels waged war, and they were not strong enough, and there was no longer a place found for them in heaven. And the great dragon was thrown down, the serpent of old who is called the devil and Satan . . .*
>
> —Rev. 12:7–9

This was a spiritual war in heaven that had natural consequences on Earth.

Many Christians have incorrectly understood this war to be a picture of what happened way back before the world was created. They use this passage to teach that Satan once was a good angel who fell from heaven thousands or even millions of years ago, but that explanation does not fit here. John wrote how the *"accuser of our brethren has been thrown down . . ."* (Rev. 12:10). This could not be referring to Satan being cast out of heaven before this world was created because the *"brethren"* did not exist at that time.

The war described in Revelation 12:7–9 happened in the first century. We know this because John was reporting things that happened after he was taken to heaven and was shown things to take place in the near future—that is, in John's future (Rev. 4:1).

During the first century, John was taken into the throne and got to see Jesus taking His position at the right hand of Father-God. John watched events that unfolded as a consequence of Jesus being enthroned as King.

Before Jesus ascended into heaven, Satan was the god of this world (2 Cor. 4:4; Eph. 2:2; John 12:31). That is why Satan was able to tempt Jesus in the wilderness by offering Jesus all the kingdoms of this world (Matt. 4:8–9).

As the god of this world, Satan influenced humanity in many ways. One of those ways was through deceiving nations (Rev. 20:3). During the first century, the strongest government in the world was the Roman government. So, Satan—in the form of the great red dragon—played a major role in manipulating and controlling humanity through the Roman government.

This does not mean that everything about the Roman Empire was evil. It simply reveals how Satan was able to influence people within and through the Roman Empire.

To see this more clearly, think in spiritual terms. The apostle John was in heaven watching spiritual dynamics that have consequences in this natural world. Hence, we understand that the dragon was not just the Roman government, but it was a spiritual force behind the Roman government.

Satan was the god of this world, but that changed when Jesus ascended into heaven. Jesus was given all authority over heaven and Earth. At that time, Satan was cast down and lost his position of authority.

Jesus Enthroned & Satan (Dragon) Was Cast Down to Earth

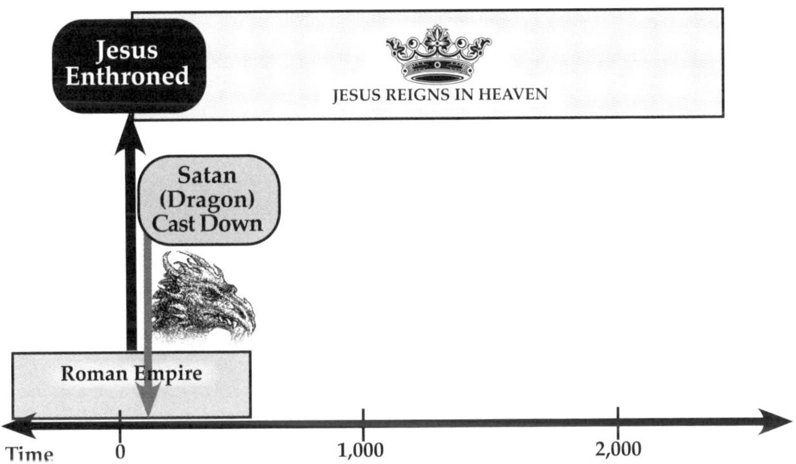

Before Jesus died, resurrected, and ascended, He told His disciples that Satan was about to be defeated:

> *Now judgment is upon this world; now the ruler of this world will be cast out.*
>
> —John 12:31

As Jesus resurrected from the dead, He conquered death. Then, as Jesus ascended into heaven, Michael and his angels waged war to dethrone the dragon. When Jesus sat down at the right hand of Father God, Satan was cast out of heaven.[51]

51. Satan is still god of this world, if we are using the word "world" to refer to the corrupt system which is still at work in the world, e.g., Rom. 12:2; 1 John 2:15; James 4:4.

After Satan and his angels were cast out, John heard a loud voice in heaven, saying:

> *Now the salvation, and the power, and the kingdom of our God and the authority of His Christ have come . . .*
>
> —Rev. 12:10

The Kingdom of God was established. Jesus began to reign.

Revelation 12:12: Satan Came to Earth

Once Satan was cast out of heaven, he was not sent to hell. Revelation 12:12b tells us that Satan came down to Earth:

> *Woe to the earth and the sea, because the devil has come down to you, having great wrath, knowing that he has only a short time.*

Satan's fall happened in the spiritual realm, but we should be able to identify events that correspond in the natural realm. No one can say with certainty what natural events were caused by specific spiritual events. Still, it is reasonable to make some association between Satan coming down to Earth and the demonic ways in which certain emperors began to act.

Any modern Christian who has studied the life of the Roman emperors and believes in the possibility of demonic possession would suspect some of the Caesars of being demon-possessed, especially those known for their evil ways, such as Nero, Caligula, and Decius.

Several Roman emperors demanded worship. Every Roman citizen had to come into the temple of Caesar on a particular day of each year, burn a pinch of incense, and then declare, "Caesar is Lord." Temples to the godhead of the emperor were constructed throughout the Empire. Some emperors took on the title Augustus or Sebastos, which meant "one to be worshiped." By the reign of Emperor Decius (AD

249–251), emperor worship was demanded of all nations within the Empire.[52]

Revelation 13:1–10: The First Beast of Revelation

Revelation 13 starts with the great dragon standing on the sand of the seashore. Corresponding to this, the Roman Empire rose out of the Mediterranean Sea upon the Italian peninsula. In prophetic language, the sea sometimes represented the mass of humanity, e.g., Rev. 17:15. Hence, we can also identify Rome and the Roman Empire arising out of the sea of humanity.

Then John described a beast in Revelation 13:1:

> *Then I saw a beast coming up out of the sea, having ten horns and seven heads . . .*

This is the first of three beasts revealed in the book of Revelation. Who is this first beast?

John explained that the dragon gave the beast *"his power and his throne and great authority"* (Rev. 13:2). This reveals an association between the dragon (Rome and the Roman Empire) and the first beast.

We are also told that the beast had *"ten horns and seven heads"* (Rev. 13:1), which is the same information we learned about the dragon (Rev. 12:3). From this, we can infer that both the beast and the dragon influenced the first seven Caesars and ten kings of the Roman Empire.

Even though this beast influenced several Roman leaders, John described specific actions of this beast that correspond perfectly with the actions of one specific Roman leader, Nero. As already mentioned, Nero was the emperor who ordered the great persecution of the early Church after the city of Rome burned in AD 64. It is more than coincidence

52 During some periods, the Jews were exempt from emperor worship.

that the first beast was given authority for 42 months, that is, three and one-half years, to blaspheme and *"to make war with the saints and to overcome them"* (Rev. 13:7). Nero's persecution of Christians lasted 42 months, from the middle of November in AD 64 to the beginning of June in 68, when he committed suicide.[53]

This does not mean we should equate the beast with Nero. Remember, we are talking about what John watched in the spiritual realm. We also saw how the beast influenced seven Caesars, not just one. It is better to think of the beast as an evil spiritual being who worked amid several Caesars to bring about his will. That beast was particularly effective in controlling Nero, and the beast's desire was most fully manifested through Nero.

It is difficult to imagine any ruler more wicked than Nero. He had many members of his own family killed, including his pregnant wife, whom he kicked to death. Nero married a boy with all the usual public ceremonies and then castrated the boy and took him as his wife. He also carried on an incestuous relationship with his mother. At times, Nero dressed up as a wild beast and attacked, raped, and murdered male and female prisoners. Nero took great pleasure in watching people being tortured and suffering the most heinous deaths. Finally, at age 31, he killed himself.[54]

Nero was so evil that some leaders outside of the Christian world referred to him as a beast. For example, Apollonius of Tyana wrote:

> In my travels, which has been wider than every man yet accomplished, I have seen many, many wild beasts of Arabia and India; but this beast, that is commonly called a Tyrant, I know not how many heads it has, nor if it be crooked of claw, and armed with horrible fangs . . . And of the wild beasts you

53. Chilton, *Paradise Restored* (Tyler, TX: Dominion Press, 1994), 179.

54. Most of what we know about Nero comes from four ancient writers, Josephus, Tacitus, Suetonius, and Cassius Dio.

> cannot say that they were ever known to eat their own mother, but Nero has gorged himself on this diet.[55]

Many leaders of the early Church believed that Nero was the beast of Revelation. Consider the quotations below.

Jerome

And there are many of our viewpoint who think that Domitius Nero was the Antichrist because of his outstanding savagery and depravity.

Cited in *In The Days of These Kings: The Book of Daniel in Preterist Perspective* by Rogers, 2017, 690

F. W. Farrar

All of the earliest Christian writers on the Apocalypse, from Irenaeus down to Victorious of Pettau and Commodian in the fourth, and Andreas in the fifth, and St. Beatus in the eighth century, connect Nero, or some Roman emperor, with the Apocalyptic Beast.

The Early Days of Christianity, 1882, 519

Revelation 13:3: Slain and Then Healed

In Revelation 13:3, John wrote more about the beast:

> *I saw one of his heads as if it had been slain, and his fatal wound was healed . . .*

55. Philostratus, *Life of Apollonius,* cited in John T. Robinson, *Redating the New Testament* (Philadelphia, PA: Westminster, 1976), 235.

The near-death experience described in this verse corresponds well with the period during which the Roman Empire was almost destroyed. Not only was a third of Rome burned to the ground in AD 64, but also in the years surrounding Nero's reign, four emperors were killed, there were three civil wars, and numerous foreign wars broke out around the Empire. Josephus wrote that Rome was near "ruin"[56] and "every part of the habitable earth under them was in an unsettled and tottering condition."[57] Tacitus further described the conditions of the Empire and wrote that it was almost the end.[58] It was not until Vespasian became emperor in AD 69 that the Roman Empire experienced a return of order.

Revelation 13:11–15: The Second Beast

After those events, John wrote that he saw a second beast in a vision. He went on to tell us that the second beast *"exercises all the authority of the first beast . . ."* (Rev. 13:12). From this, we can infer that this beast influenced several leaders similarly to how the first beast did.

What did these beasts influence the Roman leaders to do? As already mentioned, the first beast caused a Roman leader to persecute Christians for 42 months (Rev. 13:5–7). That Roman leader also blasphemed God for 42 months (Rev. 13:5–6).

John told us that the second beast gave a Roman leader the power to perform signs (Rev. 13:11–14).[59] The second beast also caused everyone to worship the first beast (Rev. 13:15). Evidence of this worship is the fact that there have been found inscriptions on coins calling Nero "Almighty God" and

56. Josephus, *Wars*, IV.xi.v.

57. Ibid., VII.iv.ii.

58. Tacitus, *Histories*, 1.11.

59. We cannot be certain what those signs were, but we do know that both Josephus and Tacitus described several signs that appeared in the sky before the Roman armies destroyed Jerusalem during the reign of Nero. Josephus, *Wars*, VI.v.iii; Tacitus, *Histories*, V.13.

"Savior." Nero enjoyed the worship people offered him and had a 120-foot-high image of himself built in Rome.

Two Beasts of Revelation Influencing Roman Leaders

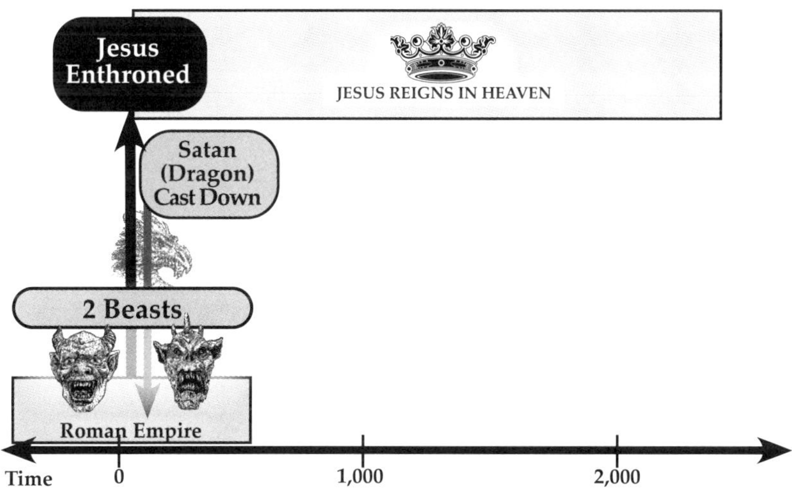

John also associated the second beast with the number 666 (Rev. 13:18), which is worth discussing next.

Revelation 13:16–18: The Mark of the Beast

The number 666 has raised tremendous interest in the modern Church and has been used by futurist preachers, writers, and moviemakers to instill fear in the hearts of millions by proposing various contemporary or future humans who could be identified with 666.

However, we should try to understand this number as it would have been understood by the people who first read the writings of John.

The letters of the Hebrew alphabet possessed numeric values. It is similar to how certain letters in the Roman alphabet are used as numerals: "I" means 1; "V" means 5; "X" means 10; "L" means 50; "C" means 100, and "D" means 500. Therefore, if we see the following Roman letters, DCLXVI, we know that this is equivalent numerically to 666. This is not difficult to figure out for anyone who understands Roman numerals. Nor was it difficult for any literate Jew to read the number of Nero's name. The Hebrew spelling of Nero Caesar was Nrwn Qsr (pronounced Neron Kesar). The Hebrew equivalent of this name is exactly 666.[60]

Why did John use 666 instead of Nero's name?

Unlike most of the information written in Revelation, John never said or implied that the number 666 was in one of his visions. John wrote the comment about the number of the beast much like an aside, giving a separate notation to the reader:

> *Here is wisdom. Let him who has understanding calculate the number of the beast, for the number is that of a man; and his number is six hundred and sixty-six.*
>
> —Rev. 13:18

John may have used the number 666 to protect the early Christians. If any Christian had been caught with any written material in which Nero was put in a bad light, that Christian could expect to be immediately hauled off to prison or sent to the coliseums. Yet, the first Christians were primarily Jewish converts, so they could easily understand the meaning of the number 666. It would have been natural for them to see that Nero was the one to whom John was referring. Nero was the one who was killing their leaders, friends, and family members.

It is worth taking a moment to talk about the modern discussions that futurists have about some contemporary person represented by the number 666. The most captivating stories are centered around the futurist teachings that soon there will be an antichrist who will take over the world's economic systems

60. Kurt Simmons, *The Consummation of the Ages* (Carlsbad, NM: Bimillennial Preterist Association, 2003), 268; R.C. Sproul, *The Last Days According to Jesus* (Grand Rapids, MI: Baker Books, 1998), 186–188.

and then control all humanity's expenditures. Many futurists say this control will be possible because the antichrist will demand that each person receives a computerized chip in their forehead or right hand.

In reality, the word "antichrist" is never mentioned even once in the book of Revelation. The only place the word "antichrist" is used is in 1 and 2 John. There is no biblical basis to equate the beast of Revelation with the antichrist mentioned in the letters of John (we will discuss the antichrist in Section Six).

Next, it is worth noting how out-of-balance futurists' teachings are about the mark of the beast. Today, a person can find many Christian books on the market that talk about the mark of the beast, with each book giving the author's interpretation of some contemporary or future antichrist figure. At the same time, we would be hard-pressed to find a Christian author who has written about the mark of God.

Did you know that the mark of God, the seal of God, and the name of God, which are written on the foreheads of His people, are mentioned in the book of Revelation the same number of times as the mark of the beast? Both are mentioned seven times. Yet, the futurists are always talking about the mark of the beast and never even mention the mark of God. As Christians, we should be more interested in the mark of God—who is alive today and active in our lives—than we are in the mark of some beast that we do not even know exists!

Furthermore, we must understand the mark of the beast from a similar frame of mind as the mark of God. By this, we mean that if the mark of the beast is to be understood literally, then we should understand the mark of God literally. On the other hand, if we take the mark of the beast spiritually, we should take the mark of God spiritually. That is simple honesty and integrity in the way we interpret Scripture. Both marks are spoken of in the book of Revelation and even together in the same chapter (chapter 14).

Then why do the futurist teachers put fear in people by talking about a computer chip being placed in the foreheads or right hands of people? Do they also believe that the mark of God will be a computer chip? Of course not. That points out the foolishness of the whole chip scare. Again, if the Scriptures talking about the mark of the beast are taken literally, then the same Scriptures talking about the mark of God should be taken literally. If one is spiritual, then the other is spiritual. We must be consistent in the way we use Scripture.

Partial preterists believe that both marks must be understood in a spiritual sense. Those people who give themselves over to the works of Satan will have the mark of evil in their thoughts and the works of their hands. Those who give themselves over to God will have the mark of God upon their minds and the works of their hands. The seal of God upon His people is His Spirit. Similarly, those who give their lives and hearts to Satan will be marked by the spirit of the evil one.

Place this discussion back in the context in which the book of Revelation was written. The apostle John was writing to real Christians who were enduring real persecution. That persecution was being carried out under a man whose name is equivalent to 666. To the first-century Christians, the meaning would have been clear.

Revelation 13:17: Unable to Buy or Sell

Consider one of the significant consequences experienced by those who did not receive the mark of the beast. John wrote that no one would *"be able to buy or sell, except the one who has the mark, either the name of the beast or the number of his name"* (Rev. 13:17).

Futurists explain this verse, saying that when the antichrist comes at some future date, Christians who refuse the mark of the beast will be unable to buy anything, including food.

Instead of seeing this as a prophecy for our future, consider how it may have been fulfilled within the Roman Empire during the first century. As mentioned earlier, the Roman government required every citizen to offer a pinch of incense to publicly acknowledge that Caesar was the supreme lord. Those who obeyed were given a certificate that had to be renewed annually.

We do not have historical documents describing what actually took place, but we know that Christians were identified by their unwillingness to offer the required incense.

Knowing this, we can understand how buying and selling could be controlled. However, "buying and selling" did not refer to purchasing food at the local grocery store. It referred to setting up a business in the marketplace.

Those who did not have the required certificate could be easily identified. At that time, the marketplace was a close-knit community. All business owners knew the people who set up businesses next to them. People who did not submit to the Empire were shunned, and people refused to do business with them.

Revelation 12–14: The Identities of Figures in Revelation

So far, we have identified several figures that are mentioned in the book of Revelation. We identified the Male Child as Jesus and the Mother of the Male Child as the Mother of Jesus. However, we have extended the definition of "Mother" to include all who believed and cooperated with God to bring the Seed into the world.

We identified the great red dragon as Satan working in and through the Roman Empire. Also, we identified the seven heads as the first seven Caesars and the ten horns as the ten senior leaders of the ten Roman provinces. Then, we identified the two beasts in Revelation 13 as evil spiritual beings that were associated with the dragon (Rome and the Roman Empire) and influenced the first seven Caesars and ten kings of the Roman Empire.

Finally, we explained how Emperor Nero most closely carried out the works of the two beasts, and his name corresponds with the number 666.

Generally, we (Eberle and Trench) agree about the identities of the figures mentioned above.[61] Our differences revolve around the identities of three other entities discussed in Revelation. Those three entities are the "great city," "Babylon," and "the harlot." We will examine these three entities in the following pages.

Does the "Great City" Refer to One or Two Cities?

All partial preterist teachers agree that *"the great city"* described in chapter 11 of Revelation refers to Jerusalem.

> *The great city which mystically is called Sodom and Egypt, where also their Lord was crucified.*
>
> —Rev. 11:8

There is no doubt that Jerusalem is the city where Jesus was crucified. Harold and Martin agree about this.[62] They also agree that Revelation 7–11 is about God's judgment of Jerusalem and the early Jews.

Of course, the judgments came upon the first-century apostate Jerusalem, which from now on we will refer to as "Old Jerusalem" to separate it from New Jerusalem, which is

61. Harold and Martin generally agree about the preceding identities, but they would use slightly different terminology to explain some details about those identities. This is because Harold's view sees the two beasts as spiritual beings that influence several human leaders, while Martin is comfortable equating a beast with Nero.

62 Two times Jerusalem is referred to as the great city by Josephus in *Wars*, VII:i:i and VII:viii:vii. Jerusalem is also referred to as "the famous city" by Tacitus in *Histories* 5:2 and Pliny in *Natural History* 5:14:70.

revealed as coming down to Earth after God forms the new heaven and Earth (Rev. 21–22).

We know *"the great city"* mentioned in Revelation 11 is Old Jerusalem. However, the terminology *"the great city"* is used several other times in the rest of Revelation.

Martin sees *"the great city"* always referring to Old Jerusalem in Revelation 7–18.

Trench's Understanding of Revelation	
Figures in Rev. 12–18	**Identity**
The Great City	Old Jerusalem

Harold believes that the terminology *"the great city"* is used to refer to two cities in Revelation 7–18: Old Jerusalem and Rome. Harold makes this distinction for several reasons.

First, he points out that referring to two cities as "great" does not make them the same city. The Greek word for great is *megas,* which is a common adjective that can describe any large city. Today, we can say that New York is a large city, and we can also say that London is a large city, but just because they are both large cities does not mean they are the same city.

Further, we know that the two great cities in the book of Revelation are not the same because the first great city, Old Jerusalem, which is discussed in Revelation 11, is referred to in the masculine gender (Rev. 11:8, 13), while the second great city, Rome, is referred to in the feminine gender (Rev. 16:19; 17:18; 18:10, 16, 18, 19, 21). This distinction cannot be seen in English translations of the Bible, but in the original Greek it is obvious.

Gender was an important distinction in ancient times, comparative to how someone today should correctly refer to you as he or she. If someone made a mistake on this, it would be significant and noted.

When *"the great city"* is referred to in Revelation 11:8, the original Greek uses the masculine gender for both the noun, city, and the adjective, great (*polous megalēs*). When referring to *"the great city"* in Revelation 14–18, the Greek uses the feminine gender for both the noun, city, and the adjective, great (*polis megalē*). So, anyone reading the original writings would see the distinction between "he" and "she."

Harold sees this distinction as critical. The two cities are not the same city. The first great city (masculine) is Old Jerusalem (Rev. 7–11), and the second great city (feminine) is Rome (Rev. 12–18).[63]

Eberle's Understanding of Revelation	
Figures in Rev. 12–18	**Identity**
The Great City (Masculine)	Old Jerusalem
The Great City (Feminine)	Rome

Several other facts support this distinction between the two cities.

Other Names of Old Jerusalem and Rome

In ancient times, it was common for people to label one city with the name of another city when the two cities were associated or shared some of the same major characteristics.

For example, Old Jerusalem was called Sodom in Revelation 11:8 and several OT passages, e.g., Deut. 32:32; Is. 1:9–10; Jer. 23:14; Ezek. 16:48–49, 53; Rev. 11:8. These references were very derogatory. It is comparable to calling modern cities "Sodom

63. John also separates Old Jerusalem from New Jerusalem. He uses the masculine to refer to Old Jerusalem, e.g., Rev. 11:8, 13, and the feminine when referring to New Jerusalem, e.g., Rev. 3:12; 20:9; 21:2, 10, 14, 15, 16, 18, 19, 21, 23; 22:14,19. John also uses the feminine when referring to Jerusalem as the holy city (Rev. 11:2; 21:2, 10) and beloved city (Rev. 20:9). There are no exceptions to John's use of these gender identifications, which tells us John was deliberate and careful in making these distinctions.

and Gomorrah." Anyone familiar with this terminology would immediately think of those modern cities as places of rampant sexual perversions.

In Revelation 11:8, Old Jerusalem was also called Egypt, which would have brought to the mind of the early Jewish readers thoughts of being slaves in Egypt. The Jews would have also remembered when the OT prophets rebuked them for trusting in Egypt rather than God, e.g., Is. 20:5, 31:1, 36:6; Jer. 42:14; Ezek. 29:16.

Old Jerusalem = Sodom & Egypt
(Rev. 11:8)

Harold and Martin agree that Old Jerusalem was called Sodom and Egypt. However, they disagree about the other great city in Revelation, which is called "Babylon."

Before we identify what "Babylon" refers to, we should exclude from our discussion any reference to the derogatory way the label "Babylon" is used today by some people who are very critical of the modern Church. When anyone uses the label Babylon to refer to the modern Church, they take it out of its context in Revelation. We will not do that because this book is a serious attempt to explain the book of Revelation in its historical setting.

In Revelation, Babylon is always referred to in the feminine gender. Harold sees this as evidence that Babylon is not Old Jerusalem, which is masculine; Babylon corresponds with Rome, which is expressed in the feminine gender.

Babylon = Rome
(feminine) (feminine)

This is where Harold and Martin see things differently. Martin sees Babylon as referring to Old Jerusalem. In other words, Martin sees Sodom, Egypt, and Babylon as different names for the same city, Old Jerusalem.

Trench's Understanding of Revelation		
Figures Rev. 12–18	**Name**	**Identity**
Great City	Sodom, Egypt, Babylon	Old Jerusalem

In contrast, Harold sees Babylon as referring to Rome. Harold sees two great cities in Revelation: Old Jerusalem, called Sodom and Egypt; Rome called Babylon.

Eberle's Understanding of Revelation		
Figures Rev. 12–18	**Name**	**Identity**
Great City (He)	Sodom & Egypt	Old Jerusalem
Great City (She)	Babylon	Rome

Is Babylon Old Jerusalem or Rome?

Does "Babylon" refer to Old Jerusalem or Rome?

Among partial preterist teachers, there are strong supporters of each view.

The view Martin favors, that Babylon refers to Old Jerusalem, is supported by some modern partial preterist writers, including Kenneth Gentry, Gary DeMar, and Peter Leithart. Because this view has recently become popular, it is sometimes referred to as the "modern partial preterist view."

The view Harold favors, that Babylon refers to Rome, may be called the "historicist partial preterist view." The association of Babylon with Rome was expressed by some of the early Church fathers, among whom was Tertullian, who wrote:

> So, again, Babylon in [the writings of] our own John, is a figure of the city of Rome. For she is equally great and proud of her sway.[64]

64. Referenced in: *A Dictionary of Early Christian Beliefs*, ed. David W. Bercot (Peabody Mass: Hendrickson Pub., 1998), 50.

Hippolytus made the same association:

> Tell me, blessed John—apostle and disciple of the Lord—what did you see and hear concerning Babylon? Arise and speak! For it [i.e., Rome] sent you into banishment.[65] [66]

Victorious agreed:

> The great overthrow of Babylon, that is, the Roman state.[67]

We have no record of any early Church father associating Babylon with Jerusalem.

The association of Babylon with Rome has been the dominant view of Christianity over the last 2,000 years. For centuries it has been held by several mainline denominations, including Roman Catholicism.[68]

The modern scholar, N.T. Wright also makes the association between Babylon and Rome:

> We know from other re-readings of Daniel in the first century, such as that of the apocryphal book known as 4 Ezra, there was no problem in deleting 'Babylon' and substituting 'Rome'.[69]

Both Judgments Were Prophesied

Although we will continue explaining both views of

65. We know it was Rome that sent John into banishment on the island of Patmos.

66. Referenced in: *A Dictionary of Early Christian Beliefs*, ed. David W. Bercot (Peabody Mass: Hendrickson Pub., 1998), 50.

67. Referenced in: *A Dictionary of Early Christian Beliefs*, ed. David W. Bercot (Peabody Mass: Hendrickson Pub., 1998), 50.

68. Three sites that offer this Roman Catholic view are:
    https://catholicstand.com/who-is-the-whore-of-babylon
    https://www.catholic.com/tract/the-whore-of-babylon
    https://www.catholic.com/tract/hunting-the-whore-of-babylon

69. N.T. Wright, *What Saint Paul Really Said* (Grand Rapids, MI: Eerdmans Pub., 1997), 26.

Babylon, Martin is graciously allowing Harold's view to be explained more fully. So, from here forward, we will discuss more evidence supporting the view that Babylon is Rome, but we will add a few comments and footnotes supporting Martin's view that Babylon refers to Jerusalem.[70] [71]

To support his view that Revelation 7–11 talks about the judgment of Old Jerusalem and Revelation 12–14 talks about the judgment of Babylon / Rome, Harold points out that there is a consistent pattern in the OT of judgment happening first to the Jews, then to the over-bearing nation that God used to judge the Jews.

For example, Habakkuk explained how God used the Chaldeans to judge Israel (Hab. 1:12), and then God judged the Chaldeans (Hab. 2:8). This pattern is what we see in Revelation, with God using the Romans to judge the Jews (Rev. 7–11), and then God judging the Romans (Rev. 12–14).

Paul explained that this is how God judges:

> *There will be tribulation and distress for every soul of mankind who does evil, <u>for the Jew first</u> and also <u>for the Greek</u>.*[72]
>
> —Rom. 2:9

We also know that it was prophesied that both the Jews and the Romans would be judged once the Kingdom of God was established. In Section One, we examined Jesus' prophecy that the early Jews and Old Jerusalem would be judged within a generation (Matt. 23). In Section Three, we examined Daniel's interpretation of King Nebuchadnezzar's dream that revealed how the Kingdom of God was destined to crush the Roman Empire (Dan. 2:36–45). Knowing these prophecies, we should

70. Kenneth Gentry argues that Babylon refers to Jerusalem at the following website: https://postmillennialworldview.com/2014/01/29babylon-is-jerusalem-in-revelation-1/

71. Martin has additional articles supporting his view that may be found at martintrench.com.

72. Paul used the title "Greeks" to refer to the citizens of the Roman Empire and the term "Gentiles" to refer to all non-Jews.

not be surprised that Revelation talks about both the judgment of Jerusalem and Babylon/Rome.

John Saw Babylon in the Spiritual Realm

To further support that Babylon refers to Rome, Harold reminds readers of how John came up with the information that he wrote in the book of Revelation. John did not makeup images and symbols that he could use to explain what was going to happen in the future. John did not decide to use the symbol of Babylon to refer to Jerusalem or Rome. That is not how John came up with his information.

John received information from the spiritual realm. In the book of Revelation, Babylon was first introduced when John saw into the spiritual realm, and an angel declared the destruction of Babylon, saying, *"Fallen, fallen is Babylon . . ."* (Rev. 14:8).

In the Spirit, John Saw Babylon Being Destroyed

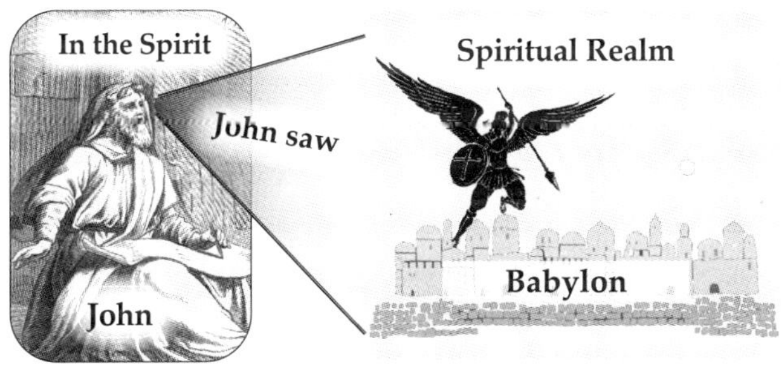

When John received that revelation, Babylon had already been destroyed. The city fell to the Persians in 539 BC, then declined until there was almost nothing left by the time of Christ. Since Babylon had already fallen, John's vision of Babylon falling had to have another meaning. John was prophesying about future events.

As explained before, spiritual realities may have different layers of meaning. Those layers comprise things that are associated or have similar purposes and characteristics. Those associations exist because of spiritual connections.

With this in mind, consider how the Babylonian Empire and the Roman Empire served parallel purposes for God. In 589 BC, Nebuchadnezzar II, the king of Babylon, laid siege to Jerusalem, resulting in the destruction of the city and its Temple. That was the most significant event that came to the Jewish mind when they thought of Babylon. They knew God had used Babylon to judge them; then God judged Babylon. Rome was used by God in a parallel fashion, judging and destroying Jerusalem and the Temple in AD 70. Then, God judged and destroyed Rome in AD 410, followed by the fall of the Roman Empire in AD 476.

John Saw in the Spirit a Vision That Rome Was like Babylon, Meaning Rome Would Judge Jerusalem, Then Be Judged by God

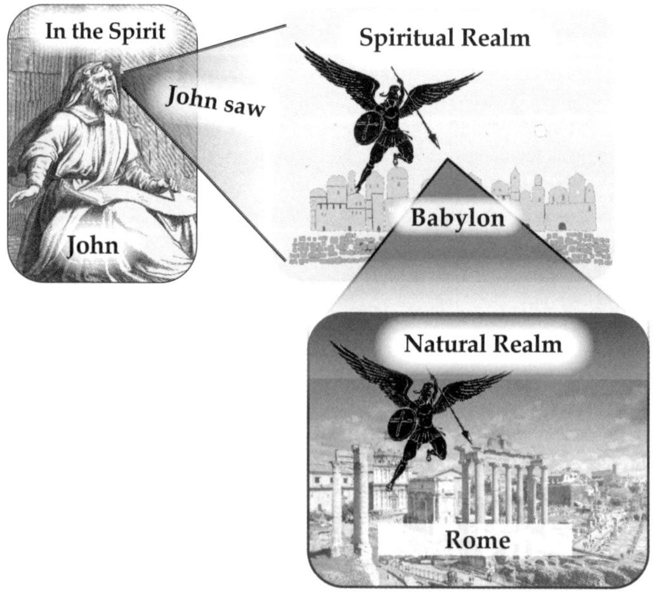

To realize how the Jews saw the judgment of Babylon and Rome as parallel events, consider how, even today, Jews around the world observe Tisha B'av, at sundown every July 29. That is the most somber of Jewish holidays, when Jews commemorate the destruction of the two Temples in Jerusalem. On that day, Jews fast and pray, seeing themselves as joined with their ancestors who experienced the destruction of Jerusalem first by the Babylonians in 586 BC[73] and then by the Romans in AD 70.

Although that way of thinking may be foreign to the modern Western mind, seeing Babylon and Rome linked would have been natural for John 2,000 years ago. John was well aware of how the Babylonians destroyed Jerusalem in 586 BC. So when John saw Babylon in a vision destroying Jerusalem, he would have made the association that another city was going to destroy Jerusalem. That city was Rome.

Rome Seduced the Nations

There are several other reasons to associate Babylon with Rome rather than Jerusalem.

After John saw the angel saying, *"Fallen, fallen is Babylon …"* (Rev. 14:8), he heard the angel describe Babylon as:

> *She who has made all the nations drink of the wine of the passion of her immorality.*

Did this apply to Rome or Old Jerusalem?

First, note that Babylon is referred to as "she." As pointed out earlier, Rome was also referred to in the female gender, while Old Jerusalem was referred to in the masculine gender.

Then the angel said the city had made *"all the nations drink of the wine of the passion of her immorality."* Harold points out that Old Jerusalem was not influential enough at that time

73. Some historians place the destruction of the first Temple at 587 BC.

in history to have *"made all the nations drink of the wine of the passion of her immorality."* In fact, several of the nations within the Roman Empire looked at the Jews with such disdain they would have nothing to do with the Jews.

In contrast, Rome was ruling over the entire Mediterranean region, forcing the nations to submit, which included worshipping the gods of the Empire. Rome was also sending captured Christians around the Empire to be killed in the public arenas. Rome made *"the nations drink of the wine of the passion of her immorality."*

Revelation 16:19: The Nations Fell When Rome Fell

Another reason to see that the second great city is Rome, rather than Old Jerusalem, is because Revelation 16:19 tells us that the city was so great that when it fell, *"the cities of the nations fell."* This was true of Rome, not Old Jerusalem.

When Old Jerusalem was destroyed in AD 70, the city of Rome prospered as the wealth of Old Jerusalem was taken to Rome. So also, many other cities within the Empire prospered because thousands of soldiers in the Roman army returned home with wealth and slaves. The nations of the earth did not fall when Jerusalem fell.

In contrast, all the nations within the Roman Empire fell, or at least suffered greatly, when Rome was conquered in AD 410. The Visigoths, Huns, Franks, and Vandals attacked and plundered Rome. Alaric, the king of the Visigoths, took two tons of gold and thirteen tons of silver from Rome. All the tribes took some of the wealth of Rome back to their homelands, leaving the economic system of the Roman Empire in shambles.

For almost a thousand years, Rome had provided law and order that disappeared when Rome fell. An entirely new social, political, and economic system known as feudalism replaced what Rome had created. Europe broke into smaller regions governed by struggling leaders fighting to establish the boundaries of their territories. The miles of Roman roads and waterways were no longer maintained. Commerce and trade quickly broke down. Such a radical change happened that historians see the fall of Rome as the transition between Classical Antiquity and the Middle Ages.

No such changes happened to the nations when Old Jerusalem fell.

Two Groups of 144,000 People

Next, consider how two different people groups were sealed by God before the first and second set of judgments.

We already discussed Revelation 7, which tells us about 144,000 people who were sealed by God before the judgments against the Jews began. Those 144,000 were Jews, 12,000 from each tribe (Rev. 7:4–8).

In contrast, Revelation 14 starts with 144,000 of God's people standing before the throne in heaven, singing a new song. We are told that:

> *These have been purchased from among men as first fruits to God and to the Lamb.*
>
> —Rev. 14:4c

We know these were early Christians because they had the name of Jesus and the name of His Father written on their foreheads (Rev. 14:1). They were the *"first fruits from the earth,"* which means they were the first ones to be born of God's Spirit and go to heaven.

Notice that this group of 144,000 differs from the first group of 144,000 reported in Revelation 7:4–8. Why is this important? Each group of 144,000 corresponds with the judgment that followed. Before the early Jews and Old Jerusalem were destroyed in AD 70, 144,000 Jews (Rev. 7:4–8) were sealed to serve as a remnant who would not be killed in the Jewish judgment. In contrast, the second group of 144,000 (Rev. 14) were Christians who had already died and were in heaven. They were mentioned before the judgment of Rome and the Roman Empire because they were looking for God's justice, having already been killed by the Roman leaders.

This leads the reader to conclude that the first and second sets of judgments were directed toward different people groups: the Jews first and the Romans second.

Rome, Not Jerusalem, Ruled Over the Kings

There is still more evidence that Babylon refers to Rome rather than Old Jerusalem.

Revelation 17:18 tells us that the second great city (Babylon) reigns over the *"kings of the earth."* Indeed, the Roman emperors did rule over kings within the Empire.

This cannot be correctly said of Old Jerusalem. During the NT period, the Jews lived as a conquered people, subject to the leaders of Rome. The Jews had lived as subjects of other nations for most of the previous 500 years. When Jesus was born, Herod was the king who reigned over Judea. Although Herod was raised in the Jewish customs, his father was an Edomite. The Jews did not rule themselves. Nor did the Jews rule over any kings.

Revelation 17:9: Rome as the City of Seven Hills

Consider another reason to see Rome as the second great city in Revelation.

In Revelation 17, Babylon is associated with a harlot who sat on seven mountains (Rev. 17:9). We will discuss the harlot later, but here consider how Rome was built on seven mountains. Rome was widely known as "The City of Seven Hills" (in antiquity, called *Septimontium*).[74]

A Roman coin minted under Emperor Vespasian (ca. AD 70) shows Rome as a woman sitting on seven hills.[75]

In contrast, the Jews proudly associated Jerusalem with one mountain called Mount Zion. "Zion" appears in the OT 152 times as a title referring to Jerusalem, e.g., 2 Kings 19:31; Is. 2:3; Joel 2:1. The writer of Hebrews encouraged believers saying, *"You have come to Mount Zion and to the city of the living God, the heavenly Jerusalem . . ."* (Heb. 12:22). Zion is even mentioned in the book of Revelation (14:1).

The Jewish Christians to whom John first wrote Revelation would have known that Jerusalem was associated with one mountain. They also would have known that Rome was the City of Seven Hills.

Rome, Not Jerusalem, Is the Second Great City

Let us summarize the differences we have thus far identified between the two large cities that were judged in Revelation.

Old Jerusalem, the first great city (talked about in Rev. 7–11), was a city:

1. that was referred to in the male gender (Rev. 11:8)
2. where Jesus was crucified (Rev. 11:8)
3. that did *not* have a history parallel to Babylon
4. that did *not* seduce the nations *"to drink of the wine of the passion of her immorality"* (Rev. 14:8)

74. A few of the ancient references to Rome being the city on seven hills include: Virgil, *Publius Vergilius Maro, Aen.* VI.783; Virgil, *Georgics,* II.534; Cicero, *Ad Att.* VI.5.2; *Tibullus,* II.5.55; Varro, *De lingua Latina,* v.41; and *Aulus Gellius,* xiii.14. "Septimontium" also referred to an ancient festival celebrated every year by the inhabitants of the seven hills of ancient Rome.

75. David Criswell, *She Who Restores the Roman Empire: The Biblical Prophecy of the Whore of Babylon.* iUniverse. 46.

5. whose fall did *not* lead to the fall of the nations (Rev. 16:19)
6. judged after 144,000 Jews were sealed (Rev. 7:3–8)
7. that did *not* rule over the kings of the earth (Rev. 17:18)
8. built on one hill called Mount Zion

Babylon, the second city (talked about in Rev. 14–18), was a city:

1. that was referred to in the female gender (Rev. 17:18)
2. where Jesus was *not* crucified (Rev. 11:8)
3. that did have a history parallel to Rome
4. that did seduce the nations *"to drink of the wine of the passion of her immorality"* (Rev. 14:8)
5. whose fall led to the fall of the nations (Rev. 16:19)
6. judged after 144,000 Christians were sealed (Rev. 14:1)
7. that did rule over the kings of the earth (Rev. 17:18)
8. built on seven hills (Rev. 17:9)

Do these two cities sound like the same city? No, they do not. The first is Old Jerusalem. The second is Rome.

Revelation 17: The Harlot as Old Jerusalem or Rome?

One's decision about the identity of the two great cities in Revelation is so determinative of one's understanding of the entire book that it is worth settling this issue.

Revelation 17–18 introduces another figure called *"the harlot."* This harlot is also associated with *"the great city"* in the feminine gender. Later, we will see the role and activity of the harlot, but now let us consider if this harlot refers to Old Jerusalem or Rome.

Since Martin sees *"the great city,"* referring to Old Jerusalem in Revelation 7–18, he sees *"the harlot"* as another label for Old Jerusalem.

Trench's Understanding of Revelation		
Figures	**Name**	**Identity**
Great City	Sodom, Egypt, Babylon, Harlot	Old Jerusalem

In contrast, Harold sees the harlot as referring to a spiritual entity that influenced Rome and the Roman Empire.

Eberle's Understanding of Revelation		
Figures Rev. 12–18	**Name**	**Identity**
Great City (He)	Sodom & Egypt	Old Jerusalem
Great City (She)	Babylon & Harlot	Rome

Is Old Jerusalem the Harlot?

Teachers who see Old Jerusalem as the harlot (Martin's view) like to support their view by quoting OT passages that refer to Old Jerusalem as a harlot. For example, Isaiah 1:21 refers to Old Jerusalem saying:

> *How the faithful city has become a prostitute* [harlot] . . .

Old Jerusalem—Harlot
(Is. 1:21)

After pointing out this OT association with a harlot, adherents will then point out verses like Revelation 17:5, which show the harlot is also associated with Babylon:

> *And on her* [the harlot's] *forehead a name was written, a mystery: "Babylon the Great . . ."*

Harlot—Babylon
(Rev. 17:5)

Teachers of this view can then connect Old Jerusalem with Babylon by connecting Isaiah 1:21 with Revelation 17:5:

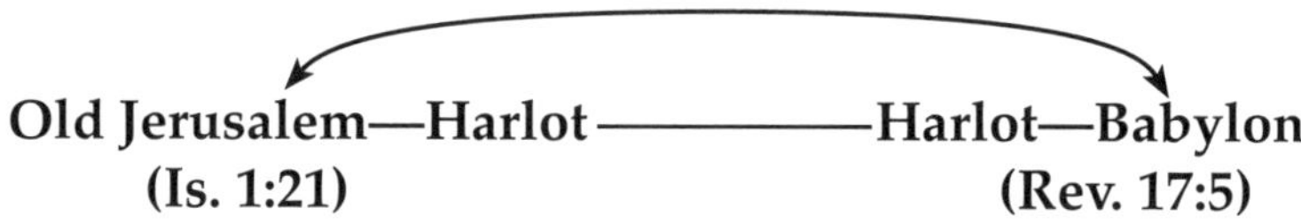

This progression of thought is used to support the view that Old Jerusalem is the harlot and Babylon in Revelation.

Old Jerusalem Is Not the Harlot or Babylon

Teachers, such as Harold Eberle, will challenge the above progression of thought. The connection that adherents try to make between Old Jerusalem and Babylon is built on the assumption that the harlot mentioned in Isaiah 1:21 is the same harlot that is mentioned in Revelation 17:5.

Showing that assumption is dubious is the fact that more than one city and nation in the OT are referred to as harlots. For example, Isaiah 23:15–17 calls the city of Tyre a harlot. The prophet Nahum recorded the words of God that referred to Nineveh as a harlot (Nahum 3:4–7). Pointing out that Tyre and Nineveh are referred to as harlots in the OT, someone could argue that these are the cities talked about in Revelation. Harold mentions this to show how finding a connection between a city and a harlot in the OT is not a solid argument for equating Jerusalem with the harlot of Revelation.

We must also look carefully at the context in which Israel is referred to as a harlot in the OT. Beginning around 930 BC, Israel was a separate kingdom from Judea. During that time,

Jerusalem was not part of the kingdom of Israel. Therefore, referring to Israel as a harlot during that time did not include Jerusalem in the label "harlot."

To confirm this, note that the primary theme of the book of Hosea is the condemnation of Israel for acting like a harlot, but that was talking about Israel during the period when the kingdom of Israel was separate from Jerusalem and Judah.

There is one place (Jer. 23) where Samaria and Jerusalem are compared and both are condemned as harlots.

Since the label "harlot" is used in the OT to refer to several cities, kingdoms, and nations, we should not think of "harlot" as the name of one particular city. Harlot is not a name. It is a descriptive term applied to any city, kingdom, or nation whose heart turned away from God.

Comparatively, we can say "large" is a descriptive term. Just because we find a large city being referred to in the OT does not mean it is the same large city referred to in Revelation.

A Bible reader who assumes Revelation is all about the judgment of Old Jerusalem may conclude that the harlot in Revelation is also Old Jerusalem. Anyone who does not make that assumption will consider the evidence that identifies the harlot in Revelation as something other than Old Jerusalem. For this reason, Harold provided eight points showing that the great city / Old Jerusalem is a different city than the great city / Babylon.

The great city / Babylon is Rome. Therefore, Rome is the city that was judged in Revelation 12–14.

Eberle's Understanding of Revelation		
Figures Rev. 12–18	**Name**	**Identity**
Great City (He)	Sodom & Egypt	Old Jerusalem
Great City (She)	Babylon & Harlot	Rome

Harold would again point out that this has been the dominant view of Christianity over the last 2,000 years.

Why Is This Discussion Important?

For most readers, whether *"the great city"* refers to one or two cities will not make any difference in their daily lives. It will not influence how they care for their family, pay their bills, or enjoy their day. Identifying the great city will not have a noticeable or immediate influence on how people live.

However, truth is always relevant. The truth about the book of Revelation does influence one's worldview, and one's worldview guides the overall direction of a person's life.

This is easy to see when we contrast the partial preterist view with the futurist view. Futurists believe all the judgments of Revelation are coming in the future, which tends to create fear and anxiety about the future. Futurists also believe the world is getting worse and worse, which causes adherents to feel hopeless about improving society. As a result, they tend to not get involved with changing society. Further, futurists who spend much time thinking about Jesus returning very soon are unlikely to make long-range plans or invest in the future.

In contrast, partial preterists see most of the judgments of God as past and, therefore, not in our future. They also have an optimistic view of the future as the Kingdom of God grows until it fills the earth. These are important issues that do influence one's day-to-day living.

However, the distinctions partial preterists make about *"the great city"* being one city or two cities will not have such a profound influence on one's life.

Still, they may influence one's attitudes and perceptions. For example, if a Christian believes all God's judgments in Revelation 7–18 were against Old Jerusalem and the Jews, that does influence what a person thinks and feels about the Jews.

On the other hand, if a Christian believes God's judgments in Revelation 7–18 were against Old Jerusalem and Rome, that causes a person to have a more critical attitude toward the values of the ancient Roman Empire and, therefore, one's desires to be like or not to be like the ancient Romans.

Truth is far-reaching. It reaches deep into crevices, out of which plants grow. We may never be able to trace the roots of all our behavior, attitudes, and perceptions, but our thoughts and values are the soil for our life.

Revelation 14: Jesus Reaped a Great Harvest

Now, let us focus on Revelation 14, which describes the fall of Babylon. While accepting Babylon as Rome (Harold's view), let us look carefully and see if any events around the fall of Babylon / Rome correspond with known historic events.

In Revelation 14:6, we see how John watched an *"angel flying in midheaven, having an eternal gospel to preach to those who live on the earth"* (Rev. 14:6). As John continued looking into the vision, he saw Jesus with a sickle in His hand (Rev. 14:14). Then an angel cried out:

> *Put in your sickle and reap, for the hour to reap has come, because the harvest of the earth is ripe.*
>
> —Rev. 14:15b

The world was ready for a great harvest:

> *Then He* [Jesus] *who sat on the cloud swung His sickle over the earth, and the earth was reaped.*
>
> —Rev. 14:16

If we are looking for historic events that correspond to a harvest and the preaching of the *"eternal gospel,"* we would expect to find thousands, perhaps millions, of people responding to the gospel.

Did anything like this ever happen in the Roman Empire? Yes, it did—one time. In AD 313, everything in the Roman Empire changed. Before that date, it was illegal to be a Christian throughout the Empire. The masses of Roman people worshipped many gods, such as Jupiter, Mars, Venus, and the emperors. Then, in AD 313, Christianity was made legal.

Constantine, the emperor, made many gifts to the Christian Church, including extensive property donations. He built the first great Christian cathedral in Rome and churches in cities around the Empire. Christianity exploded in growth during that period.

In AD 380, Christianity was made the only authorized religion of the Empire. By the end of the fifth century, the majority of the Roman Empire claimed to be Christian.[76]

REVELATION 14: JESUS REAPED A GREAT HARVEST

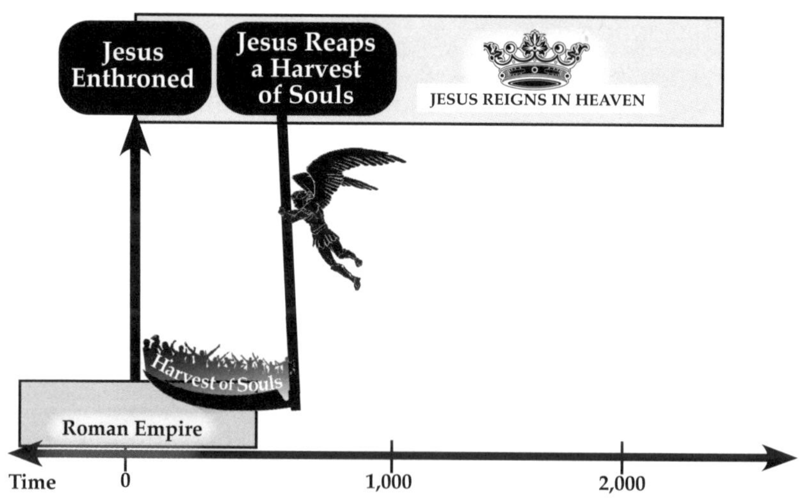

Many Christians are unaware of the incredible harvest that took place at that time. Some have only learned about the problems that arose during the Middle Ages due to the

76. Kenneth Scott Latourette, *A History of Christianity*, Vol. 1, (New York: Harper and Row, 1975), 97.

State and Church joining arms. Indeed, many power struggles occurred between the government and Church.

Yet, being more aware of those struggles than the historic harvest is similar to Christians who read the book of Revelation and are more aware of the beast than they are of Jesus. The book of Revelation is not about the beast. It is about the kingdoms of this world becoming the Kingdom of Jesus. When we read Revelation 14, we must not miss the most glorious transformation of society in which more than a million people heard the gospel and began to believe in Jesus. The world was ripe, and Jesus reaped a great harvest. This is the grandest, most important event that preceded the defeat of Rome.

Recognizing this great harvest gives us reason number nine[77] to see the great city of Babylon as Rome rather than Old Jerusalem. There was no such harvest before Old Jerusalem fell.

Old Jerusalem was a city:

9. that did not experience a great harvest before it fell.

Babylon was a city:

9. that experienced a great harvest before it fell.

In other words, Babylon was Rome.

Revelation 14: The Fall of Babylon (Rome)

Revelation 14 describes how another angel came forth and swung another sickle. That second sickle was not to reap a great harvest. It was for judgment and destruction:

> *So the angel swung his sickle to the earth and gathered the clusters from the vine of the earth, and threw them into the great wine press of the wrath of God. And the wine press*

77. The preceding eight reasons are given on pages 187 and 188.

> *was trodden outside the city, and blood came out from the wine press, up to the horses' bridles, for a distance of two hundred miles.*
>
> —Rev. 14:19–20

Throughout the fourth century, Rome declined as invaders from the North looted and killed the people of the surrounding regions. Then, in AD 378, the Goths had a decisive victory over the Roman legions. In AD 410, the Visigoths descended upon Rome and ransacked the city.

In AD 476, the Western portion of the Roman Empire collapsed.[78]

The Eastern portion survived as the Byzantine Empire until AD 1453 when the Turks captured and took control of Constantinople. Exactly as Daniel told us, the Roman Empire was crushed, and the eternal Kingdom of God continued to increase (Dan. 2:40–44).

Second Angel Swung a Sickle and the Roman Empire Fell

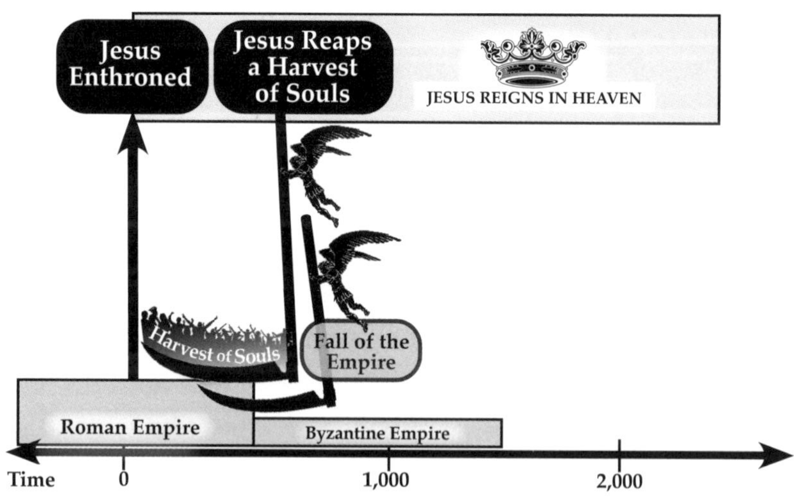

78. Because Martin Trench sees this judgment against Jerusalem rather than Rome, he says: *"They were trampled in the winepress outside the city, and blood flowed out of the press, rising as high as the horses' bridles"* speaks of the Roman armies on horseback invading Jerusalem and slaughtering those within.

Revelation 15–18:
The Third Set of Judgments

Now that we have studied the first and second sets of judgments, we will examine the third set of judgments described in Revelation 15–18.

Revelation 15–18: Third Set of Judgments Against Whom?

Since Martin Trench sees all the judgments in Revelation 7–18 as against the Jews and Old Jerusalem, he sees the third set as a continuation or repeat of the first and second sets of judgments.

All Judgments Against the Early Jews and Old Jerusalem

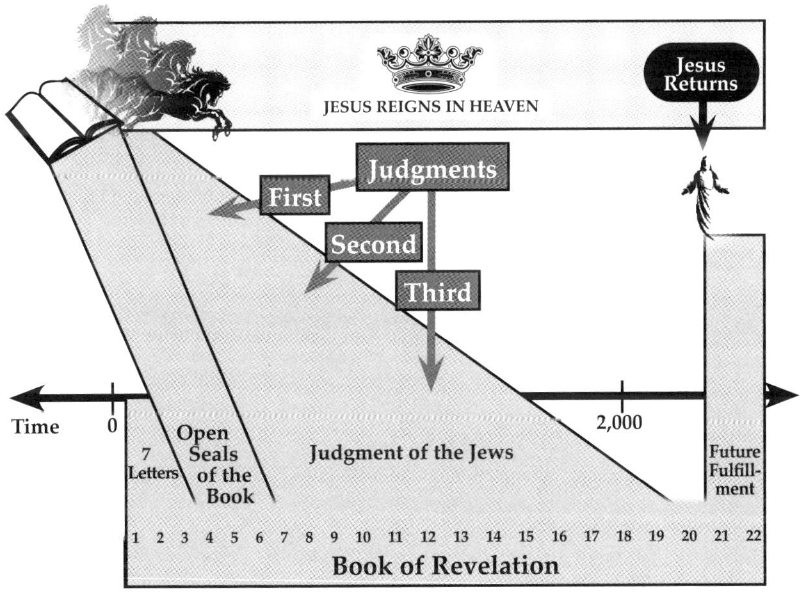

Harold Eberle sees the judgments in Revelation as sequential, with the judgment of Jerusalem first (Rev. 7–11), the judgment of the Roman Empire second (Rev. 12–14), and the judgment of the whole world third (Rev. 15–18).

Three Sets of Judgments:

> **First, Against the Early Jews and Old Jerusalem**
> **Second, Against the Roman Empire**
> **Third, Against the Whole World**[79]

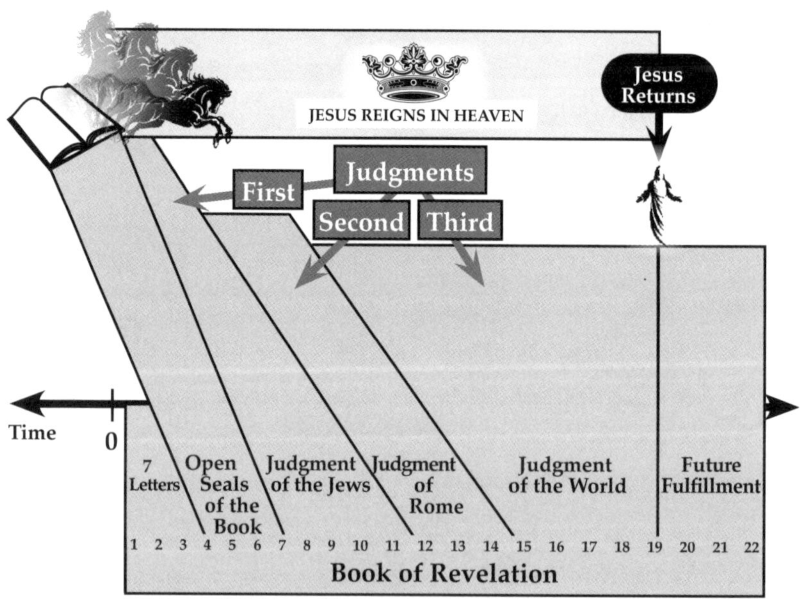

79. Although this diagram shows the three sets of judgments as consecutive, each of the sets starts over at the life of Jesus: the first set goes from Jesus in heaven (Rev. 4–6) to the destruction of Jerusalem (Rev. 11); the second goes from Jesus' birth (Rev. 12:2) to the destruction of Babylon/Rome (Rev. 14); the third set goes from Jesus' life during the Roman Empire to Jesus' return in the future (Rev. 19).

Revelation 15–18: Third Set Against the World

For the third set of judgments, John saw seven angels releasing seven plagues (Rev. 15) and pouring out seven bowls of the wrath of God (Rev. 16).

An Angel Pouring Out a Bowl of God's Wrath

As we explain how these seven bowls came upon the whole world, we are not discussing the final judgment when all the nations will stand before Jesus. That final judgment is an event discussed in Revelation 20. The judgments described in Revelation 15–18 correspond to God's actions before Jesus returns. The third set of judgments happen to all the nations until they are progressively subdued under Jesus.

This is evident as we read the song that was sung in heaven as the third set of judgments are poured out:

> *Great and marvelous are Your works,*
> *Lord God, the Almighty . . .*
> *For all the nations will come and worship before You,*
> *For Your righteous acts have been revealed.*
>
> —Rev. 15:3b–4

Songs such as these not only praised God but also gave God glory for what He was doing at that time. Here, we see God's people giving Him glory for turning the nations toward Himself. God's goal is to align the nations, then send Jesus to reign over them.

Because this view (Harold's favored view) sees the judgments of God extending over all of history from the birth of Jesus (Rev. 12:2) to the present and into the future, it is referred to as the "historicist view" of the book of Revelation. Proponents of the historicist view find historic events that correspond with each vision John saw in Revelation.

Different teachers of the historicist view may not explain the events of Revelation 7–18 exactly as Harold explains them, but historicists have in common the belief that Revelation 7–18 covers the course of history beginning with Jesus' birth.

The partial preterist view called the historicist view was the most predominant view held by the leaders of the Protestant Reformation, including Luther, Knox, Calvin, and Huss. During the Reformation, it was referred to as "the Protestant view."[80]

Finishing the Judgments of God

With the third set of judgments, we are told that *"the wrath of God is finished"* (Rev. 15:1). Corresponding to this, we are told about *seven* angels, *seven* plagues, and *seven* bowls of God's wrath. When we hear the number *seven,* we should know that the Jewish people thought of seven as the number of completion. The Jewish readers would have understood this to mean that God was executing judgments that would complete the job He set out to do.

Of course, the completion of God's judgments means something different to Martin Trench than it does to Harold Eberle. Martin associates it with the completion of God's judgment of Old Jerusalem, and Harold associates it with the completion of God's judgments to put all Jesus' enemies worldwide under His feet.

80. Although the leaders of the Reformation held to the historicist view, most of them saw the beasts, Babylon, and the harlot associated with the Roman Catholic Church, rather than the Roman Empire.

We will continue explaining the view Harold favors while inserting comments and footnotes that support Martin's view.

Third Set of Judgments: Seven Angels Pour Out Seven Bowls of Wrath

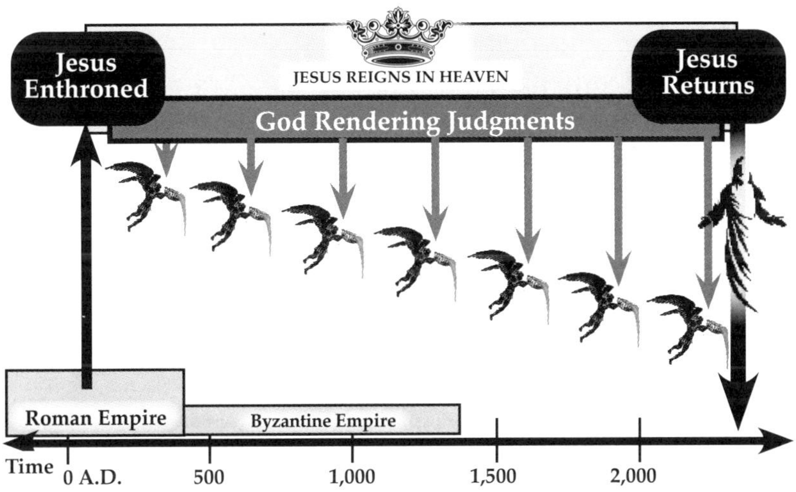

Revelation 19 starts off praising God for the completion of His judgments. Before the end of chapter 19, Jesus is declared the triumphant King (Rev. 19:16) who will rule the nations with a rod of iron (Rev. 19:15).

Revelation 17: The Third Beast of Revelation

Keeping in mind that the third set of judgments spread from the life of Jesus to His Second Coming, let us look at some events that happened during that long period.

In Revelation 17:3, a third beast comes on the scene. This third beast is referred to as *"a scarlet beast."* John wrote that the scarlet beast came out of the abyss (Rev. 17:8). This implies that this beast did not originate with the humans living on Earth.

We also know this beast was not human because it had seven heads and ten horns (Rev. 17:3, 7). This is the same information that we learned about the first two beasts. We explained that the seven heads and ten horns refer to the first seven Caesars and ten kings of the Roman Empire. This leads one to believe that all three beasts influenced and worked through multiple leaders of the Roman Empire.

The Three Beasts Influencing Leaders of the Roman Empire

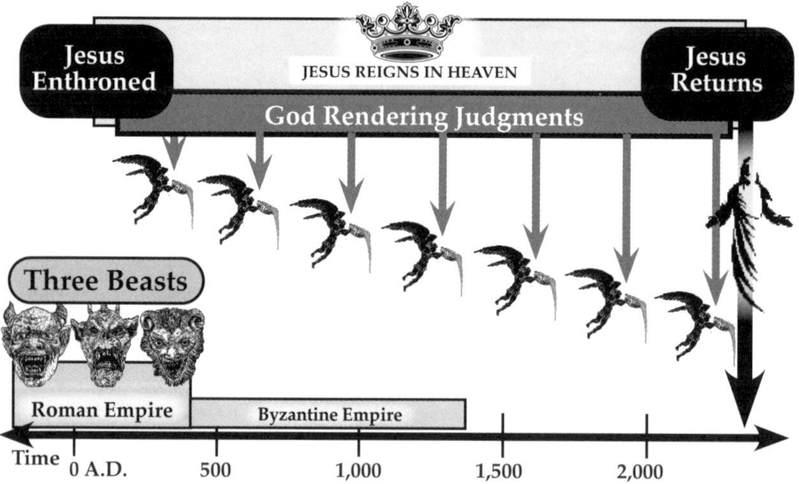

It is important to keep in mind that the three beasts are spiritual in nature. Therefore, they have been able to continue working in the world even after the Roman Empire collapsed.

Revelation 17: The Harlot Rides on the Third Beast

Alongside the third beast, John described a harlot. This harlot was riding on the back of the third beast (Rev. 17:3, 7), which implies that the scarlet beast ushered the harlot into the Roman Empire.

The harlot's relationship with Rome is evident from what John saw written on the harlot's forehead:

> *And on her* [the harlot's] *forehead a name was written, a mystery: "Babylon the Great . . ."*
>
> —Rev. 17:5

The fact that the harlot had *"Babylon . . ."* written on her forehead meant she was bonded into submission to Babylon / Rome.

The ancient Romans sometimes branded runaway slaves on their foreheads. That brand symbolized to whom the branded person belonged. We can see similar symbolism used earlier in Revelation, where we are told that the saints who had died had the name Jesus and His Father written on their foreheads (Rev. 14:1). That signified that they belonged to and were in submission to Jesus and Father-God. With "Babylon" written on the harlot's forehead, we can infer that the harlot was bonded to Babylon / Rome.

The Harlot Rode on the Third Beast

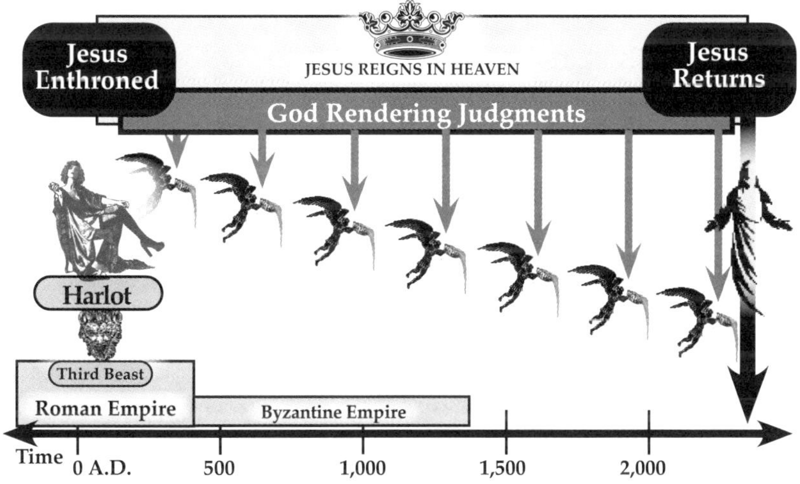

Revelation 17: Who Is the Harlot?

The most common use of the word "harlot" in the Bible was to refer to a woman who used sexual temptation to lure the hearts of men. The harlot talked about in Revelation lured people's hearts away from God.

She used sexual pleasure, lust for wealth, and other sensualities for her seductive influences (Rev. 17:2; 18:3, 9). The context of Revelation 18 also implies that she stirred lust for power, fame, and even worship.

The wealthy and powerful leaders of the Roman Empire were known for their pursuit of wealth, power, fame, comfort, and pleasure. The harlot offered what they desired:

> *The great men of the earth . . . because all the nations were deceived by your sorcery.*
>
> —Rev. 18:23

> *The merchants of the earth have become rich by the wealth of her sensuality.*
>
> —Rev. 18:3b

The harlot's temptation was similar to how Satan made an offer to Jesus, *"I will give You all this domain and its glory . . . if You worship before me . . .* (Luke 4:6–7). Many wealthy and powerful people came under her spell.

Revelation 17–18: The Harlot Is the Roman Empire

An angel told John that the harlot reigned *"over the kings of the earth"* (Rev. 17:18). With authority over many great leaders, the harlot had those leaders carry out her will.

We saw this during the Roman Empire as the harlot worked with the beasts. We already discussed how the first beast caused a Roman government leader to persecute

Christians for 42 months (Rev. 13:5–7). A second beast caused a Roman government leader to force everyone to worship him (Rev. 13:15). The third beast gave the harlot access to the Roman leaders, and the harlot turned the hearts of the leaders toward false gods, then caused the Roman leaders to kill Christians.

Revelation 17–18: Who Killed the Early Christians?

John described the harlot as follows:

> *And I saw the woman drunk with the blood of the saints, and with the blood of the witnesses of Jesus.*
>
> —Rev. 17:6a

Looking at this verse, partial preterists who see all the judgments in Revelation 7–18 as directed toward the Jews and Old Jerusalem (Martin Trench's view[81]) must see Jerusalem as the city that was *"drunk with the blood of the saints."* Adherents will refer to Matthew 23:35, where Jesus said, *"The guilt of all the righteous blood shed on earth, from the blood of righteous Abel to the blood of Zechariah"* would fall upon the Jewish religious leaders.

We have already given nine reasons[82] to associate the harlot with Rome rather than Old Jerusalem. Now, look carefully at the judgments for killing God's righteous ones (Matt. 23:35 and Rev. 17:6).

Both Matthew 23:35 and Revelation 17:6 talk about judgments for killing God's people; however, they are not talking about the same people or the same judgment. Matthew 23:35 shows us that the Jews and Jerusalem were condemned for shedding *"the blood of righteous Abel to the blood of Zechariah."* Those were OT saints. They all died before Jesus died. In

81. Martin Trench explains that the harlot is Old Jerusalem and the beast is Rome. Martin says Old Jerusalem made a pact with Rome but Rome eventually turned on Old Jerusalem and destroyed her.

82. Eight reasons are listed on pages 187 and 188. Reason number nine is on page 195.

contrast, Revelation 17:6 shows us the harlot was drunk on the *"blood of the saints, and with the blood of the witnesses of Jesus."* These are NT saints. They all died after Jesus died.

The judgment for killing OT saints came upon Old Jerusalem. The judgment for killing NT saints came upon the harlot which refers to the spiritual power that influenced Rome.

This gives us reason number ten for seeing that Old Jerusalem was not Babylon or the harlot. Old Jerusalem was a city:

10. that was judged for killing OT saints.

The Babylon/harlot/Rome was a city:

10. that was judged for killing NT saints.

This distinction is important for the historicist view.

It also corresponds with the historical evidence. It was under Roman rule, not Jewish rule, that Christians were killed. Emperor Nero blamed the burning of the city of Rome in AD 64 on the Christians, which began the horrific period of Christian persecution. The historian Tacitus (ca. AD 55–120) described how Christians were tortured, nailed to crosses, or covered in animal skins and then torn to death by dogs. The Jews were not involved.

The second major persecution took place during Domitian's reign (AD 81–96), when famine, pestilence, and earthquakes were blamed on Christians, leading to the martyrdom of untold numbers—again by Romans.

Then, the greatest and bloodiest persecution of Christians in the Roman Empire happened during the reign of Diocletian (AD 284–305), who became known in history as the "adversary of God."

The city of Rome was *"drunk with the blood of the saints, and with the blood of the witnesses of Jesus."* This is evident when we think of the tens of thousands of Christians who were slaughtered in the coliseums. Envision the Roman crowds cheering, and you will understand how they were drunk on the blood of the saints.

During all of that period, it was illegal for the Jews to put anyone to death (John 18:31). At times, Jewish mobs got out of control and stoned an individual, e.g., Acts 7:58–59, but the only way for Jews to have someone legally put to death was to go through the Roman legal system. Jews were not involved in most of the killings of Christians. The Romans were responsible.

The Harlot Continued Working After Rome Fell

The corrupt Roman Empire fell in AD 476. We discussed that fall when we studied Revelation 14, where there is a description of Babylon/Rome falling.

After the Empire fell, the harlot continued to work in the world. In chapters 17 and 18 of Revelation, we read about the harlot continuing to lure the hearts of the kings, along with the hearts of other wealthy and powerful people. The harlot's end does not come until the end of Revelation 18, just before Jesus returns in Revelation 19.

Revelation 16:13–16: The Battle of Armageddon

In a minute, we will return to the subject of the fall of the harlot, but before that, let us discuss what has become known as the "Battle of Armageddon." After the sixth bowl of wrath was poured out, but before the last bowl was poured out, John saw a vision that led to a great battle:

> *And I saw coming out of the mouth of the dragon and out of the mouth of the beast and out of the mouth of the false prophet, three unclean spirits like frogs; for they are spirits of demons . . .*
>
> —Rev. 16:13–14

John saw three *"spirits of demons"* that were like frogs. He said they came out of the mouth of the dragon, beast, and false prophet, which implied that the spirits of the demons originated from the dragon, beast, and false prophet.[83] These were the same figures that were active back in the Roman Empire.

John Saw the Spirits of Demons in the Spiritual Realm

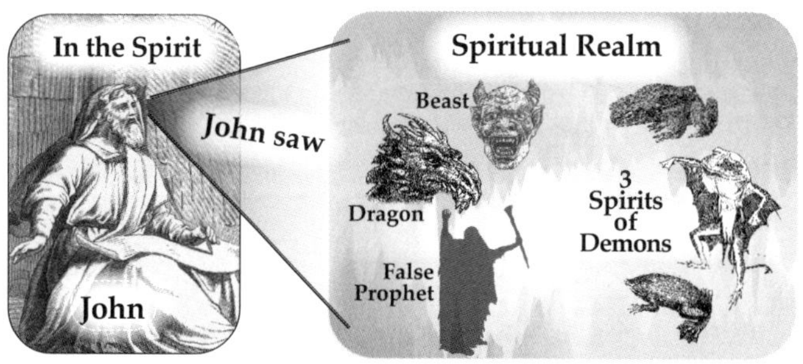

Today, many Christians are skeptical about demons or spiritual powers, so they do not like to talk about them. Because they are skeptical about the activity of demons, they cannot accept at face value what John said: *"They are spirits of demons . . ."*

In his first letter, John wrote about *"all that is in the world, the lust of the flesh and the lust of the eyes and the boastful pride of life"* (1 John 2:16). John does not connect these with the three spirits of demons in the book of Revelation, and it may just be coincidental that they are both three in number. However, no reader can accept the existence of such spirits if they do not embrace a worldview that sees spiritual entities influencing the natural realm. Without that worldview, the reader will never understand what John wrote.

After seeing the *"spirits of demons,"* John described how those demons went out to:

83. Although the prophet is mentioned here and in Rev. 19:20 and 20:10, there is no description of the nature or role of this prophet. It is reasonable to think that the prophet spoke in a fashion to further the goals of the dragon and beast.

> *The kings of the whole world, to gather them together for the war of the great day of God, the Almighty.*
> —Rev. 16:14b

John watched those demons go out into the world for the purpose of stirring in the hearts of kings to war against God.

That war is called the Battle of Armageddon. This name comes from what John wrote in Revelation 16:16:

> *And they gathered them together to the place which in Hebrew is called Har-Magedon.*

THE SPIRITS OF THE DEMONS INFLUENCE LEADERS TO WAR

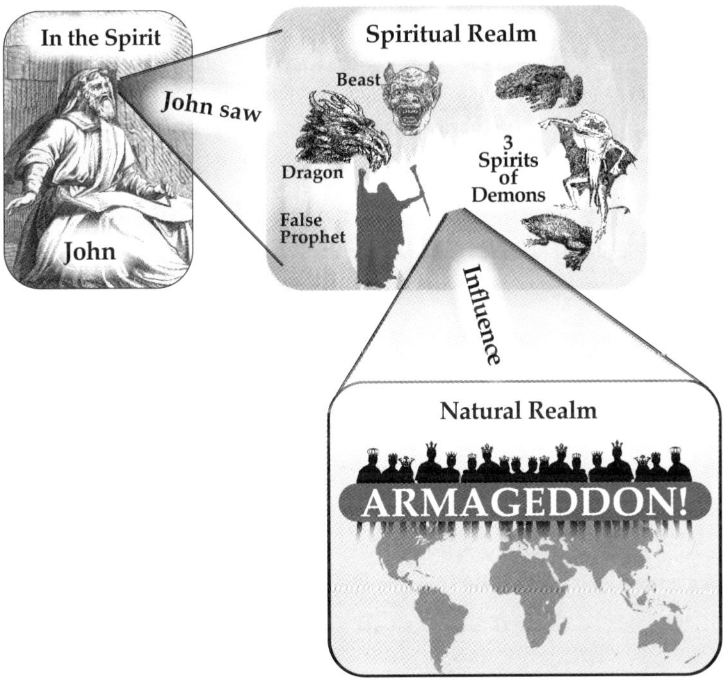

From what John wrote, we know that the *"entire world"* will be involved in this war against God. Every human being will be tempted by evil, but Revelation 17 and 18 focus primarily on leaders called kings. They will be especially targeted by evil spirits.

We should think of leaders beyond those who are called "kings" since that title is not as common today. We may infer that the demons will attempt to get many leaders in the world involved, which implies that the demons will try to influence all the people under the authority of those leaders.

We also know that that war will be close to the end just before the last angel pours out his last bowl of judgment.

Revelation 16:13–16: Confusion About Armageddon

We just examined everything the Bible says about the Battle of Armageddon. There are only four verses about the great battle (Rev. 16:13–16).

Readers who have studied other books about eschatology know that some Christian teachers have written extensively about Armageddon. Entire books have been dedicated to that subject. Since there are only four verses in the Bible about Armageddon, you can be sure that those books about Armageddon are the product of very active imaginations.

Futurists have been especially ambitious to embellish the stories about a final war. They usually portray images of millions of soldiers from Russia and China coming against Israel toward the end of a seven-year tribulation. They develop this image by taking other Bible passages that talk about various battles—particularly, those described in Ezekiel 38 and 39—and then associate them with this Battle of Armageddon. In doing so, they can develop their teachings and build in the minds of listeners images of huge destruction coming upon the world right before the end.

Discussing the battles of Ezekiel 38 and 39 should be beyond the scope of this book; however, we are forced to mention them because futurists pull these battles into their scenario of end-time events.

Ezekiel 38 and 39 never mention Armageddon. Those two chapters describe wars that took place in 175 to 164 BC with the Seleucids and Antiochus IV Epiphanes.[84] Those wars are not descriptions of modern warfare but about *"horses and horsemen, all of them magnificently dressed, a great contingent with shield and buckler, all of them wielding swords"* (Ezek. 38:4). For futurist teachers to apply those wars to modern times, they have to say that those outdated means of warfare are to be understood as symbolic, but the relevant passages give us no indication that they are symbolic or referring to some future war.

Many futurists will admit that Ezekiel was describing those wars of the second century BC, but then they say those wars foreshadow the more important war that will take place at the end of the world.

There is no reasonable or biblical basis to equate the battles of Ezekiel 38 and 39 with any future war—especially the battle of Armageddon. The enemies at war are not even the same. Ezekiel 38 and 39 tell us how Gog and Magog (whom futurists typically say mean Russia and China), and other armies from the north, come against Israel. Revelation 16 never mentions Gog, Magog,[85] or Israel. *None* of the key players are mentioned! Instead, we are told that *"the kings of the whole world"* come against God (Rev. 16:14).

Revelation 16:13–16: Armageddon as a Spiritual Battle

Once we have separated in our minds the battles described in Ezekiel 38 and 39 from the battle of Armageddon in

84. One of many places this can be researched is in *Adam Clark's Commentary,* which may be accessed at: http://www.godrules.net/library/clarke/clarkeeze38.htm

85. Gog and Magog are mentioned in Revelation 20:8 at the end of a millennial reign of Jesus.

Revelation 16, then we can read Revelation 16 and develop an understanding from what the text actually tells us.

And what do we read? Not much. Four verses are all we have.

We do know the same spiritual powers that were at work back in the Roman Empire, the Dragon, beast, and false prophet, will release demons to try to stir up a war in which the entire world will come against God.

However, we do not even know if that war will be physical in nature. We do not know if it will entail guns, tanks, aircraft, missiles, or drones. After all, physical weapons will be no good in a war against God.

There is a spiritual war that other Bible passages tell us about:

> *For our struggle is not against flesh and blood, but against the rulers, against the powers, against the world forces of this darkness, against the spiritual forces of wickedness in the heavenly places.*
>
> —Eph. 6:12

According to Paul, the real battle in life is not against other human beings. It is against evil spiritual beings.

The war that Jesus was concerned about was one in which the Kingdom of God grows until it displaces the realm of darkness.

> *The kings of the earth take their stand*
> *And the rulers conspire together*
> *Against the Lord and against His Anointed, saying,*
> *"Let's tear their shackles apart*
> *And throw their ropes away from us!"*
> *He who sits in the heavens laughs,*
> *The Lord scoffs at them.*
> *Then He will speak to them in His anger*
> *And terrify them in His fury, saying,*
> *"But as for Me, I have installed My King*
> *Upon Zion, My holy mountain."*
> *"I will announce the decree of the Lord:*

He said to Me, 'You are My Son,
Today I have fathered You.
Ask it of Me, and I will certainly give the nations as Your inheritance,
And the ends of the earth as Your possession.
You shall break them with a rod of iron,
You shall shatter them like earthenware.'"

—Ps. 2:2–9

This is the only battle that will involve every human being on Earth. This is the only battle in which all the nations will fight against God. The outcome of this battle was settled 2,000 years ago when God placed Jesus on His throne as King.

After Jesus sat down on His throne, the Father said to His Son, *"Sit at My right hand, until I make Your enemies a footstool for Your feet"* (Acts 2:34–35). It is only a matter of time until every knee bows and every tongue confesses Jesus as LORD.

It is a spiritual battle. Every person has to fight in their heart and mind. It is right versus wrong: good versus evil, the Kingdom of God against the realm of darkness.

Consider how the term "Armageddon" may have been understood by the early Jewish Christians who first read the writings of John. The term "Armageddon" was not used anywhere else in the Bible. It was taken from two Hebrew words: *Har,* meaning mountain, and *Megiddo,* referring to a city about 70 miles north of Jerusalem. In Jewish history, Megiddo was a place where many great battles had occurred. Megiddo is mentioned 11 times in the OT. We can understand this reference to be a great battleground.[86]

In modern times, we may refer to battlegrounds and apply those references to our personal lives, such as when someone says that they have "met their Waterloo," or "it is D-Day," or "remember the Alamo." Someone amid great struggles may say, "I am in the midst of a World War." For those familiar with such terminology, these phrases bring to remembrance

86. Kelley Varner, *Whose Right It Is* (Shippensburg, PA: Destiny Image Publishers, 1995), 178–179.

great battles, but they refer to present personal battles.

A helpful comparison is to the Muslims' understanding of "jihad." Many fundamentalist Muslims envision jihad as a war in which Muslims are called to kill infidels, that is, those who do not follow the teachings of Muhammad. In contrast, there are many other Muslims who understand jihad as a call for each Muslim to battle temptation and evil in their own life.

Just as jihad has two different understandings, so does the Christian battle of Armageddon.

We all have an Armageddon in our personal life. It is the war with our finances, in our neighborhoods, in our schools, and in our governments. It is in our hearts and minds. That is the only war that will encompass every human being on Earth.[87]

Revelation 18: The Harlot Falls

After Armageddon, the last enemy to be defeated is the harlot who stirs the lusts of people and seduces them to turn away from God. As the last bowl of wrath is poured out, God's people are exhorted to rejoice:

> *Rejoice over her, O heaven, and you saints and apostles and prophets, because God has pronounced judgment for you against her* [the harlot].
>
> —Rev. 18:20

This is where the harlot is defeated!

Revelation 19 starts with the celebration of the completed judgments:

87. Because Martin Trench sees all the judgments in Revelation as directed toward the destruction of old covenant Judea and Jerusalem, he sees the Battle of Armageddon as the Roman invasion of Judea and Jerusalem in AD 70. Before that battle and destruction, God's people were called to flee the city (Rev 18:4–5) exactly as Jesus told His followers to flee from Jerusalem (Matt 24:16–18). We know that there was never a time when Christians fled Rome en mass, prior to its impending destruction; however, they did flee from Jerusalem prior to its destruction.

Hallelujah! Salvation and glory and power belong to our God, because His judgments are true and righteous; for He has judged the great harlot who was corrupting the earth with her sexual immorality . . .

—Rev. 19:1b–2

THE HARLOT FALLS JUST BEFORE JESUS RETURNS

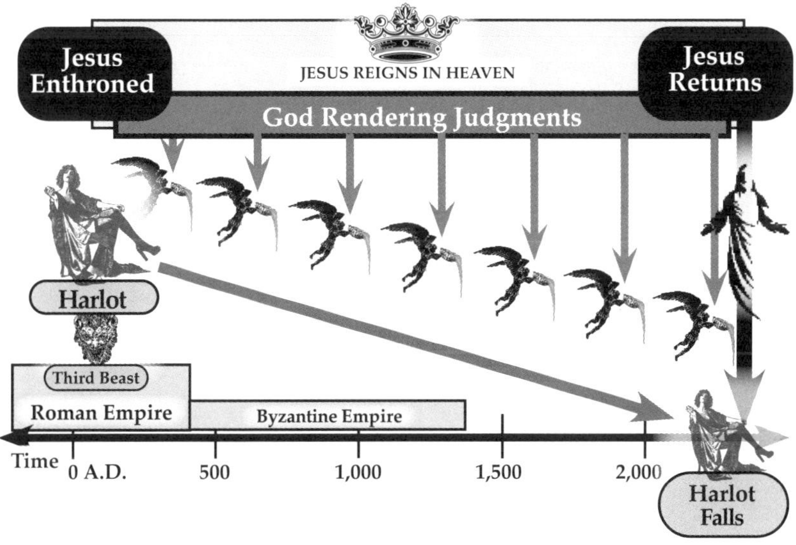

After the harlot is judged, chapter 19 tells us about Jesus' return to Earth.

The Metanarratives of the Three Partial Preterist Views

Before we complete our study of Revelation, it will be helpful to step back and see the metanarrative[88] of the entire book.

From the beginning of our study, we hope you have seen how the events prophesied in Revelation began to unfold in John's lifetime, with the judgment of the early Jews and Jerusalem in AD 70 (Rev. 7–11).

Once that truth is accepted, the futurist's understanding of Revelation must be rejected. The metanarrative of Revelation is not about God pouring out His wrath upon the world in our future.

Partial preterists understand God's judgments began to unfold in the first century. However, we have identified three partial preterist views of Revelation.

	Three Partial Preterist Views of Revelation	**Judgment against:**
View #1	All three sets of judgments against:	Jews & Old Jerusalem
View #2	First set of judgments against: Second & third set of judgments against:	Jews & Old Jerusalem Roman Empire
View #3	First set of judgments against: Second set of judgments against: Third set of judgments against:	Jews & Old Jerusalem Roman Empire World

88. By the "metanarrative of the entire book," we are referring to the big picture that ties all of Revelation together. It is the overarching story. We can identify the metanarrative by answering the question, "What was the primary message Jesus was communicating throughout the book of Revelation?"

As explained, Martin Trench favors the first view and Harold Eberle favors the third view.

Similarities in the Second and Third Views

The second and third partial preterist views are sometimes indistinguishable and may be considered variations of each other. One reason they are so close is that they require adherents of each view to come to the same conclusions about the identities of the figures in Revelation 7–18.

Second & Third Partial Preterists' Views of Revelation	
Figures in Revelation 7–18	**Identity**
Male Child	Jesus
Woman Who Birthed the Male Child	Mother of Jesus
Great Red Dragon	Satan Working through the Roman Empire
Seven Heads	Seven Caesars
Ten Horns	Ten Kings
Beast #1	Spiritual Being #1
Beast #2	Spiritual Being #2
Leader Most Ruled by the Beasts	Emperor Nero: 666
Great City (He)/Sodom/Egypt	Old Jerusalem
Great City (She)/Babylon	Rome & Roman Empire
Beast #3 Upon Which Harlot Rode	Gave Harlot Access to Rome & Roman Empire
Harlot	Spiritual Being that Worked in Rome & Whole World

There are several other reasons the second and third views are similar. The third set of judgments (Rev. 15–18) is not as clearly defined as the first (Rev. 7–11) and second (Rev. 12–14) sets. Therefore, partial preterists who hold to the second view may leave the question about the third set of judgments unanswered. Adherents may comment on how Babylon, the beasts, and the harlot influenced the Roman Empire but leave open the possibility that Babylon, the beasts, and the harlot continue working in the world until the end. That open-ended position turns the second view into the third view.

It is reasonable to see that Babylon, the beasts, and the harlot continue working in the world if one considers these figures as *spiritual entities that influenced* certain leaders, cities, and nations rather than *figures that represented* certain leaders, cities, or nations. If Babylon, the beasts, and the harlot are concrete terms that *represented* specific leaders, cities, or nations, then it is reasonable to conclude they fell when those leaders, cities, or nations fell. If that were true, it would not make sense that Babylon, the beasts, or the harlot would continue working in the world after those entities were defeated.

In contrast, readers who see Babylon, the beasts, and the harlot as spiritual entities may see Revelation 7–18 as a greater battle of good versus evil, the Kingdom of God versus the realm of darkness. That battle was not focused on Old Jerusalem or the Roman Empire. Instead, the fall of Old Jerusalem and the Roman Empire were consequences within the bigger plan of God to bring all things into submission to Jesus.

Metanarrative of the Book of Revelation

This leads us to consider the metanarrative of the whole book of Revelation. The first view is structured around one metanarrative, while the second and third are structured around a different metanarrative.

The first view (Martin's favored view), that all the judgments are against the early Jews and Old Jerusalem, is built on a metanarrative that corresponds with Covenant theology. That metanarrative is formed around the idea that God made one covenant of works and another covenant of grace. The people who tried to become God's people through a covenant of works failed miserably. The people who become God's people through a covenant of grace are pleasing to God. Therefore, God abolished His old covenant of works and everything associated with it (Rev. 7–19). Since then, God has established, confirmed, and worked with His people through His new covenant of grace (Rev. 20–22).

Because the first partial preterist view of Revelation is developed around Covenant theology, Christians already trained in Covenant theology (such as those in Presbyterian or Reformed churches) are most likely to read the book of Revelation and embrace the first view that all the judgments of God are directed toward the early Jews and Old Jerusalem.

Metanarrative Provided by Covenant Theology ⟶ **First Partial Preterist View**

In contrast, the second and third partial preterist views are built on a metanarrative corresponding with Kingdom theology. Kingdom theology is formed around the truth that Jesus was enthroned over God's Kingdom 2,000 years ago, and since then, the Kingdom has been growing and will continue growing until it fills the Earth.

The metanarrative of a growing Kingdom corresponds well with the second partial preterist view because it was inevitable that Old Jerusalem and the Roman Empire had to be judged once God's Kingdom was established. The Bible tells us that the Kingdom would be taken away from the Jews (Matt. 21:43), and Daniel interpreted King Nebuchadnezzar's dream, which revealed that the Roman Empire would be destroyed by the growing Kingdom of God (Dan. 2:36–45).

The metanarrative of a growing Kingdom also corresponds well with the third partial preterist view (Harold's favored view) because all Jesus' enemies, including Old Jerusalem, the Roman Empire, and the entire world had to be put under the feet of Jesus before He returns to reign over God's Kingdom on Earth.

Metanarrative Provided by Kingdom Theology	→	**Second Partial Preterist View**
	→	**Third Partial Preterist View**

Seeing that the second and third views are both built on a metanarrative that corresponds with the growing Kingdom reveals another reason the second and third views are similar.

The fact that each of the three views is built on a specific theological perspective does not mean the Bible reader is limited to the corresponding theological perspective. A Bible reader may believe both Covenant theology and Kingdom theology but choose to use Covenant theology as the metanarrative to understand Revelation. A different Bible reader may believe both Covenant theology and Kingdom theology but decide to use Kingdom theology as the metanarrative around which to understand Revelation.[89]

Because one's metanarrative provides the structure for one's understanding of Revelation, it is worth thinking deeply about one's metanarrative. Since Harold favors the metanarrative corresponding to Kingdom theology, he likes to point out that words associated with a kingdom, such as "throne," "king," "kings," and "kingdom," are mentioned more than 60 times in the 22 chapters of Revelation. In contrast, neither the covenant of works nor the covenant of grace is mentioned in Revelation.[90] If the frequency of mention indicates what a book is about, then Revelation is about the King and His Kingdom.

89. New Covenant theology also leads to the first partial preterist view.

90. The word "covenant" is mentioned one time in Revelation, but that one mention is in the context of identifying the "ark of the covenant" that was located in the Temple (Rev. 11:19). There is no discussion about any covenant.

The Book in Revelation 6

The two metanarratives we just explained determine how a reader understands almost all of Revelation. One clear demarcation is how the reader understands the book whose seals are broken in Revelation 6.

Teachers who structure Revelation around Covenant theology usually see the book discussed in chapter 6 of Revelation as a writ of divorce.[91] Mosaic law required that any man deciding to divorce his wife must write and give her a certificate of divorce (Deut. 24:1–4; Matt. 5:31). Knowing this, many teachers who see Revelation as God abolishing the old covenant and establishing the new covenant understand the book discussed in Revelation 6 to be the writ of divorce that God gave to the Jews to certify His divorce from them.

Partial preterists who understand Revelation is structured around Kingdom theology do not see the book in Revelation 6 as a writ of divorce. It was never referred to as that. Divorce is never mentioned in Revelation.

The book discussed in Revelation 6 is described and treated as a record of the decrees of a king. In those days, the decrees of every king were written down to make sure they were remembered and fully enforced. The book in Revelation 6 recorded the decrees of God. As each seal on the book was broken, more judgments of God were released.

Such a book of judgments was very different from a writ of divorce. A writ of divorce was given to the woman being divorced to protect her rights within society. The book in Revelation 6 was never given to the woman. It did not protect the woman. It did the opposite: the judgments written in that book destroyed her.

This subject is so important we will return to it in Section Five and examine the Scriptures in which God promised to never divorce Judah. For now, let us finish our study of Revelation.

91. Kenneth Gentry Jr. takes this view in *The Book of Revelation Made Easy*, 48–49.

Revelation 19: The Kingdom of God Is Victorious!

At what point will Jesus return? No one knows the day or the hour, but the Father told His Son to sit down on His throne until every enemy has been made a footstool for His feet. In Acts 3:21, we are also told about Jesus:

> *Whom heaven must receive until the period of restoration of all things about which God spoke by the mouth of His holy prophets from ancient times.*

Jesus will return to Earth when the world is ripe for the restoration of all things.

This does not mean all evil will be eliminated before Jesus returns. In Matthew 13:31–32, we read the parable Jesus told explaining that the Kingdom of God may be compared to the tiniest of seeds but would grow to be the biggest plant in the garden. Hence, we know that the Kingdom of God will be the most significant entity on Earth at the time of our Lord's return.

However, we know that there will still be evil on Earth, for an enemy has sown his seeds, which are also growing (Matt. 13:36–43). We know that Jesus will come in judgment to subdue all remaining enemies and separate the chaff from the wheat and the goats from the sheep (Matt. 13:24–30; 25:31–46).

Not everyone will be Christian when our Lord returns, but every person will have an opportunity to hear and respond to the gospel. There will be a tremendous worldwide revival. There will be nations bowing to the Lordship of Jesus.

This idea that nations will bow to Jesus is central to the truth of God advancing His Kingdom. For Christians who have never been exposed to this truth, it can seem almost too good to be true. The idea that nations will bow to Jesus is—to say the least—optimistic.

Both Martin and Harold hold to this optimistic view.

We did not always have such optimism. As we have mentioned, we used to hold to the futurist view, along with its belief that the antichrist will take over this world, establish one economic system, create one world religion, and cut the heads off of Christians who refuse to receive the mark of the beast. For many years, we believed and taught that the world is getting more unstable, chaotic, and evil, but a day will come when Jesus will return and save us from this terrible mess.

The transition in our thoughts required significant time and years of study. We started to hear fresh voices talk about the Church rising in glory before the return of Jesus. They often quoted Isaiah 60:1–2:

> *Arise, shine; for your light has come, and the glory of the Lord has risen upon you. For behold, darkness will cover the earth and deep darkness the peoples; but the Lord will rise upon you and His glory will appear upon you.*

This promise of God's glory rising upon His people caused our hopes to rise. We began to envision a future glorious Church amid a dark world.

Our hopes reached even higher as we dedicated ourselves to studying the Scriptures in ways we had not previously considered—ways that are presented in this book. Even the Isaiah passage that we just quoted came alive as we read the very next verse and saw the promise for the nations to respond to the light:

> *Nations will come to your light, and kings to the brightness of your rising.*
>
> —Is. 60:3

This verse leads the reader to believe that the Church will not only rise within a dark world but that the dark world will respond to the glorious Church. Nations will come to her light. This means that the world will not get darker and darker until the very end, but the world will get lighter and brighter as humanity comes to God.

Promises to this end are scattered throughout the Scriptures, but they are easy to miss until a reader embraces a new perspective. Consider what Habakkuk, the prophet, said:

> *For the earth will be filled with the knowledge of the glory of the Lord, as the waters cover the sea.*
>
> —Hab. 2:14

God declared to Moses:

> *As I live, all the earth will be filled with the glory of the Lord.*
>
> —Num. 14:21

Jacob declared:

> *The scepter will not depart from Judah, nor the ruler's staff from between his feet, until he to whom it belongs shall come and the obedience of the nations shall be his.*
>
> —Gen. 49:10, NIV

God promised His Son:

> *I will certainly give the nations as Your inheritance,*
> *And the very ends of the earth as Your possessions.*
>
> —Ps. 2:8

God will fulfill His promise to Jesus.

Revelation 19: Jesus Is Revealed as King

In Revelation 19:6, we see Jesus appearing in glory. Let the celebration begin! John wrote:

> *Then I heard something like the voice of a great multitude and like the sound of many waters, and like the sound of*

mighty peals of thunder, saying, "Hallelujah! For the Lord our God, the Almighty, reigns."

After this, the marriage feast is announced:

> *Let us rejoice and be glad and give the glory to Him, for the marriage of the Lamb has come and His bride has made herself ready.*
>
> —Rev. 19:7

Then, the Groom comes into the picture:

> *And I saw heaven opened, and behold, a white horse, and He who sat on it is called Faithful and True . . . His name is called The Word of God. And the armies which are in heaven, clothed in fine linen, white and clean, were following Him on white horses.*
>
> —Rev. 19:11–14

This is the procession of victory. It is a parade of glory. The war is over. Jesus is declared as Victor:

> *From His mouth comes a sharp sword, so that with it He may strike down the nations, and He will rule them with a rod of iron; and He treads the wine press of the fierce wrath of God, the Almighty. And on His robe and on His thigh He has a name written: "KING OF KINGS, AND LORD OF LORDS."*
>
> —Rev. 19:15–16

Jesus returns to Earth as King.[92]

---

92. With Martin Trench's view, Revelation 19 is not the final return of Christ, but rather Jesus "coming in judgment over Jerusalem." Jesus will return in the same manner as He ascended (Acts 1:11) and not riding a white horse. His name is *"The Word of God ... From His mouth comes a sharp sword"* (Rev. 19:15). This is speaking of the fulfillment of Jesus' prophetic word that Jerusalem would be surrounded by armies and destroyed, with not one stone left upon another (Matt 24). The destruction of Jerusalem and the full end of the old covenant system is followed by 1,000 years or a very long time during which the Kingdom will advance until the final return of Christ.

Revelation 20: The Millennial Reign of Jesus

In Revelation 20, we are told that Christians are raised from the dead in what is called *"the first resurrection."* Those Christians rule and reign with Jesus for 1,000 years. That 1,000-year reign is called the millennium or the millennial reign of Jesus.

To understand the millennial reign, it is essential to know that the Hebrew people did not always take numbers such as 1,000 in a literal sense as Westerners do. God owns the cattle on 1,000 hills (Ps. 50:10), but this does not mean God owns the cattle only on 1,000 hills; He owns all cattle everywhere. Similarly, the Psalmist says that one day in the house of God is better than 1,000 elsewhere (Ps. 84:10); again, we see the number 1,000 used in a non-literal sense, e.g., Ex. 20:6; Deut. 1:11; Ps. 68:17; 90:4.

The understanding of the millennial reign of Jesus being an indefinite but long period has been held by most of the great leaders in Church history, such as Augustine, Eusebius, John Calvin, John Knox, and John Wesley.[93]

Epiphanes

There is indeed a millennium mentioned by St. John; but the most, and those pious men, look upon those words as true indeed, but to be taken in a spiritual sense.

Cited in *The Literal Interpretation of Scripture Enforced* by Platt, 1831, 18

93. They understood the 1,000 years to represent an indefinite period of time; however, many of them were amillennialists.

John Calvin

But a little later there followed the chiliasts, who limited the reign of Christ to a thousand years. Now their fiction is too childish either to need or to be worth a refutation.

Institutes of the Christian Religion, vol. 2:995

How do we understand this millennial reign? When does it take place? To answer these questions, the two authors of this book, Harold Eberle and Martin Trench, must each answer for themselves. Even though we both are partial preterists, we understand the millennial reign differently.

Revelation 20: The Postmillennial View

Many partial preterists, including Martin Trench, hold to the postmillennial view. This view sees that the millennium started 2,000 years ago when Jesus ascended into heaven and sat down on His throne.[94] At that time, Jesus began ruling over heaven and Earth. Postmillennialists believe Jesus will return to Earth at the end of His millennial reign. Hence, their view is called postmillennialism, referring to Jesus' return after (post) the millennium.

Most postmillennialists say the millennium discussed in Revelation 20 refers to all the years that transpire between the first coming of Jesus and His second coming. Since we live between the first and second coming of Jesus, we are living in the millennium now.

It is common for postmillennialists to envision the Kingdom of God growing on Earth during the millennium.

94. Some postmillennialists see the millennial reign as starting, not when Jesus sat down on His throne, but when the Church has achieved significant success in spreading the gospel over the world. For them, the millennial reign may or may not have already started.

As Isaiah 9:7 said:

> *There will be no end to the increase of His government or of peace . . .*

The Kingdom of God will continue growing until it fills the earth. Then Jesus will return.

The Postmillennial View

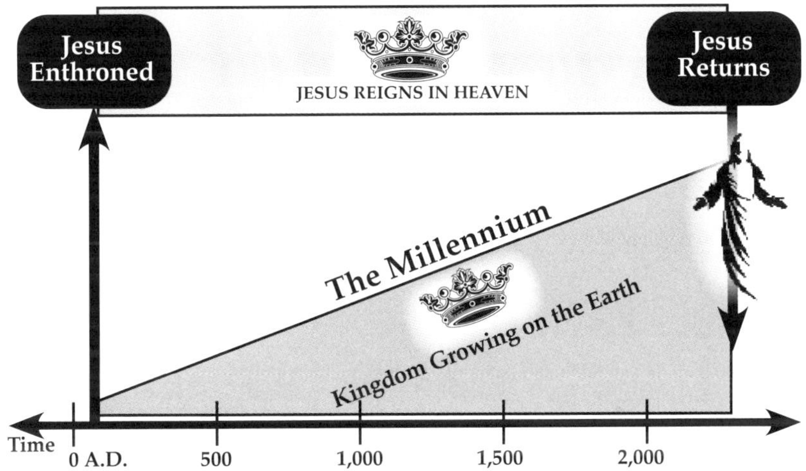

Since Revelation 20 is where the millennial reign is explained, adherents of postmillennialism see Revelation 20 as being fulfilled during the same period as Revelation 1–19. Postmillennialists say Revelation 20 is a recapitulation of the preceding 19 chapters.

The postmillennial view was the most popular view of the millennium among Evangelical Christians during the 1800s.

Revelation 20: The Premillennial View

Premillennialists identify the second coming of Jesus happening (Rev. 19) before the millennial reign of Jesus (Rev. 20). For this reason, their view is called the "premillennial view" with the return of Jesus happening before (pre) the millennium.

The Premillennial View

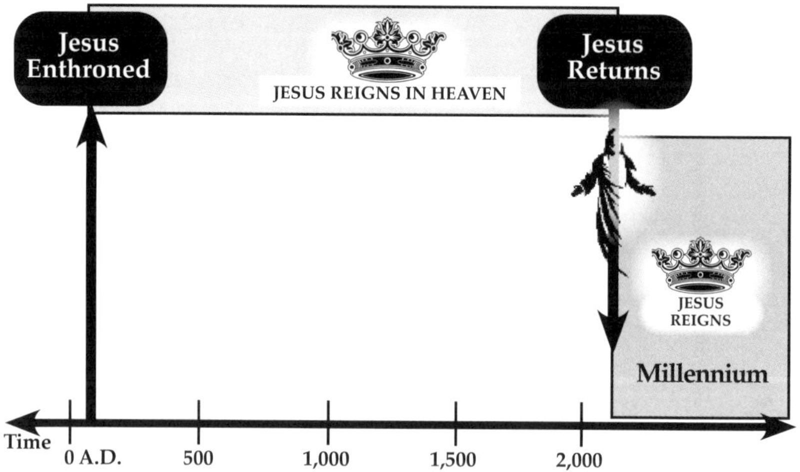

There are three different premillennial views:

1. Dispensational premillennialism
2. Historic premillennialism
3. Kingdom premillennialism

Let us look at each of these.

Revelation 20: The Dispensational Premillennial View

Dispensational premillennialism is held by today's futurists. This futurist's view is referred to as "dispensational" because it is associated with and developed out of Dispensational theology, which divides history into several periods. The *Scofield Reference Bible* is most known for popularizing this way of thinking.

Dispensational premillennialists see the events of Revelation 7–18 happening during a future seven-year tribulation. That is when they envision their end-time scenario with earthquakes, famines, antichrist, and destruction. Adherents place the seven-year tribulation after Jesus returns to rapture the Church to heaven[95] and before Jesus returns to reign over the Kingdom on Earth for 1,000 years. So, actually, they see two returns of Jesus: one at the start and one at the end of the tribulation.

Dispensational Premillennial View

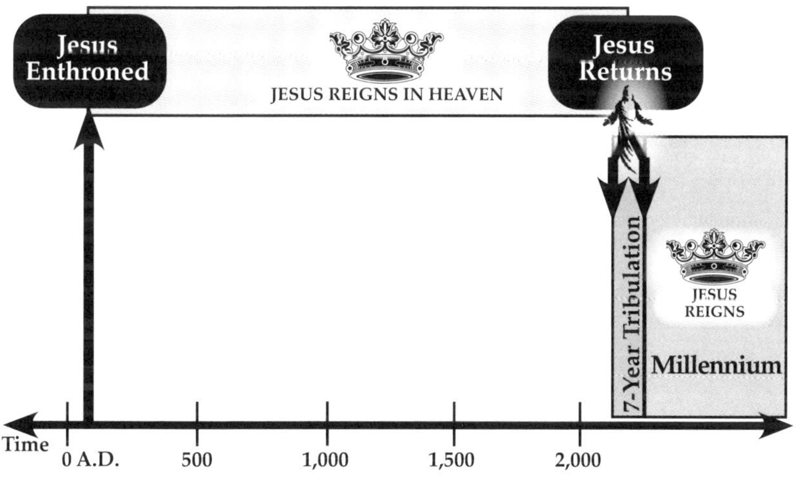

95. The rapture is explained in Section Seven.

Revelation 20: Historic Premillennial View

Historic premillennialism also sees that Jesus will return before (pre) His millennial reign, but they place a seven-year tribulation before the second coming of Jesus.

Historic Premillennial View

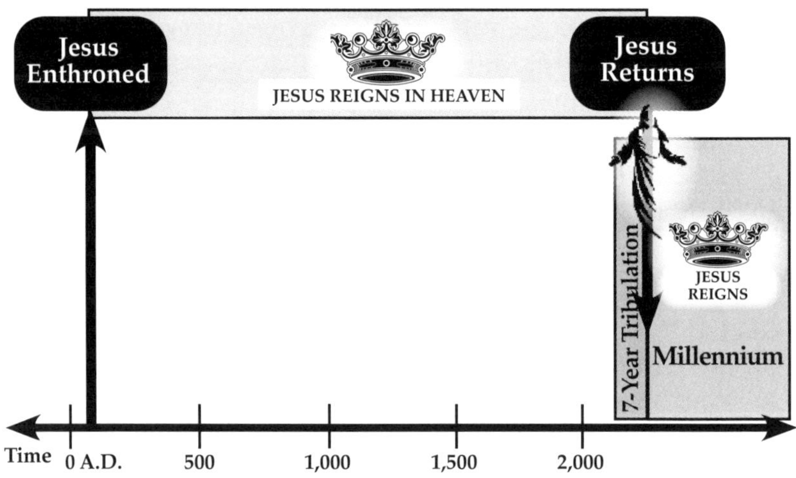

This view is called "historic" because throughout Church history we see this view appearing among various leaders, especially the early Church fathers, including Irenaeus, Justin Martyr, Papias, and Tertullian.[96]

96. Kelley Varner, *Whose Right It Is,* 137; R.C. Sproul, *The Last Days According to Jesus,* 198.

Revelation 20: Kingdom Premillennial View

We call the third form of premillennialism, "Kingdom premillennialism."

"Kingdom premillennialism" is not a commonly used label in theology today, but it is appropriate because it is associated with Kingdom theology. Kingdom theology is the view that the Kingdom of God started 2,000 years ago when Jesus sat down on His throne, and since then, it has been growing and advancing on Earth. Kingdom theology is often associated with the concept of the Kingdom being "here and coming." This refers to the Kingdom being available now for those who have faith but gradually increasing until Jesus returns to full establish it on Earth.

With Kingdom theology and kingdom premillennialism, there is no seven-year tribulation before the millennial reign of Jesus. Kingdom premillennialism is held by Harold Eberle.

Kingdom Premillennial View

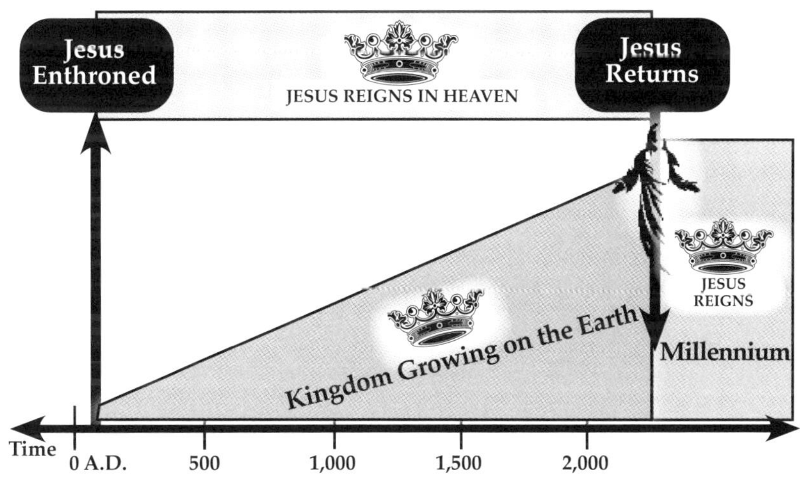

REVELATION 20: TWO VICTORIOUS VIEWS

The two views of the millennium held by Martin Trench and Harold Eberle are optimistic. Postmillennialism (Martin's view) envisions the Kingdom of God is here and growing. Kingdom premillennialism (Harold's view) also sees the Kingdom is here and growing.

Even though both views are optimistic, there is a difference in how these views envision Satan's involvement with the world. This difference exists because Revelation 20:2–3 tells us that at the beginning of the millennial reign of Jesus, an angel threw Satan *"into the abyss, and shut it and sealed it over him . . ."*

Since postmillennialists see the millennium already started, adherents see that Satan has already been thrown into the abyss.

THE POSTMILLENNIAL VIEW: SATAN THROWN INTO THE ABYSS

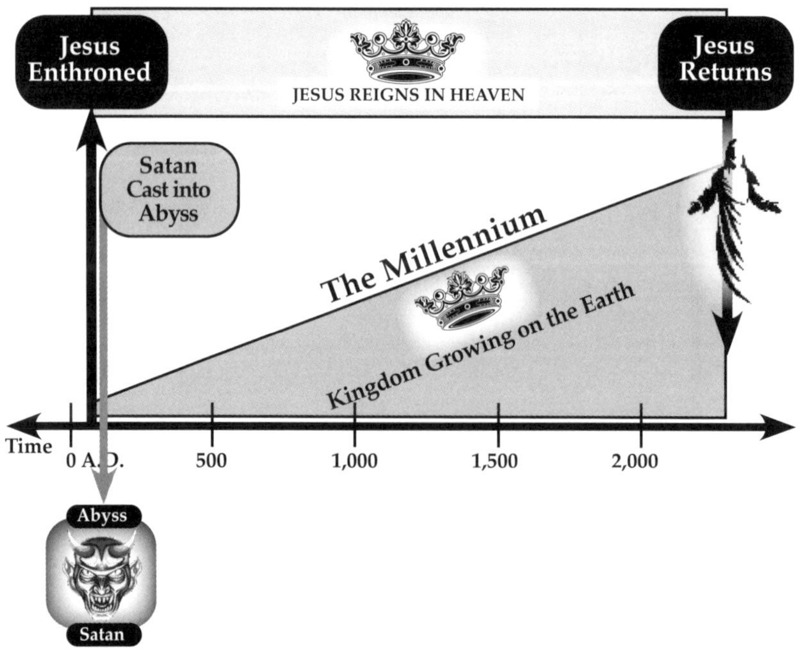

In contrast, Kingdom premillennialists see the millennial reign as starting when Jesus returns to Earth, and therefore, Satan will not be thrown into the abyss until Jesus returns. Adherents still believe Satan was dethroned when Jesus sat down on His throne. There is a difference between dethronement and being thrown into the abyss. Dethronement happened 2,000 years ago. Satan will be thrown into the abyss when Jesus returns.

**Kingdom Premillennialism:
Satan Dethroned, But Not Yet Thrown into the Abyss**

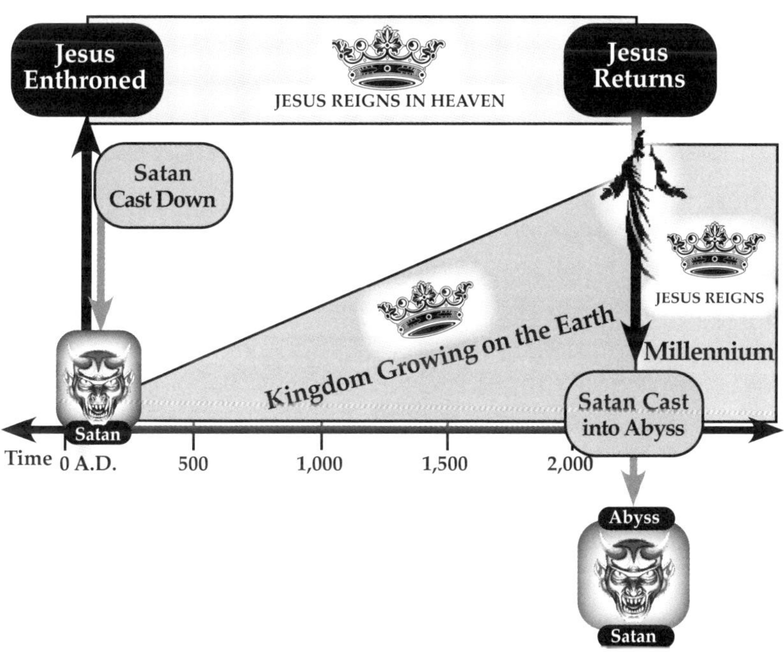

Notice with this view of Kingdom premillennialism, Satan is not god of this world, but he is in the world causing problems.

Satan's Kingdom Was Defeated

With both postmillennialism and Kingdom premillennialism, Satan was defeated 2,000 years ago. Before His death, Jesus explained:

> *Now judgment is upon this world; now the ruler of this world will be cast out.*
>
> —John 12:31

Paul explained what happened through the resurrection of Jesus:

> *When He had disarmed the rulers and authorities, He made a public display of them, having triumphed over them through Him.*
>
> —Col. 2:15

When Jesus sat down on His throne, He was given all authority. At that time, Satan was defeated and dethroned.[97]

Too many Christians, i.e., futurists, think that Satan is still in control of this world. For further evidence that Satan and his kingdom were defeated 2,000 years ago, consider the fact that the terminology "kingdom of Satan" or "Satan's kingdom," is used in only one context in the Bible. One day when Jesus was casting a demon out of a man, some Pharisees accused Him of casting out demons by the authority of Beelzebub, the ruler of demons (Matt. 12:24). Jesus responded by saying:

> *Any kingdom divided against itself is laid waste; and any city or house divided against itself will stand. If Satan casts out Satan, he is divided against himself; how then will his kingdom stand?*
>
> —Matt. 12:25–26[98]

97. It is still correct to say, "Satan is god of this world," if one is using the word "world" to refer to the corrupted system at work in the world.

98. This is the only context in which "his kingdom," that is, Satan's kingdom, is referred to, although this conversation is also recorded in Mark 3:23–27 and Luke 11:17–18.

Notice that in this context, Jesus was declaring the fall of Satan's kingdom. Our Lord went on to say:

> *But if I cast out demons by the Spirit of God, then the kingdom of God has come upon you. Or how can anyone enter the strong man's house and carry off his property, unless he first binds the strong man? And then he will plunder his house.*
>
> —Matt. 12:28–29

Two thousand years ago, the Kingdom of God came to Earth. One stronger than Satan came and dethroned him. Ever since that day, Satan's realm has been crumbling. What remains is for his house to be plundered.

In another passage, the apostle Paul explained that when people commit their life to Jesus, they are transferred from the domain, realm, or authority (Greek, *exousia*) of darkness and brought into the Kingdom of Jesus (Col. 1:13). Hence, we can appropriately call Satan's region of influence a domain, realm, or region of authority, but to call it a kingdom is to give him too much credit. Satan's demons are busy here on Earth, but Satan has no kingdom.

For this reason, we are taught to pray to God, *"For Yours is the kingdom and the power and the glory forever"* (Matt. 6:13). There is only one Kingdom now, and it is the Kingdom of God.

Because postmillennialism and Kingdom premillennialism lead Christians to see Satan as defeated and Jesus as Lord of this world, they both produce optimistic, victorious views.

Revelation 20:7–10: Satan Released

After the millennium, John explained how *"Satan will be released from his prison"* (Rev. 20:7). Then Satan will attempt one last coup by gathering many to himself so they can rebel against our Lord. This, however, will simply result in identifying those who are against Jesus. Revelation 20:9 tells us those enemies of Jesus will quickly be destroyed by fire coming out of heaven.

Revelation 20:11–15: White Throne Judgment

After the millennial reign, Jesus will take His seat on the great white throne of judgment. Then all the dead, the great and the small, will stand before Him. Books will be opened, including the Book of Life. The people then will be judged according to the things written in the books.

> *And if anyone's name was not found written in the book of life, he was thrown into the lake of fire.*
>
> —Rev. 20:15

Much could be written concerning what the great white throne judgment will entail, but here, it is enough to say that all whose names are written in the Book of Life will go on into the new heaven and Earth. The only alternative destination is the Lake of Fire, also called Hell.

REVELATION 21 & 22: THE NEW HEAVEN AND EARTH

Chapters 21 and 22 are the most glorious and thrilling passages in Revelation—perhaps in the whole Bible.

Some partial preterists who structure their understanding of Revelation according to Covenant theology see the new heaven and Earth as the Christian life within the new covenant. Therefore, they envision the new heaven and Earth as starting when Jesus resurrected 2,000 years ago. This corresponds with the Covenantal understanding of Revelation that the old covenant was destroyed and the new covenant was established by AD 70.

That is a valid understanding worth consideration. However, here we will present the view that the physical heaven and Earth that we live in now will transform into a new heaven and Earth in which God's people will live forever.[99]

Seeing the new heaven and Earth as transformed, yet physical realities, is a natural outcome of identifying a Kingdom structure throughout the book of Revelation. If God plans to redeem creation, then it is natural to envision Jesus taking over this world and completely conforming it to His will.

REVELATION 21: NEW HEAVEN AND NEW EARTH

John described the splendor and glory of a new world:

> *Then I saw a new heaven and a new earth; for the first heaven and the first earth passed away, and there is no longer any sea.*
>
> —Rev. 21:1

99. The two foundational structures for understanding Revelation, Covenant theology and Kingdom theology, were explained on pages 219–221, under the title "Metanarrative of the Book of Revelation."

In this opening verse, it is unclear whether this present world is obliterated and then a new world created or if the present heaven and Earth go through a metamorphosis like a caterpillar into a butterfly.

We have reason to believe the second is the case because several verses in the Bible indicate that Earth is eternal and will never be destroyed (Eccl. 1:4; Ps. 78:69; 104:5).

If we believe that Earth is eternal, we must explain what Peter wrote about this present world being destroyed by fire (2 Peter 3:7, 10), without going out of existence. In the context, Peter drew an analogy to how Earth was once destroyed by water in Noah's day (2 Peter 3:6). The world was purged of evil, but it was not destroyed in the sense of going out of existence. Hence, we can see how this world may be destroyed in the sense of going through a fiery purging, only to come out pure and holy. Then creation will continue to exist but be set free from all curses and death.

Revelation 21: New Jerusalem

On the center stage of the new Earth is New Jerusalem, which is lowered down out of heaven to the new Earth: *"having the glory of God. Her brilliance was like a very costly stone"* (Rev. 21:11).

This city may be understood literally and / or symbolically.

Something that leads the reader to see New Jerusalem as a literal, physical city is how it is measured with a rod *"according to human measurements, which are also angelic measurements"* (Rev. 21:17). This indicates a correspondence between the spiritual and the natural.

However, we must also see this city as symbolic, for we are told that New Jerusalem is the Bride. Furthermore, we can read throughout the NT phrases in which the Church is pictured like a building being fitly framed together, built on the foundation of apostles and prophets (Eph. 2:19–22). Paul wrote how we must all be careful how we build with gold, silver, and precious stones (1 Cor. 3:11–12). John also wrote how people who overcome will be pillars in the Temple of God, and they will not have to go out of it, but they will have written on them:

> *The name of the city of My God, the new Jerusalem, which comes down out of heaven from My God . . .*
>
> —Rev. 3:12b

John described how New Jerusalem will be lowered from heaven like a Bride adorned for Her Husband.

Revelation 21 & 22: God's Presence

Then God will dwell among His people forever, and they will see the face of our Lord (Rev. 22:4).

Selah.

Revelation 21 & 22: Our Eternal Dwelling

In chapter 22, John described a river flowing from the throne of God and the Lamb. That river will carry the life of God out toward the nations. There will also be a tree of life bearing 12 kinds of fruit, and its leaves will be for the healing of the nations. God will provide abundance, more than what we need or want.

It is worth noting that the new heaven and new Earth will be our dwelling place forever. Contrary to what many Christians have been taught, we will not float around in the clouds eternally. Instead, we will be on a real Earth, and we will have real, yet glorified bodies. Revelation 22:3 tells us that God's servants will be serving Him, implying that we will have jobs, careers, and purpose. We will not be singing praises forever, but we will have responsibilities, with some people having positions of greater authority than others (Rev. 2:26–27). We will be happy, have purpose, and be busy, forever.

Summary

If you come to believe the partial preterist view of the book of Revelation, then you may embrace many ideas that may be new to you. One of the most important is that God has been rendering judgments since Jesus sat down on His throne. God is continuing to extend His Kingdom throughout the whole earth. We are partners with Him in that venture.

Also, you will understand that there will be no future seven-year Great Tribulation. Futurists develop their belief in a future Great Tribulation by squeezing Revelation 7–18 into a future seven-year period during which God will pour out His wrath upon the world. Futurists also teach their doctrine of a future Great Tribulation by presenting Matthew 24 and Daniel 9:27 as fulfilled during that future seven-year period. Section One explained how the tribulation described in Matthew 24:4–18 was fulfilled in the first century as God judged the Jews. Section Three explained how Daniel's seventieth week was also fulfilled during the first century. Other than those passages, there is no Bible verse that futurists can use to build their doctrine of a future seven-year tribulation.

Of course, there will be tribulations and troubles in the future. Jesus explained how His disciples would always have difficult times (John 15:18–20). Indeed, many Christians around the world are experiencing terrible persecution even now. Until the day Jesus returns, there will be struggles between the righteous and the unrighteous.

However, there is no biblical basis to say there will be a future, seven-year Great Tribulation.

Futurist Christians often argue about pre-trib, mid-trib, or post-trib doctrines, meaning they question whether there will be a rapture of the Church before a tribulation, in the middle of a tribulation, or at the end of it. Partial preterists are not pre-trib, mid-trib, or post-trib. We are no-trib, meaning we do not believe there will be any seven-year tribulation period in the future.

Instead, we believe the kingdoms of this world are becoming the Kingdom of our God and we will be with the Father, Son, and Holy Spirit here forever.

Section Five
The Jews, Israel, and the Temple

Issues concerning the future of the Jews are central to our eschatology. The related topics are seen very differently by those holding to the futurist view and those holding to the partial preterist view.

The Jews Were Judged but Not Rejected

There is no doubt that the Jews were judged in AD 70. They were judged for rejecting and killing the righteous ones, who were sent by God (Matt. 23:35–36). The Kingdom of God was taken away from them (Matt. 21:43).

This truth that the Kingdom of God was taken away from the Jews is difficult for futurist Christians to accept because they continue to look for God to restore Israel and use the Jews to usher in the Kingdom of God here on Earth.

Partial preterists are much more aware of God's judgment of the Jews. They also understand that the Kingdom of God is already here and available to believers on Earth.

Different partial preterist teachers have various views about the extent of God's judgment. Their different views about the Jewish judgment in AD 70 determine much about their eschatology and what they believe about the future of the world.

The Abrahamic Covenant Is an Everlasting Covenant

Some partial preterist teachers believe that when God judged the Jews, He ended His covenant with them. Here, we will not be supporting that view. Instead, we will explain the partial preterist view that God punished the Jews, but He did not end His covenant with them.

Those who claim that God's covenant with the Jews ended typically refer to Hebrews 8:13, which says:

> *When He said, "A new covenant," He has made the first obsolete. But whatever is becoming obsolete and growing old is ready to disappear.*

Indeed, this verse does tell us that the first was made obsolete.

However, we must determine what the "first" means in this verse. When Christians read Hebrews 8:13, they often insert the word "covenant" after the word "first." This leads them to conclude that the first covenant was made obsolete. In reality, the word "covenant" does not follow the word "first" in the Greek manuscripts of Hebrews 8:13. We should also question the idea that the first covenant was made obsolete because God's covenant with Adam, Noah, and Abraham were not made obsolete.

Anyone who reads the context of Hebrews 8:13 (i.e., chapters 7 through 9) will see that the writer was talking about the Jewish Laws and religious system that God established through Moses. The writer was contrasting the Mosaic Law and religious system with the new covenant established through Jesus. In that context, the writer said the first was made obsolete.

Paul confirmed that the Mosaic Law was made obsolete through Jesus:

> *For He* [Jesus] *Himself is our peace, who made both groups into one and broke down the barrier of the dividing wall, by abolishing in His flesh the enmity, which is the Law of commandments contained in ordinances.*
>
> —Eph. 2:14–15

The Mosaic Law was never established to last forever. Paul said it was only meant to last until Jesus came (Gal. 3:19).

Even though the Law was temporary, the Abrahamic covenant is everlasting. To see this, we must separate the Mosaic Law from the Abrahamic covenant. Paul explained that the Mosaic Law came 430 years after the Abrahamic covenant was established (Gal. 3:17).

When we refer to the Abrahamic covenant, we are referring to God's commitment to Abraham and his descendants. In various ways, God said, "I will be your God and you will be My people" (e.g., Gen. 17:7; Ex. 6:7). This was a commitment to a relationship. Accompanying the covenant relationship were specific promises, such as ownership of the land given to Abraham and the release of God's blessing to every family on Earth.

Several Bible passages tell us that the Abrahamic covenant was established as an everlasting covenant. God said to Abraham:

> *I will establish My covenant between Me and you and your descendants after you throughout their generations for an everlasting covenant, to be God to you and to your descendants after you.*
>
> —Gen. 17:7

Other Bible passages confirm that the Abrahamic covenant was an *"everlasting covenant."* For example, the Psalmist wrote:

> *He has remembered His covenant forever,*
> *The word which He commanded to a thousand generations,*
> *The covenant which He made with Abraham,*
> *And His oath to Isaac.*
> *Then He confirmed it to Jacob as a statute,*
> *To Israel as an everlasting covenant.*
>
> —Ps. 105:8–10, see also Gen. 17:13, 19

This means the Abrahamic covenant is still valid today.

Extent of Judgment Determined by the Metanarrative

The truth that the Jews still have a covenant with God is incompatible with some partial preterist views.

When we studied the book of Revelation in Section Four, we explained that some partial preterists structure their understanding of Revelation around Covenant theology.[100] Those partial preterists usually understand Revelation as the

100. This is explained on pages 219–221, under the title "Metanarrative of the Book of Revelation."

abolishing of the old covenant that God had with the Jews and the establishing of the new covenant that God made through Jesus. Most partial preterists who understand Revelation that way believe God's judgment of the Jews included His rejection of them.

Their error results from confusing the Abrahamic covenant with the Mosaic Law and religious system. As discussed in the previous point, the Abrahamic covenant is everlasting, while the Mosaic Law and religious system were temporary. It was the Mosaic Law and religious system that became obsolete when the new covenant was established.

God Did Not Divorce Judah

Some partial preterists who structure their understanding of Revelation around Covenant theology go so far as to say God divorced the Jews. This corresponds to what we explained earlier about some partial preterists equating the book mentioned in Revelation 6 with a writ of divorce. Earlier,[101] we explained how the book in Revelation 6 was a record of God's kingly judgments, not a writ of divorce.

To see that God did not divorce the Jews, we must talk about Israel and Judah separately. As already mentioned, they were separate kingdoms beginning about 930 BC. The people of Israel lived north of Judah and were known for having intermarried with the Gentiles. Israel was exiled from the Promised Land into Assyria around 732 BC. In contrast, the people of Judah[102] were exiled from the Promised Land into Babylon about 586 BC. The critical point is that Israel and Judah were separate groups.

God divorced Israel, but not Judah.

When Israel was exiled in 732 BC, God divorced them:

101. This is explained on page 222.

102. Although there had been some intermarriage between tribes, the Southern tribes consisted primarily of Judah, Benjamin, and some Levites.

And I saw that for all the adulteries of faithless Israel, I had sent her away and given her a certificate of divorce.
—Jer. 3:8a

Contend with your mother, contend,
For she is not my wife, and I am not her husband.
—Hosea 2:2a

Even though God divorced Israel,[103] He explained in Hosea 1:6b–7a that He was dealing with Judah differently than He dealt with Israel:

For I will no longer have compassion on the house of Israel, that I would ever forgive them. But I will have compassion on the house of Judah and deliver them by the Lord their God.

Even though Judah committed sins similar to those of Israel, God punished and then forgave Judah. They were exiled from the Promised Land, but He did not divorce them.

Isaiah spoke for the Lord concerning Judah:

This is what the Lord says:
"Where is the certificate of divorce
By which I have sent your mother away?
Or to whom of My creditors did I sell you?
Behold, you were sold for your wrongdoings,
And for your wrongful acts your mother was sent away."
—Is. 50:1

When God asked, "Where is the certificate of divorce?" it was in the sense of saying that there was no certificate! The Jews from Judah were sent into exile for their sins, but not because God divorced them.

God did not divorce Judah; corresponding to this, the Abrahamic covenant promises went to Judah, not Israel.

103. In Hosea 2:14–23, God keeps the hope before Israel that He is able to someday take them back as His wife. This may be referring to the hope in Jesus as Savior.

This is easier to understand once we realize that God never promised that the Abrahamic covenant would extend to all of Abraham's descendants. We can see this when we recognize how the covenant promises went to Abraham's son Isaac rather than Ishmael (Gen. 21:12; Gal. 4:22–28). Then, from Isaac, the covenant promises went to Jacob rather than his brother Esau (Gen. 27). Knowing this, we can see how the Abrahamic covenant was everlasting, but it was never meant to go to all of Abraham's descendants. After Judah and Israel separated, the covenant went to Judah.

The Abrahamic Covenant Promises Went to the Jews

It is helpful to know that the label "Jew" was primarily used to refer to the people of Judah after they were separated from Israel. Still, it did not come into common usage until after the people of Judah were exiled into Babylon and then returned to the Promised Land.

While Judah was in exile, the Jews thought God had abandoned them:

> *Zion said, "The Lord has abandoned me,*
> *And the Lord has forgotten me."*
>
> —Is. 49:14

God corrected them, saying:

> *Can a woman forget her nursing child*
> *And have no compassion on the son of her womb?*
> *Even these may forget, but I will not forget you.*
> *Behold, I have inscribed you on the palms of My hands.*
>
> —Is. 49:15–16a

God said He would *never* abandon Zion (which refers to Jerusalem, the capital of Judah) any more than a mother could abandon her nursing child.

Remember, God said His covenant with Abraham was an *"everlasting covenant,"* e.g., Gen. 17:7, 13, 19; Ps. 105:8–10. That everlasting covenant went to the descendants of Abraham, called the Jews.[104]

Jesus Brought the Abrahamic Covenant to Christians

Jesus, a descendant of Judah, became an avenue through which the Abrahamic blessings were made available to Christians. Paul explained how Jesus made this possible:

> *In order that in Christ Jesus the blessing of Abraham might come to the Gentiles . . .*
>
> —Gal. 3:14

Those who believe in Jesus become Abraham's descendants:

> *And if you belong to Christ, then you are Abraham's descendants, heirs according to promise.*
>
> —Gal. 3:29

As believers in Jesus are brought into the blessings of the Abrahamic covenant, the Jews are not pushed out. Paul explained that Christians are brought into the Abrahamic covenant in the sense of becoming joined to the Jews:

> *Remember that you* [the Gentiles] *were . . . separate from Christ, excluded from the commonwealth of Israel, and strangers to the covenants of promise, having no hope and without God in the world. But now in Christ Jesus you who formerly were far off have been brought near by the blood of Christ. For He Himself is our peace, who made both groups into one and broke down the barrier of the dividing wall.*
>
> —Eph. 2:12–14

104. Today, the label "Jew" is used more loosely and may be associated with anyone who practices the religion of Judaism or is a descendant of Abraham, Isaac, and Jacob.

Even though Jews and Gentiles are one as children of Abraham, this does not mean Jews are saved and going to heaven. With the Abrahamic covenant, there was no promise of eternal life. Only under the new covenant established through Jesus is there a promise of eternal life.

It is helpful to think of the major promises and covenants God made and to whom He gave them:

> 1. God promised Eve that one of her descendants would crush the head of the enemy. This promise is for all of Adam and Eve's descendants, which means all of humanity.
>
> 2. God promised Noah that He would never destroy humanity again with a flood; He also promised that seasons would always continue for planting and harvesting (Gen. 8:21–22). These promises are for all of Noah's descendants, which means all people who have lived since Noah.
>
> 3. God promised Abraham that He would be God to Abraham's descendants and they would be His people. This applies to Abraham's descendants, including Jews and believing Gentiles.
>
> 4. God promised salvation and eternal life to all who believe in Jesus. This applies to all who have become children of God by believing in Jesus.

Although Jews are children of Abraham, they must become children of God through faith in Jesus to be saved.

Christians are children of Abraham and children of God through faith in Jesus.

Children receive an inheritance. Jews and Christians are heirs of the promises given to Abraham. Christians are also *"heirs of God and fellow heirs with Christ"* (Rom. 8:17). Hence, Christians are children of God who inherit eternal life.

The new covenant has better promises than the Abrahamic covenant, but both covenants are everlasting.

The Jews Still Are God's Covenant People

Although Jews will only be saved and have eternal life if they put their faith in Jesus, they still have a covenant (the Abrahamic covenant) with God. This is despite the fact that most of them rejected Jesus. Paul asked and then answered a question:

> *I say then, they did not stumble so as to fall, did they? Far from it!*
>
> —Rom. 11:11a

Even though the Jews rejected Jesus, God did not reject them:

> *I say then, God has not rejected His people, has He? Far from it!*
>
> —Rom. 11:1a

> *God has not rejected His people whom He foreknew.*
>
> —Rom. 11:2a

Paul also explained that the Jews were still God's chosen people:

> *In relation to the gospel they are enemies on your account, but in relation to God's choice they are beloved on account of the fathers.*
>
> —Rom. 11:28

Notice Paul was talking about the Jews who had rejected Jesus—the *"enemies"* of the gospel. Paul referred to the enemies of the gospel as *"God's choice."* This should not surprise us because we know God is sovereign, choosing whomever He wants, whenever He wants (Rom. 9:6–18). After saying the Jews are God's choice, Paul stated that *"the gifts and the calling of God are irrevocable"* (Rom. 11:29). According to Paul, the Jews who rejected Jesus still have a calling from God.

The Jews Still Have a Unique Place in God's Heart

The natural descendants of Abraham, Isaac, and Jacob, known in the OT as Judah and in the NT as Jews, still have a unique place in God's heart and plan.[105]

This does *not* mean God will raise the Jews to usher in the Kingdom of God on Earth, as futurist teachers claim. Nor does it mean that the Jews will lead the Kingdom during a future millennial reign as the futurists teach.

The Kingdom was taken away from the Jews (Matt. 21:43). Besides, the Kingdom is already here. All who are born of God are citizens of that Kingdom (Col. 1:13), and unless a person is born of God, they cannot be a part of that Kingdom (John 3:3, 5).

Although the Jews lost their right to be the leaders of the Kingdom of God on Earth, they do have a promise because of God's faithfulness to their forefathers. We will look more carefully at that promise as we continue.

What we have learned about the Jews influences our attitude toward them as a people. Modern individuals who think God rejected and divorced the Jews tend to think negatively about them. Some of those individuals may soften their negative attitude by saying the Jews are no different than any other people group—lost and needing Jesus as their Savior. However, saying this does not undo an underlying false belief that God divorced the Jews.

On the other hand, individuals who believe God did not divorce the Jews will inevitably hold the Jews in a place of honor—not because the Jews are better than other people groups, but because of their forefathers (Rom. 11:18, 28). Also, believing the Jews still have a unique calling from God causes Christians to watch with expectation to see how God will work among them in the future.

105. The Northern tribes, previously known as Israel, lost their identity while they were in exile. By the NT times, the labels "Israelites" (i.e., Rom. 9:4) and "Israel" (i.e., Rom. 9:6) were sometimes used to refer to the Jews.

The Coming Jewish Awakening

The natural descendants of Abraham, Isaac, and Jacob, who are the Jews, still have a covenant with God that assures them a unique opportunity in the future.

Paul explained in Romans 11:25b:

> *That a partial hardening has happened to Israel*[106] *until the fullness of the Gentiles has come in.*

From this phrase *"partial hardening,"* we can expect some Jews to believe in Jesus, but the majority will remain in unbelief until the *"fullness"* of Gentiles is saved. When God is satisfied with the Gentile harvest, He will open the eyes of the Jews, and then there will be a great awakening among the Jews before Jesus returns (Rom. 11:23–29).

That awakening among the Jews will trigger a greater awakening among the Gentiles. Paul explained this when he wrote that the Jews were hardened for a time in order that the Gentiles might be brought in, but if the Jewish *"rejection is the reconciliation of the world, what will their acceptance be but life from the dead?"* (Rom 11:15). Indeed, when the Jews get saved, it will cause the faith of multitudes to come alive in a way unknown before.

Charles H. Spurgeon

I think we do not attach sufficient importance to the restoration of the Jews. We do not think enough of it. But certainly, if there is anything promised in the Bible it is this.

From first volume of *Sermons*, 1855, as cited in Iain Murray, *The Puritan Hope*, 1998, 256

106. Here, Paul uses "Israel" to refer to the Jews who rejected Jesus.

Charles H. Spurgeon

The day shall yet come when the Jews, who were the first apostles to the Gentiles, the first missionaries to us who were afar off, shall be gathered in again . . . Matchless benefits to the world are bound up with the restoration of Israel; their gathering in shall be as life from the dead.

Cited in Murray, *The Puritan Hope,* 1998, 256

Jonathan Edwards

Nothing is more certainly foretold than this national conversion of the Jews in Romans 11.

The History of Redemption in The Works of Jonathan Edwards, vol. 1, *Banner of Truth,* reprint, 1976, 607

Charles Hodge

The second great event, which, according to the common faith of the Church, is to precede the second advent of Christ, is the national conversion of the Jews . . . That there is to be such a national conversion may be argued . . . from the original call and destination of that people.

Charles Hodge, *Systematic Theology,* vol. 3, James Clark & Co. 1960, 805

WHAT ABOUT THE LAND OF ISRAEL?

Since Jerusalem was destroyed in AD 70, the Jews have had almost no governmental authority in the land of Israel (which today refers to much of the ancient lands of Israel and Judah). The city was destroyed, and the Jews were scattered, precisely as Jesus had prophesied:

> *And they will fall by the edge of the sword, and will be led captive into all the nations; and Jerusalem will be trampled underfoot by the Gentiles until the times of the Gentiles are fulfilled.*
>
> —Luke 21:24

For almost 2,000 years, Jerusalem has been trampled underfoot by Gentiles. The whole land of Israel has experienced many wars and has been under the control of various people groups. It was not until 1948 that Israel became a sovereign nation under the control of Jewish leaders.

Some Christians believe that 1948 was the historic fulfillment of God's timetable when Jerusalem no longer would be trampled underfoot and *"the times of the Gentiles"* had been fulfilled. Perhaps that date is indeed upon us, but there is reason to doubt it because Jerusalem, to some extent, is still being trampled underfoot by non-Jewish people. Though Jews hold the political control, other people groups—in particular, Arabs in that region—battle for control of the area. In addition, the Muslim temple known as the Dome of the Rock stands where the Jewish Temple stood 2,000 years ago. This Dome of the Rock is the third most holy site for Muslims, but it is an abomination in the sight of Jews.

There is also reason to doubt that the times of the Gentiles have been fulfilled because God is continuing to work powerfully among the Gentiles. In fact, more Gentiles are becoming born-again Christians today than at any time in history (approximately 200,000 per day). The facts do not support the idea that God has shifted His attention from Gentiles to

Jews, who, for the most part, remain hardened to the gospel, with only a small percentage believing Jesus is the Messiah.

When the times of the Gentiles are truly fulfilled, what will happen to the land of Israel? Those who hold to the futurist view believe God will fulfill His promise to give the land back to the natural descendants of Abraham. They cite the promise that God made to Abraham many years ago:

> *On that day the Lord made a covenant with Abram, saying, "To your descendants I have given this land, From the river of Egypt as far as the great river, the river Euphrates."*
>
> —Gen. 15:18

Adherents of the futurist view believe that God will cause the Jews who have been scattered around the world to migrate back to Israel (a migration called *Aliyah*) and then establish them as a nation that will be a light to the world. The Jews will experience God's blessings, and they will be elevated as a nation to a position of great authority on Earth.

Adherents of the partial preterist view see a different future for the Jews and Israel. As explained (Section Three), God's 490 years of Jewish favor have passed. The Jews will experience a future awakening, but the land will *not* be brought back under the exclusive control of the Jews. Allow us to explain.

Futurist teachers often state or imply that Jews are presently migrating from all over the world back to Israel, and thus, God must be fulfilling His promise to Abraham. It is true that approximately 800,000 Jews have emigrated from Russia to Israel in recent years; however, a large percentage of them have used Israel as a transfer station to gain entrance into the USA. Jews have been migrating from other locations as well, but the Israeli daily, *Yediot Ahronot,* reported on April 4, 2007, that there is a net exodus of people from the country.[107]

107. The following source reports that the Jewish population grew by 1.8 percent in 2011: Schneider, Aviel. "The Nation Grows Despite the Threats." Israel Today, November 1, 2012.

There are more Jews in the USA today than in Israel, and the largest population gathered in any one location is in New York City. The idea that Jews are now returning en masse to Israel is a myth.

To understand what God intends for the Middle East, it is important to point out that God's promise to Abraham was not only for the land that today is known as Israel. God promised all the land, *"From the river of Egypt as far as the great river, the river Euphrates"* (Gen. 15:18). The Euphrates River runs through present-day Syria, Iraq, and Kuwait. The land God promised to Abraham also includes Jordan and Lebanon, along with parts of Egypt and Saudi Arabia. If God is going to give the land promised to Abraham to the modern Jews, as futurist teachers say, then the Jews will have to possess all the land between the two great rivers.

Yet the Bible tells us of the most significant future transformation that will happen in that region. Isaiah prophesied:

> *Thus the Lord will make Himself known to Egypt, and the Egyptians will know the Lord on that day . . . In that day there will be a highway from Egypt to Assyria, and the Assyrians will come into Egypt and the Egyptians into Assyria; and the Egyptians will worship with the Assyrians. In that day Israel will be the third party to Egypt and Assyria, a blessing in the midst of the earth, whom the Lord of armies has blessed, saying, "Blessed is Egypt My people, and Assyria the work of My hands, and Israel My inheritance."*
>
> —Is. 19:21–25

This passage reveals how a day will come when the people of Egypt, Assyria, and Israel will worship the true God together.

Isaiah's prophecy sounds almost too good to be true! The people groups that he mentioned have battled with each other for generations. Egypt and Assyria lie at the foundations of the Arab and Muslim world. Yet, Isaiah said that Egyptians, Assyrians, and Jews will be worshipping together.

Isaiah's prophecy also reveals God's heart for Egypt and Assyria, for God called Egypt *"My people"* and Assyria *"the work of My hands."* To hear God speak this way can be difficult for Christians (and Jews) who think of the Jews as God's chosen ones. Of course, God did choose the Jewish people, but it never was His intention to make them the only humans to receive His favor. Instead, God chose them as a light to the nations. With the same love that God dealt with the Jews, He has always desired to deal with every people group. He loves the world. The Jews were not the only ones chosen, but they were the first fruits of the earth to reveal God's heart to all people.

Jesus told us of a day when He will gather people from outside of the Jews to Himself:

> *I have other sheep, which are not of this fold; I must bring them also, and they will listen My voice; and they will become one flock with one shepherd.*
>
> —John 10:16

We are waiting to see God fulfill this promise—one flock consisting of many people groups.

Where will this happen? All over the world, but most prominently in the Promised Land. God will take the most tumultuous region of the world and make it His showcase, where different people groups will become one flock with Jesus Christ as their Shepherd.

God is not giving the land that He promised to Abraham exclusively to the Jews. He is going to give it to all His children. Paul made this clear in Galatians 3:16 when he wrote:

> *Now the promises were spoken to Abraham and to his seed. He does not say, "And to seeds," as one would in referring to many, but rather as in referring to one, "And to your seed," that is, Christ.*

Paul explained how the promises were not for Abraham

and his descendants (plural). They were given by God to Abraham and his descendant (singular)—Jesus Christ. Paul further explained how all who put their faith in Jesus will inherit the blessings promised to Abraham:

> *Therefore, be sure that it is those who are of faith who are sons of Abraham . . . There is neither Jew nor Greek, there is neither slave nor free man, there is neither male nor female; for you are all one in Christ Jesus. And if you belong to Christ, then you are Abraham's descendants, heirs according to promise.*
>
> —Gal. 3:7–29

Paul is giving us the proper way to understand the promises of God to Abraham. To whom does the Promised Land belong? Who are the heirs of the land between the river of Egypt and the river Euphrates? All who put their faith in Jesus Christ.

What, then, should we expect for the Promised Land? We know that the Jews must have a significant presence there because Isaiah prophesied that the Jews would worship God together with the neighboring countries. However, it is also true that God is giving the land to His children who have been born of the Seed—Jesus. Therefore, we should expect many people groups to settle in that region. As all those people bow to the lordship of Jesus Christ, they will be a light to the nations, for that region shall be the most visible place on Earth where various people groups will come together under one Shepherd, Jesus Christ.

What About the Temple in Jerusalem?

Futurists believe that the Jewish Temple in Jerusalem must be rebuilt. This fits their understanding of end-time events because they believe that in the middle of a seven-year tribulation, the antichrist will put an end to the Jewish offerings and sacrifices. According to the Jewish religious system, those offerings and sacrifices must be accompanied by certain religious practices that can only be performed in the Temple. Because of this, believers of the futurist view teach that the Temple in Jerusalem must be rebuilt before or soon into a Great Tribulation.

Those embracing the partial preterist view have different expectations. The Temple was destroyed in AD 70, and God has no intentions of allowing the Temple to be rebuilt. Jesus declared to the Jews, *"Behold, your house is being left to you desolate!"* (Matt. 23:38). That Temple was meant to be left desolate. God does not want to see the Jewish religious system reconstructed. He destroyed it. He does not want people to approach Him through animal sacrifices or a high priest in the Jerusalem Temple. He does not want that to happen—ever again. Jesus is the only mediator between God and humanity (1 Tim. 2:5).

We can gain further confirmation of this by considering how Jesus and the apostles viewed the Temple. The only Temple in which they were interested was the new Temple of Christians who the Holy Spirit indwelled. Nowhere can we find any statement indicating or implying that the Temple in Jerusalem would ever be rebuilt. In fact, both Jesus and Stephen were sentenced to death, and central to triggering their deaths were their bold declarations that God did not dwell in stone temples, that the Jewish Temple would be destroyed, and a new spiritual Temple would be raised (John 2:19; Mark 14:58; Acts 6:13–14, 7:44–50).

The NT writers' understanding of the future Temple must

be our understanding of the Temple. We believe they were inspired by the Holy Spirit; therefore, we need to embrace their understanding of how God will fulfill His promises.

Paul talked about the new Temple consisting of both Jews and Gentiles being fitly framed together to become a dwelling place for God. That Temple, Paul explained, is being built on the foundation of the apostles and prophets with Jesus Christ as the cornerstone (Eph. 2:11–22). That is the Temple that Jesus is building, and the gates of hades shall not prevail against it (Matt. 16:18)!

SUMMARY

Some readers may confuse the view of the Jews that we are presenting with a teaching called *replacement theology*. That would be a mistake. Replacement theology teaches that God has ended His covenant relationship with the Jews, and Christians have replaced the Jews in reference to inheriting all the promises that God originally made to Abraham.

At the other extreme of replacement theology is *Zionism*, which envisions God favoring the Jews to such an extent that He will cause them to migrate back to Israel, rebuild the Temple, and become a nation dominant on Earth. The futurists hold to Zionism and call it *Christian Zionism*.

We are not teaching either Replacement Theology or Christian Zionism. We are teaching *One New Man*, which is the view that sees God still having a covenant with the Jews, a covenant ensuring them of a future spiritual awakening. However, God's promises to Abraham concerning the land are available to all who believe in Jesus. The ultimate end will be to make Jews and Gentiles into one new man, worshipping God together (John 10:16; Eph. 2:11–22).

1. **Replacement Theology:** Christians have replaced the Jews in reference to all the promises God made to the Jews, including the land promises.
2. **One New Man:** God still has a covenant with the Jews that assures them of a future awakening; however, the promises God made to Abraham, including the land promises, are available to all God's people.
3. **Christian Zionism:** The Jews will still see the fulfillment of all God's promises to them, including the land promised to Abraham.

Christian Zionists show great loyalty to the Jews and the nation of Israel. It should be no surprise that Christians love the Jews since Judaism forms the foundation of Christianity and God will mold the hearts of Jews and Gentiles together in the final great revival. However, partial preterists see Christian Zionism as a misunderstanding of how God will fulfill His promises.

Most importantly, the land promised to Abraham will never be possessed exclusively by the Jews. Like branches cut off from the tree, the Jews were severed from the blessings promised to Abraham (Rom. 11:17–19). A day will come when those Jews who receive Jesus as Messiah will be grafted back in (Rom. 11:24), but they will be joined with all believers in Jesus. Hence, Christian Jews and Gentiles will possess the land together.

If you embrace the view we have been explaining, you will anticipate a great harvest of souls as the times of Gentiles are fulfilled. That harvest will trigger jealousy in the hearts of Jews, who will then respond to the gospel. Then, Jews and Gentiles will worship Jesus Christ together. Then, there will be peace in Jerusalem. Pray for that day to come quickly.

Section Six
The Antichrist

When Christians raised with the futurist view hear the word "antichrist," images come into their minds of an evil ruler possessed by Satan who will soon take control of the world by establishing one world government, a united economic system, and a false religious system.[108]

Is this view of the antichrist really in the Bible?

108. Noted futurist teacher, Jack Van Impe, writes, "Logic dictates that this man is alive today, waiting to make his move." *Millennium: Beginning or End?* (Nashville, TN: Word Publishing, 1999), 5.

Pertinent Passages About the Antichrist

The word "antichrist" is mentioned in only four passages of the Bible. All four are in 1 and 2 John. We will look briefly at each of those passages to learn what the Bible says about the antichrist, but first, you should realize how little the Bible has to say about this topic.

Some Christians trained with the futurist view think that the book of Revelation is about the coming antichrist and his activity in the world during the end days. In truth, the word "antichrist" is never mentioned in the book of Revelation. This fact can be shocking to Christians who have sat for years under futuristic teachings. The antichrist is discussed extensively in those circles, and much of their discussion results from equating the antichrist with the beast mentioned in Revelation. As we studied in Section Four, the beast is more accurately associated with the Roman Empire. As partial preterists, we see no justifiable basis for associating the antichrist mentioned in 1 and 2 John with the beast of Revelation. As we will see in the coming pages, the Bible's description of the antichrist is very different from the description of the beast of Revelation.

Futurists also like to associate the antichrist with the person mentioned in Daniel 9:27, who put an end to sacrifice and grain offerings. The antichrist is never mentioned in Daniel 9, and as we discussed in Section Three, it is more accurate to understand that Jesus is the One who put a stop to the sacrifices and grain offerings of the Jewish religious system.

Futurists also like to see the antichrist in Matthew 24:15, where Jesus referred to the abomination of desolation. As we studied in Section One, the abomination of desolation is more accurately understood as the Roman armies surrounding Jerusalem. In fact, Luke recorded the same discussion of our Lord and told us that the abomination of desolation referred to those armies (compare Matt. 24:15 with Luke 21:20).

The only other Bible passage that futurists typically use to teach about the antichrist is 2 Thessalonians 2:3–10, where Paul talks about the man of lawlessness (also called the man of sin or son of perdition in some translations). This passage also has nothing to do with a future antichrist, as we will see. This issue is so crucial that we will include a discussion about the man of lawlessness in this section, but first, let us examine the four Bible passages where the word "antichrist" actually appears.

John's Description of the Antichrist

As we mentioned, there are only four passages in the Bible where the word "antichrist" can be found, and all four are in 1 and 2 John. To understand how John uses this term, we must identify the historical setting in which John was living and the people to whom he was writing his letters.

John's primary ministry was in Asia Minor, the center of Gnosticism, an aberrant version of Christianity. To understand John's ministry, we must understand this first-century cult.

First-Century Gnosticism

At the foundation of first-century Gnosticism was a worldview in which the spiritual world was distinctly separated from the natural world. The spiritual world was considered good, and the natural world was considered corrupt. As leaders with this worldview attempted to embrace Christianity, they concluded that God could not have taken on flesh or come into this corrupt world in the form of Jesus. This led to several false teachings about the nature of Jesus (some of which we discuss below). Thinking of this natural world as corrupt also led them to believe that a person must be very spirit-conscious to be a good Christian. Hence, they developed some mystical understandings and taught that a person must have secret knowledge to know God. From this, the word Gnosticism came, for it literally means "knowledge."

During the first century, Gnosticism took many forms, but one of the most influential Gnostic groups completely rejected the OT. They declared that the God of the OT was the devil and Jesus had come to reveal an "unknown Father" to us. Other Gnostics taught that the OT rituals were still valid for Christians. Some were hyper-ascetic and taught vegetarianism and were opposed to any sexual expression—even within marriage—while others taught "freedom" from all laws and held orgies as part of their rituals.

One of the most prominent Gnostic teachers was a man called Cerinthus. He was a Jew who lived in Asia Minor, teaching that Jesus was the son of Joseph and Mary (not born of a virgin)—an ordinary man. A heavenly spirit called "the Christ" came upon Jesus at His baptism and left Him at the crucifixion. Jesus had brought secret teachings that would enable people to overcome enslavement to the physical world, but the Jewish customs also had to be observed. Those who proved faithful to these teachings and observances would live for a 1,000 years of sensual pleasures. These teachings of Cerinthus flourished throughout Asia Minor.

Historical records tell us that John was so horrified at Cerinthus' teachings that on one occasion, when John walked into the public baths with his disciples at Ephesus, he saw Cerinthus and ran out of the bathhouse, warning his disciples that the house may fall because "Cerinthus, the enemy of the truth, is inside."[109]

This is the setting in which John ministered. History tells us that by AD 150, one-third of all Christians were under the influence of Gnosticism. It was a huge cult and a primary concern of the Church fathers. John was on the frontlines of that battle.

John Wrote to Correct Gnostic Teachings

As soon as we learn about the historical setting in which John ministered, we can understand his writings. For example, his Gospel starts off by saying:

> *In the beginning was the Word, and the Word was with God, and the Word was God . . . And the Word became*

109. Pamphilius Eusebius, *The History of the Church* (London, England: Penguin Books, 1965), III, 28.

> *flesh, and dwelt among us; and we saw His glory.*
>
> —John 1:1–14a

Do you see how profound this statement is? Because the Gnostics thought of the natural world as evil, they could not believe that Jesus could have been God and, at the same time, have taken on human flesh. John boldly told the reader that he saw Jesus. Jesus was real and came into this world. John declared that Jesus is God and that Jesus took on flesh.

In his first two epistles, John also countered Gnosticism. First John starts with a declaration that is diametrically opposed to the Gnostic view of Jesus:

> *What was from the beginning, what we have heard, what we have seen with our eyes, what we have looked at and touched with our hands, concerning the Word of Life—and the life was manifested, and we have seen and testify and proclaim to you the eternal life, which was with the Father and was manifested to us.*
>
> —1 John 1:1–2

John said that he and the other apostles heard Jesus, saw Him, and touched Him with their hands. Jesus manifested Himself in this world. He was God, and He took on flesh.

This battle that John had with Gnosticism is common knowledge among Bible scholars. Any student serious about understanding John's writings must be conscious of this fact.

The Antichrist in 1 and 2 John

It is with this historical understanding that we must read John's writings. Toward the middle of his first letter, John warned about the false prophets of Gnosticism:

> *Beloved, do not believe every spirit, but test the spirits to see whether they are from God, because many false prophets*

> *have gone out into the world. By this you know the Spirit of God: every spirit that confesses that Jesus Christ has come in the flesh is from God; and every spirit that does not confess Jesus is not from God; this is the spirit of the antichrist, of which you have heard that it is coming, and now it is already in the world.*
>
> —1 John 4:1–3

Knowing that John was addressing his letter to first-century Christians who were being influenced by Gnostic thought and culture, we can understand his warning to judge various teachers. John declared that the most fundamental basis for judging them pertains to what they teach about Jesus Christ. The true prophets and teachers will confess *"that Jesus Christ has come in the flesh."* The false will deny this and / or deny that Jesus is from God.

This is the spirit that John referred to as the antichrist. According to John, the antichrist is a spirit or being which has a spirit that does not confess that Jesus has come in the flesh or Jesus is from God.

According to John's words, when was this antichrist active on Earth? John said that it was *"already in the world,"* that is, it was active in the first century while John was alive. More specifically, John was attributing the antichrist's activity to the *"many false prophets* [who] *have gone out into the world."* According to John, these false prophets were active during his lifetime.

Accepting these time references is difficult for modern futurists. Remember how we discussed earlier (Section Two) how futurists must force every end-time passage into their presupposition that it all must happen in the future? In contrast, partial preterists are not obligated to fit any specific passage into the future or the past. They try to understand each passage in its own context and historical setting. Partial preterists look for indications within the text as to when the passage applies. Then partial preterists consider the historical record to see if any clear historic events—and in this case, individuals—correspond to the biblical reference.

If we take this perspective as we read the passage from 1 John 4, we note the two time references that John gave in the text:

1. *"have gone out into the world"*
2. *"now it is already in the world"*

Suppose we are going to read these references without trying to force them into our preconceived time references. In that case, there is no question that John was writing about an antichrist active during his lifetime.

Now, let us examine the other passages that mention the antichrist.

First John 2:18a tells us:

> *Children, it is the last hour; and just as you heard that antichrist is coming, even now many antichrists have appeared.*

In this verse, John does not describe or define the antichrist, but he does expand our understanding, telling us that there are many antichrists, not just one. Further, he tells us that they already *"have appeared"* in John's lifetime.

First John 2:22 adds to our understanding:

> *Who is the liar but the one who denies that Jesus is the Christ? This is the antichrist, the one who denies the Father and the Son.*

This description of the antichrist is similar to that which we have already seen. The antichrist is the one who denies that Jesus is the Christ and denies the Father and the Son.

Finally, let us look at the fourth and last passage in which the antichrist is mentioned:

> *For many deceivers have gone out into the world, those who do not acknowledge Jesus Christ as coming in the flesh. This is the deceiver and the antichrist.*
>
> —2 John 1:7

Notice John's description of the antichrist: the deceiver who does *"not acknowledge Jesus Christ as coming in the flesh."* Do you see how clearly John is fighting the first-century heretical teaching of Gnosticism? John was speaking of a deceiver that was active in his lifetime.

That is it! No other passage in the Bible uses the word "antichrist."

For Christians who have studied the historical setting of John's writings, it is obvious that he is speaking of the Gnostic teachers with whom he was battling during the first century. In three of the four passages in which John referred to the antichrists, he described them as those who deny Jesus as coming from God or deny that Jesus came in the flesh. Furthermore, in three of the four passages, John specifically told the reader that the antichrist was active during his lifetime in the first century:

1. *"now many antichrists have appeared"* — 1 John 2:18
2. *"now it is already in the world"* — 1 John 4:3
3. *"have gone out into the world"* — 1 John 4:1
4. *"have gone out into the world"* — 2 John 1:7

This can be very disturbing to Christians who have been indoctrinated into futuristic teachings. One minister friend who was presenting the truths of 1 and 2 John to a congregation had a woman speak out in protest, demanding, "Don't take my antichrist from me!" It is sad, but it is true. Some Christians have their faith so bound up with the futuristic teachings of the antichrist that they cannot bear to have them challenged.

The Man of Lawlessness

Futurist teachers like to equate the antichrist with the man of lawlessness (also called the man of sin or son of perdition) mentioned in 2 Thessalonians 2, but there is no justification for this.

People come to the Scriptures with all kinds of predetermined understandings, and so we must be careful in examining what is actually stated about this man of lawlessness:

> *Let no one in any way deceive you, for it will not come unless the apostasy comes first, and the man of lawlessness is revealed, the son of destruction, who opposes and exalts himself above every so-called god or object of worship, so that he takes his seat in the temple of God, displaying himself as being God. . . . the one whose coming is in accord with the activity of Satan, with all power and signs and false wonders, and with all the deception of wickedness for those who perish, because they did not receive the love of the truth so as to be saved.*
>
> —2 Thess. 2:3–10

To understand who this is, consider the historical setting of Paul's words. To whom was Paul writing? He was writing to the Christians who lived in Thessalonica. Paul had a relationship with these people. They were people who Paul knew would understand his words. He was not writing mysterious messages that would have baffled their minds. Paul indicates (2 Thess. 2:5) that he is clarifying things about which he had previously taught them orally while present with them. How would they have understood his words?

Key to our understanding is the time when this man of lawlessness was active. Paul said that the apostasy must come first, but as discussed in Section One, the apostasy came during the first century.

Cyril of Jerusalem (c. 313–386)
The majority have fallen away from the sound doctrines and are readier to choose what is bad than to prefer what is good. So there you have the "falling away," and the coming of the enemy is to be expected next.

Ancient Christian Commentary, 2000, XI, 109

Paul gave us other time references for the man of lawlessness when he wrote:

> *And you know what restrains him now, so that in his time he will be revealed. For the mystery of lawlessness is already at work; only he who now restrains will do so until he is taken out of the way.*
>
> —2 Thess. 2:6–7

There are three time references here in these two verses that tell us that the man of lawlessness was around during Paul's lifetime:

1. *"what restrains him now"*
2. *"already at work"*
3. *"now restrains"*

Paul also told the Thessalonians, *"You know what restrains him,"* implying that they were familiar with this man of lawlessness and that it had to do with things happening around them at that time.

Further, we know that Paul was put to death around AD 68, so he must have been writing about some ruler at that time.

To whom, then, does this man of lawlessness refer? We must give you three answers. Of course, we know this would be much easier if we had only one answer to offer, but dozens—perhaps hundreds—of individuals have been proposed throughout Church history as this man of lawlessness. After extensive study, we have concluded that three different answers have significant credibility.

Because this is only a side issue and this book is not concentrating on the man of lawlessness, we will only briefly discuss each of the three options. More information can be found in the books listed in the bibliography.

Emperor Nero as the Man of Lawlessness

First, we must consider who would have come to the minds of the people to whom Paul wrote his letter. Remember that Paul was writing to real people who lived in Asia Minor. Of course, today, we accept 2 Thessalonians as part of the sacred Scripture, and therefore, we can apply its teachings to our lives. However, we must keep in mind the historical setting. Two thousand years ago when Paul was writing, he addressed his letter to friends and disciples who were going through difficult times.

Putting ourselves in the shoes of those first-century Christians, it is possible we would have equated the man of lawlessness with Emperor Nero. It is difficult to imagine any person more lawless than he was. As we explained, he killed many of his family members, including kicking his pregnant wife to death. He tortured and murdered Christians in great numbers and demanded to be worshiped as god. Some inscriptions from that time period referred to Nero as "Almighty God" and "Savior." In light of this, it seems that the Thessalonians who first read Paul's letter may have concluded that the man of lawlessness was Nero.

Many preterist teachers would agree that Nero was the man of lawlessness. Perhaps most noted would be Kenneth

Gentry, Jr., who has written extensively on this subject. The bibliography lists two of his books.

John Chrysostom

"For the mystery of lawlessness does already work." He speaks here of Nero . . .

Ancient Christian Commentary, 2000, XI, 111

Augustine

What means the declaration, that the mystery of iniquity already works? . . . he always expected that what he said would be understood as applying to Nero.

Cited in *A Commentary on the Apocalypse* by Stuart, 1845, 441

John Levi as the Man of Lawlessness

John Bray, another respected eschatology teacher and author, strongly argues that the man of lawlessness was a first-century man named John Levi of Gischala.[110]

John Levi was a leader among the Zealots, a Jewish sect trying to overthrow the Roman government. He was lawless in the sense that he rebelled against both Jewish and Roman rule. When Paul wrote his letter to the Thessalonians, John Levi was active in Jerusalem stirring up the Jews to rebel against Rome. Still, he was restrained because of the priests and, in particular, Ananus the high priest. John incited the Idumaeans to come against Jerusalem with 20,000 soldiers.

110. John Bray, *The Man of Sin of II Thessalonians 2,* (Lakeland, FL: John Bray Ministry, 1997), 27–41.

They led a great massacre, killing more than 8,000, including the high priest.

Once the high priest, that is, the restrainer, was killed, John stirred up the Zealots, along with many other Jews, to rebel against the Roman government. It was that rebellion—prevalent among many Jews and further stirred up by John Levi—that caused Rome to descend upon Jerusalem and destroy it in AD 70.

John also had the city's supply of corn burned, along with other provisions, and as a result, the famine came and thousands of Jerusalem dwellers starved to death while the Roman armies had the city enclosed. As the city was attacked, John Levi and his followers took control of the Temple. John had the Temple defiled by using the sacred vessels and stopping the Jewish sacrifices. In this sense, John was taking the place of God while he was in the Temple.

John was taken away as the Temple was burning to the ground. John Bray taught that that was the time when Jesus came in judgment and slew that man of lawlessness.

The Carnal Man as the Man of Lawlessness

One other reasonable explanation of Paul's man of lawlessness is not an individual but humanity as a whole in its carnal, sinful state. When Christians first hear this, they often have a difficult time even conceiving of it because they have always thought of an individual when thinking of the man of lawlessness. However, it can make a lot of sense once a person allows their mind to think along these lines.

To consider this explanation, we must see humanity as divided into two groups—the unsaved and the saved, those in Adam and those in Christ, the old man and the new man, those who are lawless and those who are righteous. It is reasonable for us to think of people in these two groups because the apostle Paul sometimes talked about people not as individuals but collectively as corporate bodies with all the other individuals who are in a similar spiritual condition, e.g., Rom. 5:12–21; 6:5–6; 1 Cor. 2:14; 3:1, 16; 12:12–14; 2 Cor. 6:14–16; Eph. 2:19–22; 4:22–24; Col. 3:5–11. So then, the whole collective body of Adam may be the man of sin in 2 Thessalonians. In contrast, the collective body of Christ is the Temple of God. The man of sin is everyone who is dead in sin. The body of Christ is everyone who is alive in Christ. Since Paul used this terminology in some of his writings, it is worth asking if he was using the same ideas when writing to the Thessalonians.

With this understanding, we can read Paul's description of the man of lawlessness:

> *Who opposes and exalts himself above every so-called god or object of worship, so that he takes his seat in the temple of God, displaying himself as being God.*
>
> —2 Thess. 2:4

Paul may be explaining how carnal people reject the true God and set themselves up as god.

In the above passage, Paul also writes how the carnal man is being restrained. This may be understood as the effect that Christians have upon the world since they are the salt of the earth and the light of the world. A day will come when Jesus returns, and then the true believers will be caught up with Him. At that time Jesus will remove the restrainer, and hence, there will be a revealing of the carnal man. It will be like the separation of the sheep from the goats or the wheat from the chaff. Once God's people are removed, the lawless one will be revealed.

Paul then wrote:

> *Then that lawless one will be revealed whom the Lord will slay with the breath of His mouth and bring to an end by the appearance of His coming.*
>
> —2 Thess. 2:8

At His second coming, Jesus will appear in glory; then He will slay the wicked and do away with carnality.

Who Was the Man of Lawlessness?

Even though we may prefer one explanation over another, no one knows with certainty who the man of lawlessness was. Realize that our source of information about this man was written about 2,000 years ago, and there is no other written source of information. That information is only a few sentences long, and Paul was commenting on a conversation he had with his audience at some earlier date. No one knows what that earlier conversation entailed. The full context is not available to us.

We know that the time references within the text make it clear that the man of lawlessness was alive while Paul was writing his letter. As discussed, it could refer to humanity as a whole in its carnal, sinful state. It could also be some leader such as Nero or John Levi. Historically, we know that it was a difficult time with evil, oppressive leaders at many levels of government. It could have been any of them and even some unknown government leader who operated at a very local level and with whom the Thessalonians had to deal.

Summary

In recent years, hundreds of books, movies, and videos have developed the image of a soon-coming world leader called the "Antichrist." Active imaginations have been at work building one idea upon another until a fully developed evil legendary figure has taken hold of the minds of millions of modern-day Christians.

That legendary figure has been built on the mistake of equating the antichrist of 1 and 2 John, the beast of Revelation, and the man of lawlessness of 2 Thessalonians. As we discussed, there is no biblical basis for equating these. Indeed, they are each evil, but that is no reason to equate them any more than a person today would equate Hitler, Stalin, and Osama bin Laden.

Furthermore, the biblical descriptions of the antichrist, the beast, and the man of lawlessness are very different from one another. The antichrist of John's letters was a leader or spirit that denied that Jesus came in the flesh. The beast of the Revelation was a leader of the Roman Empire and most likely Emperor Nero. The man of lawlessness could be one of several entities, but there were hundreds of evil leaders during the first century. There is no reasonable basis to claim that the antichrist, the beast, and the man of lawlessness were the same individual.

Concerning the antichrist(s), there are only four verses in the Bible which even mention it(them), and all four verses state or imply that the antichrist(s) was (were) alive during the first century. Furthermore, when we understand the early Church's historical struggle against Gnosticism, we realize that those brief comments about the antichrist(s) were in reference to false prophets and teachers who promoted that heretical way of thinking.

Of course, Christians today can accept the historical evidence of those antichrists in the first century and still imagine some antichrist coming in the future. However, people can imagine anything they want, but it is clearly wrong to say that there is any biblical evidence telling us that there will be some antichrist coming in our future.

We boldly challenge any futurist to write in the line below any Bible verse that states or implies that there will be a future antichrist:

____

Forgive us for being melodramatic. Unless people are made to face reality, they have difficulty giving up cherished beliefs and doctrines. In truth, no one can fill in the blank because there is no Bible verse telling us there will be a future antichrist.

Section Seven

The Rapture

Both the futurists and partial preterists believe Jesus will return to Earth and appear in the sky in power and glory. Also, futurists and partial preterists believe Christians will be caught up to meet Jesus when He appears in the sky.

However, they disagree on how and when that catching up to meet Jesus will happen.

The futurists refer to the event when Christians are caught up to heaven as the "rapture." Some partial preterists will also refer to that event as the rapture, but many do not like to use that word because it has been closely associated with the futurists' understanding of that event.

Before we explain the differences between the futurists' and partial preterists' understanding, it is helpful to point out that the word "rapture" is never used in the Bible. It is an English transliteration of the Latin word *rapio*. That Latin word appears in 1 Thessalonians 4:17 in the Latin translation of the Bible. The Greek word used in the early manuscripts is *harpazo*, which is accurately translated "caught up."

We will use the words "rapture" and "caught up" interchangeably; however, the term "caught up" best conveys the literal meaning intended by the Bible writers.

Futurist View of the Second Coming

The futurist view usually depicts the rapture in the following way. Very soon Jesus will return and secretly appear in the sky so only believers can see Him. Then all the believers will vanish from planet Earth, being "caught up" to meet the Lord in the air. Cars will crash as Christian drivers disappear. Piles of clothes will be left behind as Christians vacate this habitation. Also, the bodies of dead believers suddenly will vanish from their graves, being taken up to Jesus.

Then Jesus will take all the believers to heaven for seven years. During that period in heaven, they will enjoy the marriage banquet of the Lamb, which is the feast of the wedding between Jesus and His Bride.

During those seven years, the antichrist will rule on Earth, and most of humanity will follow him. Then there will be a time of tribulation as the events of Revelation 4 through 18 occur and God pours out His wrath, destroying much of the earth, including one-third of all the people.

Now, here is where it gets a bit confusing: Although futurist teachers say the rapture is the second coming of Jesus, it will be only part one of the Second Coming; seven years later, at the end of the heavenly banquet and earthly tribulation, part two of the Second Coming will take place. Teachers of the futurist view say that Jesus will return again, bringing all the believers with Him. This time, His return will not be secret; every eye shall see Him. He will come in judgment, and His army will conquer His enemies at the battle of Armageddon.

This view has slight variations among futurist teachers, but this is the most popular version.

THE FUTURIST VIEW WITH
TWO PARTS TO THE SECOND COMING OF JESUS

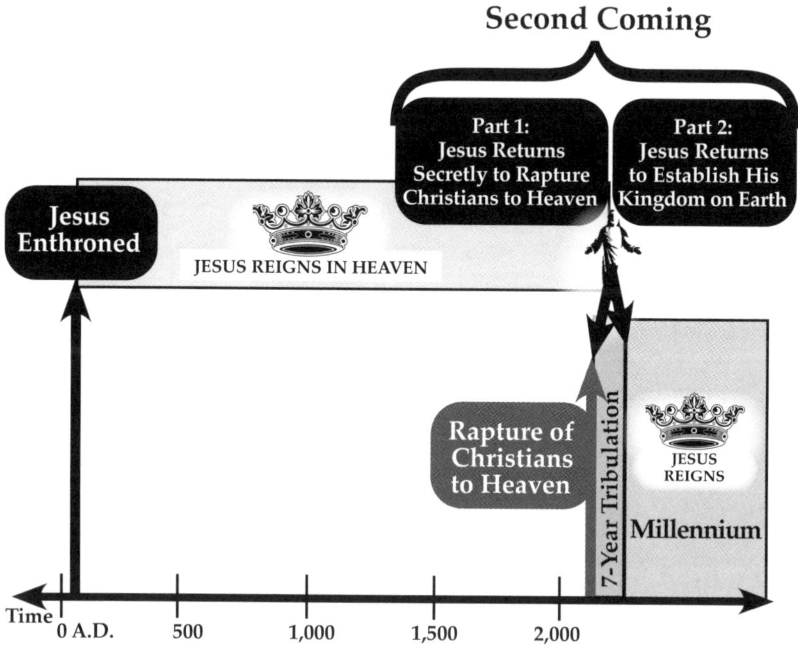

This view—that the Second Coming will happen in two events separated by seven years of tribulation on Earth—was relatively unknown before the nineteenth century. The only earlier historical references to that doctrine have been found in the writings of Dr. John Gill (1748) and Morgan Edwards (1788).

The futurists' view of the rapture happening at the start of the tribulation was not accepted by any known group until a British religious leader named John Nelson Darby publicly brought it up at the Powerscourt Conference in Ireland in 1830. Along with other leaders, Darby formed the Plymouth Brethren movement, which became the strongest advocate of the "any moment" doctrine, which refers to their belief that the rapture could happen at any moment.

Darby brought this view to America when he visited around 1864. It grew in acceptance in the United States after the Civil War when William E. Blackstone wrote *Jesus Is Coming*. D. L. Moody was a supporter of this doctrine; however, it did not become popular until after Darby's thoughts were inserted into the footnotes of the famous *Scofield Reference Bible,* first published in 1909.[111]

Darby and Scofield's view developed into the modern futurist's view. The seven-year period of Christians in heaven is where the futurist teachers place Daniel's seventieth week, which we discussed earlier (Section Three). While the Christians are in heaven, God will give the Jewish people seven years of favor, during which time they will be given a place of prominence in world events and government. In the middle of the seven years, futurist teachers say that the antichrist will break his covenant with the Jews, walk into a rebuilt Temple in Jerusalem, and declare himself as god. At that time, God will begin pouring out His wrath upon the world, and a great tribulation will occur on the whole earth. At the end of the seven years, part two of the Second Coming will happen, as Jesus returns to Earth.

111. Kelley Varner, *Whose Right It Is,* 143–145.

Partial Preterist View of the Second Coming

As explained earlier (Section Three), teachers of the partial preterist view believe that Daniel's seventieth week was completed during the first century, immediately following the 69 weeks revealed in Daniel 9. Therefore, they do not envision any special seven-year period in the future. They do not see two parts to the Second Coming, separated by seven years. Instead, they see Jesus coming in one grand event.

Partial preterists understand that Jesus will continue to build His Church, and although Christians will face many trials and setbacks, they will experience more successes than failures. This progressive building will continue until the "last day," a day that only God knows. On that day, without any warning signs, Jesus Christ will return in the clouds, and every eye will see Him. All believers—living and dead—will be "caught up" to meet Him in the air.

In that "catching up," Christians will not be taken away to heaven for seven years. They will be "caught up," as a hen would gather her chicks under her wings. Jesus will protect His people while He purges Earth of evil, then bring the believers down to Earth with Him. For this reason, we earlier stated that the Greek word *harpazo* is accurately translated "caught up" rather than "caught away." Christians will not be taken away into heaven, but they will be caught up to meet the Lord in the air and then continue with Him as He descends back to Earth to rule and reign.

Teachers of the partial preterist view will compare this catching up with people who are going to meet a friend who just arrived at the local airport. When their friend arrives, they may come to meet him. They will not fly away with him in another airplane, but they will accompany him as he comes to their home. Similarly, Jesus is returning, not to take believers away, but to be with them on Earth. Christians will meet Him in the air, and they will hesitate in that place only for as long as it takes for Jesus to purge the Earth of evil—a process that will be instantaneous, or almost so, because His glorious appearing will transform everything.[112]

Partial Preterist View of the Second Coming

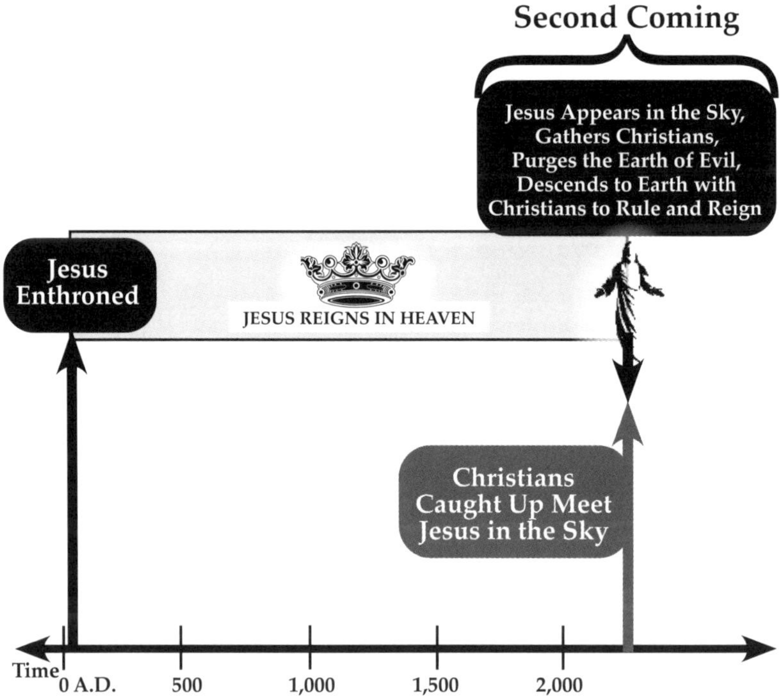

112. Since Martin Trench holds to postmillennialism, he sees this event as the Day of Judgment. In contrast, Harold Eberle holds to Kingdom premillennialism, and therefore, he sees a second judgment day at the end of the millennial reign of Jesus.

Examining Pertinent Passages

Let us show you why the partial preterists' view of the catching up is more Scriptural than the futurists' view. Although several Scripture passages speak of the return of Christ, there are three main passages (and a controversial fourth passage) that are usually referred to when discussing the rapture.

The first two passages speak about Christians receiving glorified bodies:

> *Behold, I tell you a mystery; we will not all sleep, but we will all be changed, in a moment, in the twinkling of an eye, at the last trumpet; for the trumpet will sound, and the dead will be raised imperishable, and we will be changed.*
>
> —1 Cor. 15:51–52

> *We eagerly wait for a Savior, the Lord Jesus Christ; who will transform the body of our humble state into conformity with the body of His glory, by the exertion of the power that He has even to subject all things to Himself.*
>
> —Phil. 3:20–21

These passages speak about our new bodies and do not deal with the "catching up" aspect of the rapture. Since both the futurists and the partial preterists see Christians being transformed instantaneously at the catching up, these Scriptures can be used to support either view.

A third passage used to teach about the catching up is 1 Thessalonians 4:16–17:

> *For the Lord Himself will descend from heaven with a shout, with the voice of the archangel and with the trumpet of God, and the dead in Christ will rise first. Then we who are alive and remain will be caught up together with them in the clouds to meet the Lord in the air, and so we shall always be with the Lord.*

This is the key passage. It is the only one that speaks of us being "caught up" to meet the Lord in the air. As noted earlier, it does not say we will be "caught away" to heaven for seven years. It says we will be "caught up" to "meet" the Lord in the air.

This same term "meet" (Greek, *apantesis*) is used when Paul was traveling to Rome:

> *And the brethren, when they heard about us, came from there as far as the Market of Appius and Three Inns to meet us; and when Paul saw them, he thanked God and took courage. When he entered Rome . . .*
>
> —Acts 28:15–16

Notice that the disciples met Paul, but then Paul did not reverse directions and go away from Rome. He continued on to Rome with the disciples accompanying him.

Similarly, the word "meet" is used twice in the parable of the ten virgins (Matt. 25:1–13). There, we read how five wise virgins went out to "meet" the bridegroom. They did not go with him to fly away to another location. Instead, they met and welcomed him.

In this same sense, Christians will meet the Lord in the air—not to fly away with Him—but to welcome Him and then accompany Him back down to Earth. In other words, Jesus is indeed coming back to Earth.

We also mentioned a fourth passage of Scripture usually discussed in connection with the rapture, but most scholars who teach the futurists' view readily admit that this passage is misused by the more popular "science fiction" type of futurist teachers and novelists. It is the famous "Left Behind" passage in Matthew 24:

> *For the coming of the Son of Man will be just like the days of Noah. . . . there will be two men in the field; one will be taken and one will be left. Two women will be grinding at the mill; one will be taken and one will be left. Therefore*

> *be on the alert, for you do not know which day your Lord is coming.*
>
> —Matt. 24:37–42

When we discussed Matthew 24 in Section One, we explained how this passage is not talking about a secret rapture of Christians but the second coming of Jesus, when He will wipe the unbelievers off the earth.

To confirm this, we can note that the ones taken away in this passage are not believers, as some futurist teachers say. Jesus is explaining just the opposite. In Noah's day, judgment came suddenly and swept the ungodly away. Noah and his family were left behind to inherit the earth. If we apply this, as Jesus did to His coming in judgment, we will see Christians being protected in the arms of Jesus, as Noah was protected in the ark. Then, the ungodly are swept away. After that, the righteous are "left behind" to rule and reign with Jesus on Earth.

This is what Jesus had taught His disciples in Matthew 13 in the parable of the wheat and tares:

> *So just as the weeds are gathered up and burned with fire, so shall it be at the end of the age. The Son of Man will send forth His angels, and they will gather out of His kingdom all stumbling blocks, and those who commit lawlessness, and will throw them into the furnace of fire; in that place there will be weeping and gnashing of teeth. Then the righteous will shine forth like the sun in the kingdom of their Father.*
>
> —Matt. 13:40–43a

Jesus is clear. It is the ungodly who will be removed, gathered, taken. The righteous will be left behind to shine as the sun.

Contrary to what the futurists would have Christians believe, we want to be "left behind" so we can rule and reign with Jesus in His Kingdom on Earth. Or, as Matthew 5:5 tells us, the meek will inherit Earth.

Summary

If you embrace the partial preterists' understanding of the second coming of Jesus, you will not see it happening in two parts. You will see that there is no seven-year period during which Christians are in heaven while God pours out His wrath on Earth. When Jesus returns, He will literally return to Earth.

Another significant difference between the futurists' and partial preterists' views is the focus on what will happen in the near future. The futurist teachers emphasize the coming rapture so much that it remains at the forefront of the listeners' minds; it is the next great event to which they are eagerly looking forward. In contrast, Christians who embrace the partial preterists' view believe in a catching up, but their main focus is on the Church rising in glory with a great harvest of souls across the world.

Most futurist teachers will also say that they are looking for a great harvest, but they contradict themselves because their understanding of Matthew 24 necessitates a great falling away. Their view also dictates a belief that the world is going to get worse and worse, the antichrist will take over, and Jesus will rapture them away before God pours out His wrath on Earth. Many futurist teachers try to hold to both views, even though they contradict each another.

The futurist teachers are most conscious of their soon-coming escape by way of the rapture. Partial preterists are most conscious of the Church arising and the coming great harvest.

Section Eight

The End Times

The following terms are used interchangeably:

end times
end days
last days
latter days

Since the plural form is used in each of these, we can gather that the related events will not happen in a single day but will extend over a period.

When the Bible speaks of "the day" in its singular form, it usually refers to the final great Judgment Day, in which all people will be gathered before the Lord for judgment. "The day," or what is also called "the day of the Lord," will be the climax of history and should be distinguished from the end times.

In the discussion to follow, we will not be talking about "the day of the Lord," but we will examine the Bible's use of "end times," "end days," "last days," and "latter days."

The Apostles Believed They Were in the End Times

Several Bible passages reveal that the first-century apostles believed they were living in the end times. For example, when Peter preached on Pentecost day, he quoted from the book of Joel, applying the term *"last days"* to the experience of the Holy Spirit being poured out at that time in their lives:

> *For these men are not drunk, as you suppose . . . but this is what has been spoken through the prophet Joel: "And it shall be in the last days," God says, "That I will pour forth of My Spirit on all mankind . . ."*
>
> —Acts 2:15–17

Peter was convinced that he was living in the last days, and he was so confident of this that he quoted a passage from Joel declaring that it was being fulfilled on the day of Pentecost.

Peter also wrote in his first letter with this understanding that he was living in the last times:

> *For He was foreknown before the foundation of the world, but has appeared in these last times for the sake of you.*
>
> —1 Peter 1:20

Note how Peter defined the last times as when Jesus appeared to them during their lifetime.

Paul also spoke in such terms as he explained how we should learn from the events that happened in the OT:

> *Now these things happened to them as an example, and they were written for our instruction, upon whom the ends of the ages have come.*
>
> —1 Cor. 10:11

Was Paul wrong? Was Peter wrong? Were they confused?

If we study the teachings of other NT writers, we learn that they, too, believed they were living in the last days.

The writer of Hebrews wrote:

> *God, after He spoke long ago to the fathers in the prophets in many portions and in many ways, in these last days has spoken to us in His Son.*
>
> —Heb. 1:1–2a

The writer was convinced that he was living in the last days, and he defined the last days as the period during which God spoke through Jesus while Jesus was alive on Earth.

We see that James had the same belief when we read how he rebuked some greedy people, telling them of the destruction about to come upon them, saying:

> *It is in the last days that you have stored up your treasure!*
>
> —James 5:3b

James believed that the "last days" were then, at that time in history during the first century.

The apostle John stated this belief with even greater conviction:

> *Children, it is the last hour; and just as you heard that antichrist is coming, even now many antichrists have appeared; from this we know that it is the last hour.*
>
> —1 John 2:18

John was convinced that he was living in the last hour based on the presence of antichrists. John expected his disciples to realize this, as well.

Were the NT writers wrong? Did they live in the end times? Or are the end times coming in our future? Did the apostles miss it by 2,000 years or more?

The Futurist View of the End Times

A major point of the futurist teachers is that we—living 2,000 years after the first-century apostles—are in the last days, or at least approaching closely to those days. When they talk about the last days or end times, they refer to the scenario of events that they believe will culminate in the second coming of Jesus. Whenever the futurist teachers speak of the rapture, the great tribulation, the antichrist, and the end of the world, they refer to the end-time period. They also speak of the signs of the end times, including earthquakes, famines, disasters, and people falling away from the faith. Futurists discuss all these things in the context of the end times as a period that will come in the near future or perhaps has recently begun.

The End Times According to the Futurist View

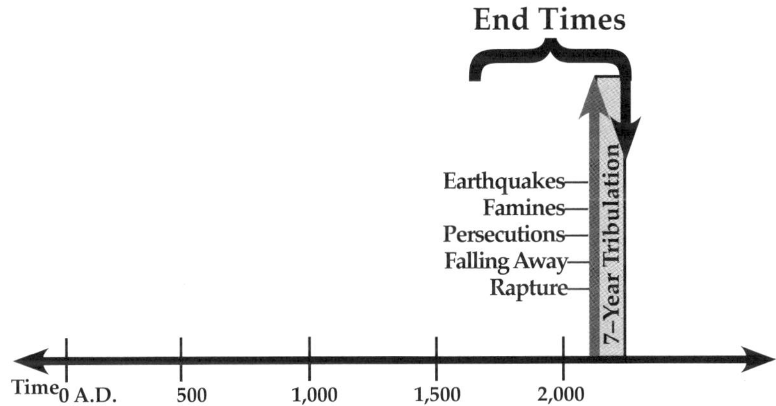

If a futurist teacher is pressed on the point that the NT writers believed they were in the last days, the futurist will concede and then say that the apostles missed it, or they will say that the end times is the period from the resurrection of Jesus to the end of the world. They will say that the last days have extended for about 2,000 years. Although they make this adjustment in their definition of the end times when necessary, they will quickly return to their discussions about the end times being the few short years right before the end of the world.

The Partial Preterist View of the End Times

Teachers holding to the partial preterists' view believe the words of the NT writers literally. Peter, Paul, James, and John were not wrong. The apostles were living in the last days. We do not live in the end times.

Please allow us to explain.

First, we must define what the Bible meant by the end times or last days.

Joel defined the last days as when the Holy Spirit would be poured out on the world. Peter accepted Joel's definition and believed it was fulfilled on Pentecost Day (Acts 2:16–17).

Peter also identified the last days as the period Jesus walked on Earth (1 Peter 1:20).

James understood the last days to be in his lifetime when destruction was about to come upon his generation (James 5:3).

John defined the last hour as the period during which antichrists were active, and John believed those antichrists were active in his lifetime (1 John 2:18).

The writer of Hebrews used the terminology *"last days"* to refer to the period in which God spoke to humanity through Jesus Christ while Jesus was alive on Earth 2,000 years ago (Heb. 1:1–2).

According to every one of these definitions of "end times," the apostles did live in the end times.

If we believe God inspired the Bible writers to write what they wrote, then we cannot say that they missed it. For example, John emphatically said, *"It is the last hour"* (1 John 2:18). Since we believe God inspired John, we must conclude that God believed—knew—it was the last hour 2,000 years ago.

Partial preterists agree with what the Bible clearly says. The end times took place during the first century.

How could the period called the end times be in the first century?

Put yourselves in the shoes of the Jewish people in the days of Jesus. Those who knew their Scriptures—the OT—knew the promises of God. The most hopeful promises centered on a coming Messiah, a new Kingdom, and God making a new covenant with His people. Devout Jews centered their lives around these promises. So important were these promises that they were always looking for the days promised to them by the OT prophets.

When Jesus came, He brought in the new Kingdom. He established the new covenant. The Temple was destroyed. The old religious system ended. The end of the old came in the first century. That was the end times. It ended the old. The end times was the period during which God abolished the old by establishing the new. It went from the day Jesus revealed Himself as Messiah to the destruction of the Temple in Jerusalem in AD 70. The apostles were not wrong. They did live in the end times. We live in new times! In a new Kingdom and a new covenant!

The End Times According to the Partial Preterist View

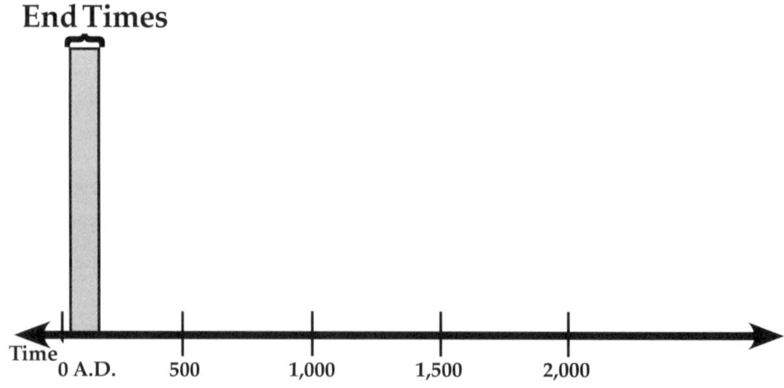

This understanding can be shocking and unsettling when first heard by Christians trained under the futurist view. They have listened to the terms "end times" and "last days" used so many times in reference to the end of the world that they cannot conceive of so great an error in their thinking.

Yet, if we are going to interpret Scripture with any sense of integrity, we must see it in its historical setting. As we have emphasized, we must look within the context of a passage for time references:

1. *"but this is what has been spoken through the prophet Joel: 'And it shall be in the last days' . . ."* —Acts 2:16–17
2. *"in these last times . . ."* —1 Peter 1:20
3. *"the ends of the ages have come."* —1 Cor. 10:11
4. *"in these last days . . ."* —Heb. 1:2
5. *"It is in the last days . . ."* —James 5:3b
6. *"it is the last hour . . ."* —1 John 2:18a
7. *"we know that it is the last hour."* —1 John 2:18b

If we read any of these Bible passages without the preconceived idea that they have to fit into the future, there is no question that the time references refer to the past, and in particular, to the period during which the first apostles lived.

This issue is critical not only for Christians but also for our defense of the faith before non-Christians. One of the most influential atheists of modern times was a scholar named Bertrand Russell. In his book, *Why I Am Not a Christian,* Russell points out how wrong and misled the disciples were by believing that they were living in end times.[113] More importantly, Russell declared that Jesus was a false prophet since the events of Matthew 24 (at least to his understanding) did not happen within a generation. Russell and other influential atheists have ridiculed Christianity, pointing out how wrong Jesus and the disciples were to believe that they were living in the end times.

113. Bertrand Russell, *Why I Am Not a Christian and other Essays on Religion and Related Subjects,* Paul Edwards, editor (New York: Simon & Schuster, 1957), vi.

Instead of making excuses for our Lord and the disciples, let us believe them. Let us accept the fact that they did live in the end times, and we do not.[114]

114. In some contexts, partial preterist teachers may use the terms "end times" or "last days" to refer to the future period during which Jesus returns. However, they do not confuse that future reference with how the terminology is used in the Bible to refer to the first-century transition from old to new.

Summary

If we shift our understanding of the end times from being in our future to our past, we will also change our expectations of the future spiritual and moral conditions of the Church and the world.

This change in expectation is because one Bible passage tells us that in the latter days many will fall away from the faith, i.e., 1 Tim. 4:1 (quoted below). Then another passage talks about evil people increasing in the last times, i.e., Jude 1:18 (quoted below). Since futurist teachers maintain that the latter days are coming in our future, before the end of the world, they teach from these two Bible passages that the world will get worse and worse, spiritually and morally.

In reality, the Bible writers were not talking about our future but rather the end times in which they were living, which is evident when we read the context in which they wrote. Paul wrote to Timothy:

> *But the Spirit explicitly says that in later times some will fall away from the faith, paying attention to deceitful spirits and doctrines of demons.*
>
> —1 Tim. 4:1

Paul was exhorting Timothy that he should not be surprised at the surrounding evil, for indeed, the Holy Spirit had revealed to them that such things would happen in latter times—that is, in their times.

Jude wrote similarly in his letter, explaining that the evil people that they were facing should be expected since the apostles had warned about the evil people who would come in the last times.

> *In the last time there will be mockers, following after their own ungodly lusts.*
>
> —Jude 1:18b

Jude was not talking about mockers to come 2,000 years later.

He was referring to the mockers living in his day with whom he had to deal.

This makes perfect sense when we recognize the terrible spiritual and moral conditions of the people under the rule of Rome during the first century. The Jewish people were known for their depravity. The Jewish historian Josephus described the conditions of his own people, that is, the generation that witnessed the destruction of Jerusalem:

> Neither did any other city ever suffer such miseries, nor did any age ever breed a generation more fruitful in wickedness than this was, from the beginning of the world.[115]

Add to this picture the cruel persecutions that were going on, with Christians being tortured and killed by the Jews and Romans. Also, many people were being taken in by false messiahs, prophets, and teachers. That was a deceived and corrupt generation.

If we recognize the spiritual and moral conditions of the time, we can easily understand the two NT passages that warn of mockers and evil people during the end times. When we study the time references and contexts of both passages, we cannot deny that the authors were talking about evil people active in the first century.

This understanding is key because it disarms futurist teachers who misuse these two Bible passages to say that evil will increase as we approach the return of Jesus Christ.

Partial preterist teachers do not negatively view the future or the world. They believe that we live in the new times and that, in these new times, the Church is being raised to a position of unity, maturity, and glory. Furthermore, the Kingdom of God will continue to grow until it fills the earth.

115. *The Wars of the Jews*, 1998, V:x:5.

Conclusion

This book may leave some unanswered questions in the minds of readers who have never been exposed to the partial preterist view. We can assure you that there are victorious ways of understanding each Bible passage, and we have listed in the bibliography books that offer those views.

We are not concerned that you understand every Bible passage the way we do. We realize that many scholarly teachers who hold to the partial preterist view explain various verses in slightly different ways than we do. However, our primary concern is that you embrace a victorious view of the future.

The most fundamental characteristics of a victorious view are an understanding that Jesus is King, there will be no end to the increase of His government (Is. 9:7), and His Kingdom will continue to grow until it fills the earth (Dan. 2:35, 44).

Christians who are settled about this understanding of God's growing Kingdom will never be shaken by what is going on in the world around them. No matter what events are happening, they know the will of God is progressively advancing on the earth.

Unfortunately, many Christians learn about the Kingdom takeover that is in process, but then they revert to fear and pessimism every time some tragic event happens. Whenever the news media shifts into high gear, sensationalizing all the negative things happening in the world, the Christians who tune in to it abandon the biblical worldview and return to living as if they are slaves in Egypt. Rather than living as children of the victorious King, they choose to live in fear, seeing themselves as grasshoppers facing giants (Numb. 13:33).

On the other hand, Christians who are confident in the promises of God become giants in the land. They are unshaken by the surrounding events. They continue to plan for the future, move ahead with courage, invest in the next generation, and believe God for greater things yet to come. Satan is not taking over this world. Jesus Christ is Lord, and He will rule until every enemy is put under His feet.

Appendix A: Bios of Church Leaders

Below, are short bios of historic Church leaders quoted within this book to support various aspects of the partial preterist view.

Arethas of Caesarea (c. 860–c. 944) was made Archbishop of Caesarea in 903. He is known as one of the most scholarly theologians of the Greek Orthodox Church.

Augustine (354–430) was a theologian, philosopher, and bishop of Hippo in North Africa. He is often considered the Church father who most influenced Western Christianity. Among his many works are *The City of God, Confessions,* and *On Christian Doctrine.*

The Venerable Bede (c. 672–735) was an English Benedictine monk known as a teacher and author. His most famous work is *Ecclesiastical History of the English People.*

John Calvin (1509–1564) was a French theologian and pastor who played a key role in the Protestant Reformation. He developed the system of Christian theology, later called Calvinism, which emphasizes the absolute sovereignty of God. His most well-known work is entitled, *Institutes of the Christian Religion*.

John Chrysostom (c. 347–407) was an influential early Church father who served as the archbishop of Constantinople. In Greek, *Chrysostom* means "golden-mouthed," denoting his celebrated eloquence.

Cyril of Jerusalem (c. 313–386) was appointed the bishop of Jerusalem in AD 350. Today, he is venerated as a saint within the Roman Catholic and Eastern Orthodox Churches.

Jonathan Edwards (1703–1758) is widely regarded as one of America's most important theologians and philosophers. While a minister of the Congregationalist Protestant Church, Jonathan was a stimulator of the revival known as the "First Great Awakening."

Epiphanes (late first century–early second century) is given credit for writing *On Righteousness*; however, some scholars doubt that Epiphanes wrote this, and little is known about his life.

Eusebius (c. 260–339) became the bishop of Caesarea Maritiam about AD 314. He was a historian of Christianity, most known for writing, *The History of the Church.*

F. W. Farrar (1831–1903) was a schoolteacher and cleric of the Church of England. He spent much of his career associated with Westminster Abbey and became an influential author.

Charles Hodge (1797–1878) achieved distinction as a teacher, exegete, preacher, and systematic theologian. He was a Presbyterian theologian and principal of Princeton Theological Seminary between 1851 and 1878.

Jerome (c. 342–420) was a Latin priest, theologian, and historian. He is best known for his Latin translation of the Bible, known as the *Vulgate.*

Justin Martyr (c. 100–c. 165) was an early Christian philosopher and author. He moved to Rome and founded a Christian school. In defense of Christianity, he wrote two bold apologies.

Origen of Alexandria (c. 185–c. 254) studied and taught in Alexandria. He is considered the first systematic theologian and philosopher of the Christian Church, even though he held to several doctrines now regarded as heretical. Origen was a prolific writer, with his most known work, *On First Principles.*

Charles Spurgeon (1834–1892) was an English Particular Baptist preacher known as the "Prince of Preachers." Spurgeon remains very respected and influential among Christians of various denominations today.

Tertullian (c. 155–c. 240) was an early Christian apologist and a polemicist against heresy who lived in Carthage, North Africa. Tertullian has been called "the father of Latin Christianity" even though he adopted some of the unorthodox views of Montanism.

John Wesley (1703–1791) was ordained as an Anglican priest in 1728, and then became known as a theologian and evangelist. Wesley was a leader of a revival movement within the Church of England known as Methodism.

Appendix B: Bibliography

The following books were used in gathering information for *Victorious Eschatology*.

Aquinas, Thomas. *Golden Chain*. Mowbray, 1956.

Athanasius. *On the Incarnation*. Translated and edited by Sister Penelope Lawson, S.C.M.V. Macmillan Publishing Co., 1946.

Augustine. *Confessions*. Translated by Maria Boulding. Vintage Spiritual Classics, 1998.

Bray, John. *Matthew 24 Fulfilled*. John Bray, 1996.

Bray, John. *The Man of Sin of II Thessalonians 2*. John Bray, 1997.

Calvin, John. *Calvin's Commentaries* (1847). Baker Book House, 1984.

Calvin, John. *Commentary on a Harmony of the Evangelists, Matthew, Mark, and Luke*. Translated by William Pringle. Eerdmans, 1949.

Chilton, David. *Paradise Restored*. Dominion Press, 1994.

Chilton, David. *The Days of Vengeance: An Exposition of the Book of Revelation*. Dominion, 1987.

Coontz, Stephanie. *The Way We Never Were: American Families and the Nostalgia Trap*. Basic Books, 1992.

Currie, David. *Rapture: The End-times Error That Leaves the Bible Behind*. Sophia Institute Press, 2003.

DeMar, Gary. *Last Days Madness: Obsession of the Modern Church.* 3rd Ed. American Vision, 1997.

D'Emilio, John and Estelle Freedman. *Intimate Matters: A History of Sexuality in America.* Harper and Row, 1988.

Edwards, Jonathan. *The Works of Jonathan Edwards* (1834). Edited by Edward Hickman. 2 volumes. Banner of Truth, 1974.

Epiphanius, *The Panarion of St. Epiphanius of Salamis.* E. J. Brill, 1987.

Eusebius, Pamphilius. *The History of the Church.* Penguin Press, 1965.

Eusebius, Pamphilius. *The Proof of the Gospel* (c. AD 300). Translated by W. J. Ferrar. The Macmillan Co., 1920.

Farrar, Frederick. *The Early Days of Christianity.* Al Burt, 1884.

Gentry, Kenneth L., Jr. *Before Jerusalem Fell.* Institute for Christian Economics, 1989.

Gentry, Kenneth L., Jr. *The Beast of Revelation.* Institute for Christian Economics, 1989.

Gentry, Kenneth L., Jr. *The Book of Revelation Made Easy.* American Vision Press, 2008.

Gorday, Peter, ed. *Ancient Christian Commentary on Scripture: New Testament IX.* InterVarsity Press, 2000.

Hagee, John. *Jerusalem Countdown.* Frontline, 2006.

Hamon, Bill. *The Eternal Church.* Christian International Publishers, 1981.

Hutchins, Robert Maynard, ed. *Great Books of the Western World. Volume 15, Tactius' Annals and Histories.* Encyclopedia Britannica, Inc., 1952.

Josephus, Flavius. *Josephus: The Complete Works.* Translated by William Whiston. Thomas Nelson Publishers, 1998.

Kik, J. Marcellus. *An Eschatology of Victory.* Presbyterian and Reformed Publishing Co., 1971.

Krupp, Nate. *The Church Triumphant.* Destiny Image Publishers, 1988.

Ladd, George Eldon. *The Gospel of the Kingdom.* Eerdmans Publishing Co., 1959.

Latourette, Kenneth Scott. *A History of Christianity,* Vol. 1, Harper and Row, 1975.

Lindsey, Hal. *The Late Great Planet Earth.* Zondervan Publishing, 1975.

Mauro, Philip. *The Seventy Weeks and the Great Tribulation.* Emissary Publications, 1921.

Merrill, Dean. *Sinners in the Hands of an Angry Church.* Zondervan Publishing, 1997.

Murray, Iain H. *The Puritan Hope.* Banner of Truth, 1998.

Newton, Stan. *Glorious Kingdom.* Vision Publishing, 2012.

Noe, John. *Shattering the Left Behind Delusion*. International Preterist Association, 2000.

Origen. *Origen Against Celsus*. Translated by James Bellamy. B. Mills, 1660.

Pate, Marvin C., ed. *Four Views on the Book of Revelation*. Zondervan, 1998.

Pike, G. Holden. *The Life and Work of Charles Haddon Spurgeon*. Funk and Wagnalls Co., 1992.

Platt, T. Pell. *The Literal Interpretation of Scripture Enforced*. Seeley and Sons, 1831.

Roberts, Alexander, and James Donaldson, eds. *The Ante-Nicene Fathers: Translations of the Writings of the Fathers Down to AD 325*. 10 volumes. Eerdmans Publishing Co., 1989.

Rogers, Jay. *In the Days of the These Kings: The Book of Daniel in Preterist Perspective*. Media House International, 2017.

Russell, Bertrand. *Why I Am Not a Christian and Other Essays on Religion and Related Subjects*. Simon & Schuster, 1957.

Russell, James Stuart. *The Parousia*. International Preterist Assoc., 2003.

Simmons, Kurt. *The Consummation of the Ages*. Bimillennial Preterist Association, 2003.

Simonetti, Manlio, ed. *Ancient Christian Commentary on Scripture: New Testament Ib*. InterVarsity Press, 2002.

Sproul, R.C. *The Last Days According to Jesus*. Baker Books, 1998.

Spurgeon, Charles. *Spurgeon's Popular Exposition of Matthew.* Baker Book House, 1979.

Spurgeon, Charles. *The Gospel of the Kingdom.* Pilgrim Publications, 1974.

Stuart, Moses. *A Commentary on the Apocalypse—Volume I.* M. H. Newman & Co., 1845.

Tacitus, Cornelis. *Annals of Imperial Rome.* Penguin Books, 1989.

Tertullian. *Apologetic and Practical Treatises.* Translated by C. Dodgson. Parker, 1842.

Van Impe, Jack. *Millennium: Beginning or End?* Word Publishing, 1999.

Varner, Kelley. *Whose Right It Is.* Destiny Image Publishers, 1995.

Weed, Robert. *The Book of Revelation, A Heavenly Worship Service.* 2016.

Wells, Ronald A. *History Through the Eyes of Faith.* HarperCollins Publishers, 1989.

Welton, Jonathan. *Raptureless,* 3rd ed. Welton Academy, 2015.

Wesley, John. *The Works of John Wesley.* Edited by Albert C. Outler. Abingdon, 1985.

Wesley, John. *Wesley's Notes on the Bible—The New Testament.* Devoted Publishing, 2017.

Wright, N.T. *What Paul Really Said.* Eerdmans Pub., 1997.

Recommended Reading

The Comings of Christ

Why I Am a Partial Preterist, Not a Full Preterist

Third Edition

Dr. Eberle has crafted this book as a follow-up to *Victorious Eschatology*. If you found valuable insights in the first book, you are in for an even deeper exploration with this new installment.

While *Victorious Eschatology* provided an explanation of the partial preterist view, it left some readers curious about the full preterist view. *The Comings of Christ* is here to address those questions and shed light on the reasons behind the disagreements between proponents of the two views. By grasping these differences, you will enhance your understanding of partial preterism and learn why it is crucial to steer clear of the pitfalls associated with full preterism.

Achieving clarity on these topics will not only enlighten you on related matters but also refine your comprehension of Scripture as a whole. Engaging with *The Comings of Christ* will help you piece together the gaps in your eschatological framework, providing a comprehensive vision of God's future plans.

Dr. Eberle's Most Important Theological Work

Father-Son Theology

Biblical Theology Presented in a Systematic Way

Twelve Volumes in Three Books

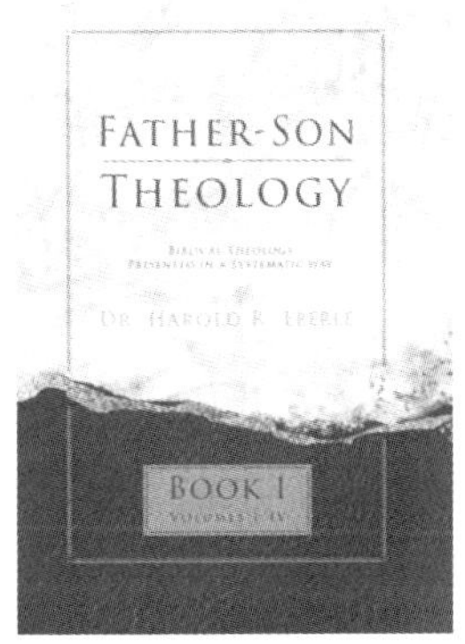

Book 1: Vols. I–IV

Father-Son theology is biblical Christianity.

This first book separates Christianity from the shackles of Western philosophy and restores us to a profound, yet simple understanding of God as our Father and ourselves as His children.

Book 2: Vols. V–VIII

Understanding God as Father, rather than Judge, changes everything. This second book focuses on humanity's problems and God's answers. Finally, a biblical theology that is logically consistent and easy to read!

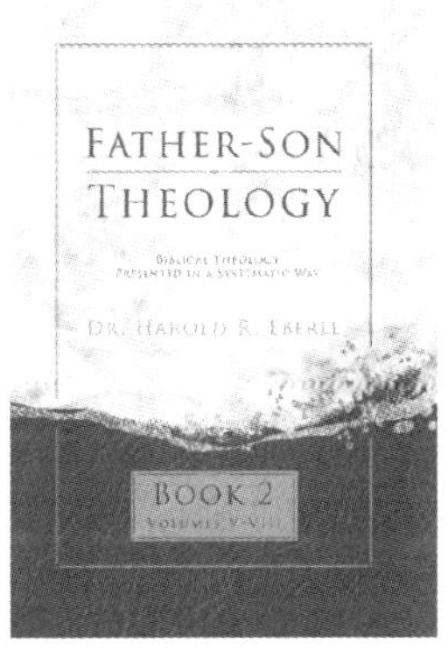

Book 3: Vols. IX–XII

If God is our Father, what does this mean for our understanding of eschatology, the Trinity, the nature of Christ, the work of the Holy Spirit, and the fundamentals of the Christian life?

More Books by Dr. Harold R. Eberle

Has God Proven His Existence?

Ever wonder how intelligent people can reach opposite conclusions about the most vital question of life: Does God Exist? Dr. Harold R. Eberle explains how a person's starting assumptions determine their end conclusion. If you examine your assumptions, you can know with certainty if God exists or not.

Christianity Unshackled

Are You a Truth Seeker?

Christians in the Western world have no idea how profoundly their beliefs have been formed by Western culture. What would Christianity be like if it was separated from Western thought?

After traveling the world and untangling the Western traditions of the last 2,000 years of Church history, Dr. Harold Eberle offers a Christian worldview that is clear, concise, and liberating. This will shake you to the core and then leave you standing on a firm foundation!

Church History, Simply Stated

First Edition, Revised

How did the Church get to where She is today? Who were the leaders who formed our thoughts? How did we get so many denominations? Where is the Church going?

To answer these questions requires a knowledge of the past. Here is a simple, concise explanation of Church history. Anyone can develop a clear picture of our Christian heritage with a little reading.

The Spiritual, Mystical, and Supernatural

SECOND EDITION

The first five volumes of Dr. Harold R. Eberle's series of books entitled, *Spiritual Realities*, have been condensed into this one volume, 372 pages in length. Topics include how the spiritual and natural worlds are related, angelic and demonic manifestations, signs and wonders, miracles and healing, the anointing, good or evil spiritual practices, how people are created by God to access the spiritual realm, how the spirits of people interact, how people sense things in the spirit realm, and much more.

Jesus Gave Five

Apostles, Prophets, Evangelists, Pastors, and Teachers

FIFTH EDITION

EARLIER EDITIONS PUBLISHED UNDER THE TITLE: *THE COMPLETE WINESKIN*

God is pouring out His Holy Spirit, and our wineskins must be changed to handle the new wine. Will the Church come together in unity? How does the anointing of God work, and what is your role? What is the 5-fold ministry? How are apostles, prophets, evangelists, pastors, and teachers going to rise and work together? Where do small group meetings fit in? This book puts into words what you have been sensing in your spirit.

Grace...the Power to Reign

The Light Shining from Romans 5–8

We struggle against sin and yearn for God's highest. Yet, on a bad day, it is as if we are fighting against gravity. Questions go unanswered:

- Where is the power to overcome temptations?
- Is God really willing and able to breathe into us so that our dry bones can live and we can stand strong?

For anyone who has ever struggled to live godly, here are some answers.

Compassionate Capitalism

A Judeo-Christian Value

Learn how capitalism first developed as God worked among the Hebrew people in the Old Testament. The resulting economic principles then transformed Western society as they spread with Christianity. However, our present form of capitalism is different from that which God instilled in Hebrew society. Dr. Eberle explains those differences, helping the reader understand why capitalism must be governed wisely and applied with compassion.

Thy Kingdom Come

The gospel Jesus and His disciples preached is not what we preach today. They preached, "Repent, for the Kingdom of God is at hand." We preach, "You are a sinner; Jesus died for your sins, and if you accept Jesus as Savior, you will be saved."

Why are these two gospels different? Who might be closer to the truth? Let us revisit Jesus' gospel and understand how to truly bring people into God's Kingdom.

Why Theology Matters

Understanding How Your Theology Changes the Way You Live

Everyone is a theologian, because everyone thinks about God. Right or wrong, theology influences your every thought, desire, and action. It determines what you think about yourself and your neighbor. It steers how you spend money, treat your family, and relate to society. Theology shapes your relationships and the world around you. So we need get it right.

God's Leaders for Tomorrow's World

REVISED / EXPANDED THIRD EDITION

You sense the call to leadership, but questions persist: "Does God want me to rise up? Do I truly know where to lead others? Is this pride? How can I influence people?" Through an understanding of leadership dynamics, learn how to develop godly charisma. Confusion will melt into order when you see the God-ordained lines of authority. Fear of leadership will change to confidence as you learn to handle power struggles. It is time to move into your "metron," that is, your God-given sphere of authority.

Hell: God's Justice, God's Mercy

Rethinking the Traditional View of Eternal Torment

SECOND EDITION

The traditional view of hell tells us that wicked people will suffer forever and forever, but what kind of God would torture people forever? Doesn't that scare you? Jesus said, "Fear Him who is able to destroy both soul and body in hell" (Matt. 10:28). Perhaps, then, God will actually destroy the soul and body of the wicked in hell. Let us talk about it.

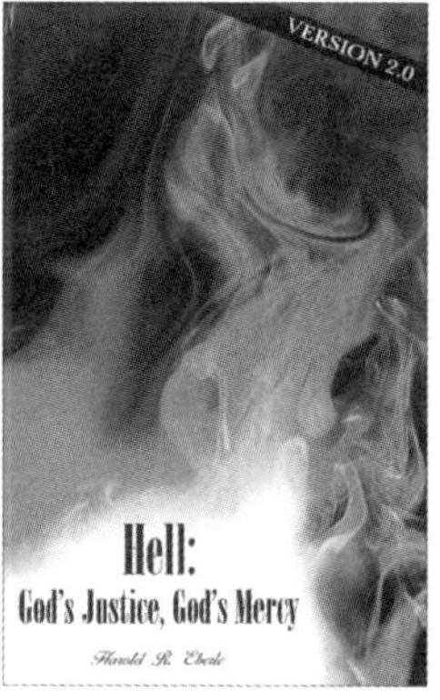

Developing a Prosperous Soul

Vol. I: How to Overcome a Poverty Mind-set

Vol. II: How to Move into God's Financial Blessings

There are fundamental changes you can make in the way you think that will help you release God's blessings. This is a balanced look at the promises of God with practical steps you can take to move into financial freedom. It is time for Christians to recapture the financial arena.

Jesus Came Out of the Tomb . . . So Can You!

An Explanation of Resurrection-based Christianity

Forgiveness of sins is at the cross. Power over sin is in the resurrection and ascension. Yet, most Christians have no idea how to access the benefits of our Lord's resurrection and ascension. They are locked into death-centered Christianity rather than life-centered Christianity. This book empowers the reader to make the transition and "come out of the tomb."

Who Is God?

The answer you give to this question will have a profound impact upon your life. It establishes the sense of security, confidence, and purpose in which you live. It influences every decision you make and every prayer you say. It determines how you see yourself and how you treat others. Your concept of God is at the foundation of everything you believe and everything you do.

Read this book and your foundation will shift. Your beliefs will be challenged. Your life will change. In the end, God will be more real and personal to you.

If God Is Good, Why Is There So Much Suffering and Pain?

Life isn't fair! Pandemics. Terrorist bombings. Ethnic cleansing. Murder. Child abuse. Natural disasters. Genetic maladies. These travesties, global and seemingly relentless, drive us to the limits of our reasoning. We attempt to garner some comfort from the worn out but inaccurate cliché: God is in control. When pain and suffering invade our well-laid plans for a good life, we ask the gut questions: "Why, God why? Why do You allow this? Why don't You do something? What kind of God are You?

Two Become One

Releasing God's Power for Romance, Sexual Freedom, and Blessings in Marriage

FOURTH EDITION

Ever wonder what happily married couples have going for them? They understand the principles of the vibrant union God intended. Let Harold and Linda Eberle explain these principles to you as they apply decades of practical experience that will help any marriage.

Two Become One has been written for individual use, couples together, or for small groups, with questions for discussion at the end of each chapter.

Releasing Kings for Ministry in the Marketplace

John S. Garfield and Harold R. Eberle

"Kings" are Christian leaders who have embraced the call of God upon their lives to work in the marketplace and transform society from that position. This book explains how marketplace ministry will operate in your community in concert with local churches and pastors. It provides a Scriptural basis for expanding of the Kingdom of God into all areas of society.

Living and Dying with the King James Bible

FIRST EDITION, REVISED

The King James Version (KJV) has been a gift of God to the Body of Christ. It has been the standard of truth and inspiration which has stabilized the Protestant Church and blessed millions of people. Still, someone needs to say it: the KJV is an inferior translation. In these pages, Dr. Harold R. Eberle clearly shows the errors and biases of the KJV, hoping that you will consider the advantages of more modern translations.

Leader Shifting

Turning a Church Over from One Senior Leader to Another

Leader shifting can be glorious or gruesome, successful or fraught with mistakes that result in devastating lives. Success requires understanding basic relational and authority dynamics then following well-thought-out steps for a smooth succession.

Precious in His Sight

A Fresh Look at the Nature of Humanity

THIRD EDITION

How evil are we? How can I love myself if I am evil? What happened when Adam sinned? How does that sin influence us? Where do babies go when they die? This book has implications for our understanding of sin, salvation, who God is, evangelism, and how we live the victorious Christian life.

About the Authors

After pastoring a church in the Northwest USA for six years, **Dr. Harold Eberle** embarked on a traveling ministry, during which he has influenced leaders worldwide. During 45–plus years of ministry, he authored over 30 books and helped build 15 Bible colleges in the Philippines, Pakistan, and seven African countries.

Dr. Eberle ministers with his wife, Linda, to whom he has been married since 1978. They raised three children in Yakima, Washington, which serves as headquarters for their ministry, Worldcast Ministries® and Worldcast Publishing.®

[Portrait by Suzette Allen at suzetteallen.com]

worldcastministries.com®

Dr. Martin Trench is an author, pastor, speaker, and consultant. Originally from Scotland, Martin has lived in Canada since 2009, where he is the Lead Pastor of The Church At South Edmonton. He is a popular inspirational speaker and Bible teacher. Martin coaches other churches and leaders on spiritual health, growth, and innovation.

martintrench.com

All Creation is longing for us to know God as Father! As we get to better know Him, join us at:

FatherSonTheology.com®

Find additional resources for personal and group study. Share Father-Son theology® with your family, friends, and local church. Share how knowing God as Father has affected your life.

- Community Discussions
- Small-Group Study Materials
- Videos for Introducing Father-Son Theology
- Resources for Personal Study
- Teaching Videos
- And Much More!